'n
ı

FAILURE

to

PROTECT

America's Sexual Predator
Laws and the Rise of the
Preventive State

ERIC S. JANUS

Cornell University Press

Ithaca and London

First published 2006 by Cornell University Press

Printed in the United States of America

Library of Congress Cataloging-in-Publication Data

Janus, Eric S.
    Failure to protect : America's sexual predator laws and the rise of the preventive state / Eric S. Janus.
        p.   cm.
    Includes bibliographical references and index.
    ISBN-13: 978-0-8014-4378-7 (cloth : alk. paper)
    ISBN-10: 0-8014-4378-4 (cloth : alk. paper)
    1. Sex offenders—Legal status, laws, etc.—United States.   2. Civil commitment of sex offenders—United States.   3. Sex crimes—United States.   4. Preventive detention—United States.   I. Title.
    KF9325.J36   2006
    345.73′0253—dc22   2006017142

Cornell University Press strives to use environmentally responsible suppliers and materials to the fullest extent possible in the publishing of its books. Such materials include vegetable-based, low-VOC inks and acid-free papers that are recycled, totally chlorine-free, or partly composed of nonwood fibers. For further information, visit our website at www.cornellpress.cornell.edu.

Cloth printing   10 9 8 7 6 5 4 3 2 1

ROPER: You would give the devil the benefit of law.

SIR THOMAS MORE: Yes, what would you do? Cut a great road through the law to get at the devil?

ROPER: I would cut down every law in England to do that.

SIR THOMAS MORE: And when the law was down and the devil turned around on you, where would you hide; the laws being all flat? This country's planted thick with laws from coast to coast, and if you cut them down, do you think you could stand in the winds that would blow through them?

ROBERT BOLT, *A Man for All Seasons*

CONTENTS

Acknowledgments   ix

Introduction: The Worst of the Worst?   1

Part I **Fateful Choices**
1. New Legislative Approaches   13
2. Judicial Promises and Betrayals   25
3. A Factual Primer on Sexual Violence   42
4. Benefits and Costs   60

Part II **Consequences**
5. Feminism, the Culture Wars, and Sexual Violence   75
6. Harbinger of the Preventive State?   93

Part III **Course Corrections**
7. There Are Alternatives   113
8. The Politics of Sexual Violence   130
9. Righting Public Policy against Sexual Violence   145

Notes   161
Index   181

ACKNOWLEDGMENTS

This book is the culmination of more than a decade of work on the legal and policy issues underlying our societal fight against sexual violence, and there are many people who have contributed in a wide variety of ways along that journey. Thanks to Liz Nudell, with whom I worked as co-counsel in the twelve-year constitutional litigation challenging Minnesota's sex offender commitment laws. I also thank Professor Sara Evans of the University of Minnesota and Professor Wayne Logan of William Mitchell College of Law for their comments and advice on the manuscript. Many others have encouraged and advised me, including Chuck Dayton, Robert Prentky, Carol Chalmers, Jim Chalmers, Kathleen Graham, and Dorothy Sauber. I thank William Mitchell College of Law for the support it has given me as I've worked on this project, especially Sean Felhofer for his work creating the index, and my research assistants David Arons, Paul Hemming, Kristopher Lee, Jeff Muszynski, Rändi Setter, Travis Thompson, and Terri Port Wright. The most important help came from my wife, Carolyn Chalmers, who has had a huge role in helping me conceive this book, write it, edit it, and get it done.

FAILURE
to
PROTECT

Introduction: The Worst of the Worst?

We keep getting sidetracked with issues like castration and pink license plates for sex offenders, as if they can't borrow or drive another car. . . . Don't get me wrong, we need extreme vigilance for some. But these people are coming from us—society—and we have to stop the hemorrhage. We have to stop pretending that these people are coming from other planets.

—NANCY SABIN, executive director
of the Jacob Wetterling Foundation

Dru Sjodin was last seen on November 22, 2003. Age twenty-two and a senior at the University of North Dakota, she was apparently abducted from the parking lot of a shopping center in Grand Forks on a busy Saturday afternoon. Ten days later, Alfonso Rodriguez Jr. was arrested and charged with her kidnapping. Rodriguez had been released from prison seven months earlier at the age of fifty. He had just served a twenty-three-year sentence as a repeat sex offender, a sexual predator who attacked strangers. Though he was classified as a level 3 offender, the highest risk category for released sex offenders, officials decided not to take the extraordinary step of seeking his civil commitment to a secure treatment facility as a "sexually dangerous person." Dru Sjodin's body was not found until the snow melted in April 2004. Rodriguez has pleaded not guilty, and his trial for capital murder was still pending as of March 2006.

Sjodin's death reminds us of the list of young women and children who have been sexually assaulted and murdered by repeat sex offenders following their

Epigraph is from Rubén Rosario, "GPS No 'Silver Bullet' for Sex-Offender Problem," *St. Paul Pioneer Press*, July 8, 2005, B1.

release from prison. In Minnesota alone, at least ten women have died over the past two decades, victims of released sex offenders. And throughout the nation, the headlines tell the same tragic story: nineteen-year-old Katie Poirier of Moose Lake, Minnesota, nine-year-old Dylan Groene of Coeur d'Alene, Idaho, thirteen-year-old Sarah Lunde of Hillsborough County, Florida, nine-year-old Jessica Lunsford of Homosassa, Florida, and eleven-year-old Carlie Brucia of Sarasota. With almost clockwork regularity yet another young innocent is found dead.

Who are the accused? They are men with long criminal records of violence and sexual assault, released from prison only to prey again. Poirier's confessed killer is Donald Blom, who had six felony convictions including sexual assault and kidnapping. Dylan Groene's accused killer is Joseph Edward Duncan III. He was released from prison in 2000, after serving a twenty-year sentence for raping and torturing a fourteen-year-old Tacoma, Washington, boy. Jessica Lunsford's accused killer, John Evander Couey, had a long criminal record of violence and sexual assault. So did Joseph P. Smith, the accused killer of Carlie Brucia. David Onstott, who has been charged with Sarah Lunde's murder, is a convicted rapist.

The recidivist crimes the men are accused of mark them as the "worst of the worst." These are the criminals we have come to call "sexual predators"—the most dangerous sex offenders, those who seem to be pathologically different from the rest of us. Punished severely for prior sexual assaults, sexual predators seem undeterred by the prospect of returning to prison. It seems that no sooner are they released from prison than they revert to their sick predilections, satisfying their deviant urges on the most vulnerable and innocent. These are the men who lurk in the bushes and parking lots, attacking strangers without provocation or warning. They often seem to lack the essential empathy and conscience that mark human beings. They are "monsters" and "beasts."

But sexual predators—and our powerful reaction to them—are doing another form of damage as well. We have come to think of these men as archetypical sex offenders and have shaped our public policy responses as if all sex offenders fit this mold. We are blind to the true nature of sexual violence in our society, which is far different from what we think it is. Rape-murders are exceedingly rare, and sexual predators represent but a small fraction—a thin sliver—of the sexual criminals in our country. In the 1980s and 1990s feminist scholars such as Florence Rush, Mary Koss, and Diana Russell have shown us that most sexual violence is perpetrated by acquaintances and intimates and family, not by strangers lurking in the dark.[1] But this clear view is being obscured by new legal initiatives and media spotlights on "the sexual predator."

Sexual predators—and our response to them—are in many ways the subject of this book. Decent people naturally feel outrage when horrible crimes are committed by recently released sexual predators. The outrage is directed not simply at the criminals but also at a system that seems incapable of protecting the most vulnerable among us. These rapists, after all, were safely locked up before being released. In hindsight, the warning signs of future tragedy seemed plain—if only state officials would have looked.

This outrage has been translated into a set of aggressive new laws aimed at disabling sexual predators before they strike. The touchstone of the new predator laws is regulatory prevention. Two legislative innovations of the early 1990s provide the focus for this book's inquiry. The first is the use of "civil commitment" to lock up "mentally disordered" dangerous sex offenders after they have finished serving their criminal sentences but before they have committed a new crime. The second is "Megan's law," named after seven-year-old Megan Kanka, a New Jersey girl who was raped and killed by a convicted pedophile who had moved into the neighborhood without her parents' knowledge. In the aftermath of the tragedy, the Kankas led a campaign to require authorities to warn communities about sex offenders in the area. All states now have a form of Megan's law.

Both of these laws impose a restraint on sex offenders before a new crime is committed. These new laws are based on the same power states use to warn consumers of the dangers of tobacco or alcohol and to manage the risk of nuclear waste by storing it in remote deserts. This regulatory power is now directed at protecting us from high-risk criminals. Yet these new tools were inadequate to save the lives of Dru Sjodin, Dylan Groene, Jessica Lunsford, Sarah Lunde, and Carlie Brucia.

A major thesis of this book is that these new laws—although well intentioned—are ill-conceived, bad policy. They were sold as innovative approaches to finding and incapacitating the worst of the worst, but there is little evidence they have succeeded in that important task. It is not simply that these new laws haven't been able to solve the problem of sexual violence. It is that our way of thinking about sexual violence is increasingly distorted. The distortion has led us to the predator laws, and the predator laws strengthen the distortion. We are in a vicious cycle of bad policy, and we need to find a way out if we want to fight sexual violence more effectively.

The distortion is straightforward. We have substituted a part of the problem for the whole. Sexual predators are rare, atypical sex offenders. But because of the intense focus of the media and these new laws, predators have become archetypical. In the headlines, and in these laws, sexual predators have come to symbolize the essence of the problem of sexual violence. In the process, the thousands of women and children whose victimization does not fit this paradigm—only recently made visible through the work of feminist scholars—are at risk of becoming invisible once again.

The origins of the predator archetype are not hard to discern. The stories of Sjodin and Rodriguez, Lunsford and Couey, although awaiting proof in courts of law, sear our consciousness. We are horrified at the cruelty, randomness, and unpredictability of these cases. They symbolize a danger that we all dread. We must not minimize the reality that a small percentage of sex offenders are psychopaths with deviant sexual urges and that they do pose a high risk of repeat violence. But we distort this reality if we magnify this small part of the problem of sexual violence and come to think of it as the whole of the problem.

By distorting the real nature of sexual violence we will hurt our efforts to fight sexual violence in four important ways. First, our focus on the sexual predator will lead us to put more and more resources into trying to do the impossible—prevent the rare but horrible crimes committed by the worst of the worst. And every time our efforts fail—as inevitably they will—we will redouble the effort we put into our faulty strategy.

Second, the spotlight on sexual predators will push the great bulk of sexual aggression—crimes that do not fit the sexual predator paradigm—into relative obscurity, ignored in the allocation of societal resources for fighting sexual violence.

Third, we will begin to think that we can fulfill our societal responsibility by excising a discrete "cancer"—the sexual predator. But, through the work of feminist reformers, we now are aware that sexual violence not only is more common than we once thought but that it is part of the fabric of our society, which includes the tacit approval of sexism and violence in everyday life. While we all are repulsed by the rapist-murderer, tolerant attitudes toward acquaintance rape are common. The sexual predator template encourages us to think that by exiling this monster we have acquitted our responsibility, yet as a larger society we will not have changed the circumstances that allow sexual violence to flourish.

Fourth, we should fear the sexual predator archetype as much as, if not more than, the sexual predator himself because this template has led to extraordinary legal measures that have embraced legal principles that are harbingers of a "preventive state."[2] The preventive state claims the right to deprive people of liberty before criminal action is afoot. Under this approach, it is enough that there is a potential for harm, that the individual's psychological makeup—or political inclinations—poses a grave risk. This attitude rips a large hole in the fabric of our American concept of justice.

With the advent of the "war on terror," there is increasing pressure to expand the preventive actions of the government. Claiming the right of preemptive attack, the Bush administration launched a preventive war in Iraq. The administration detains "enemy combatants" indefinitely, without charge. Threats of bioterrorism have triggered a reinvigoration of the assertion of state power to quarantine and forcibly treat citizens. The USA Patriot Act as renewed in 2006 expands the government's right to conduct surveillance, collecting information even when no specific crime is suspected. The government claims the right to wiretap international messages without even the modest protections of a warrant from the secret Foreign Intelligence Surveillance Act court. The horrors of September 11 are putting pressure on the delicate balance between security and liberty.

It is a truism that liberty is at the heart of our national self-identity. But many of the freedoms we take for granted today have been won through two centuries of hard-fought legal battles. The state can deprive a person of liberty only under the strictest of circumstances. In general, this means only when he or she has been charged and then convicted (beyond a reasonable doubt) of having actually committed (at a specified time and place in the past) a specified crime. We do not allow incarceration for the propensity to commit a crime. In our system, the punishment should never precede the crime.

Yet this is precisely what the predator laws seem to do—except that they do not call the deprivation of liberty "punishment." The predator laws pick out a group of people and place them in a specially degraded legal status that allows the state to treat them in ways that no other person can be treated. Sexual predators are relegated, as it were, to a "reduced-rights zone."

How can the law justify treating one particular group in a legally degraded way? If the government can lock up sexual predators in advance of their (predicted) crimes, why not other criminals? Why not terrorists? Why not political subversives? What is to stop the state from assessing all of us for "risk" and locking up prophylactically those whose RQ—risk quotient—is assessed above an arbitrary threshold?

We are confident that our fundamental principles of justice, enshrined in the Constitution, do not allow this kind of preventive detention. But the legal protections against the preventive state are fragile. The predator laws provide a template for a radical assault on those protections in a two-step process. First, the predator laws resurrect a concept that has properly fallen out of favor in U.S. law: the notion of the "degraded other." In the past, we have used categories such as race, gender, national origin, sexual orientation, and disability to put people into reduced-rights zones. But the courts have, for the most part, put a stop to that. Now, the predator laws have reversed that trend, reintroducing into our legal vocabulary the notion that we can designate a group to be put into this alternate legal universe where fundamental rights are diminished. The second step is the introduction of "risk" as a basis for putting people into the degraded status. Sexual predators are placed in the reduced-rights zone not because they have been convicted of a heinous crime but because we think they are at risk of committing one. Taken together, these two aspects of the predator template provide a formula for radically altering the balance between security and liberty.

How we conceptualize the scourge of sexual violence matters. The conceptual architecture we embrace will shape the legal and public policy choices we make. These, in turn, will determine whether we are spending our resources effectively or wastefully. And, because sexual violence carries such a powerful social meaning, the choices we make in this arena will have broad reverberations that shape our reactions to other threats to our security.

At the risk of oversimplification, we can identify two distinct and influential approaches to sexual violence that have emerged in the past several decades. One approach examines sexual violence at a societal level, asking which aspects of our society facilitate or inhibit the sexual victimization of women and children. The second approach looks at the individual sex offender and asks what biological or psychological factors are associated with sexual violence. The first approach will help us understand what societal changes we might take to prevent sexual violence. The second will prompt us to examine interventions at an individual level.

Prominent in the first approach have been feminist theorists and reformers. Law professor Catharine MacKinnon, for example, argues that sexual violence is "socially not biologically impelled." It is "an act not of [biological] difference but of dominance . . . of gender hierarchy." Sexual violence "flourishes with social support, enforcing and expressing" the socially imposed inferiority of women.[3] This theoretical orientation leads MacKinnon, like other feminist reformers, to understand sexual violence as a widespread feature of our society, thriving in intimate relationships and families, on dates, and between acquaintances. If sexual aggression is nourished by a widespread socially sanctioned hierarchy of gender, then solutions must also be widespread, and they must seek to dismantle the hierarchy.

Feminist ideas have had a powerful—but limited—influence in reshaping our approaches to sexual violence. That sexual aggression is relatively widespread has received broad acceptance, but the underlying implication—that sexual violence flourishes because of a sexist society—remains the subject of intense controversy.

The second approach to sexual violence is exemplified by the work of R.

Karl Hanson, a social science researcher with the Canadian government. Hanson is among the leading experts worldwide in the empirical analysis of sexual offending. He has put together massive databases about sexual offending and sex offenders, crossing continents and spanning decades. Using sophisticated statistical analysis, he mines these data. He is looking for "predictors" of sexual recidivism, measurable facts about individuals that correlate with recidivism. From this research, Hanson constructs and validates "actuarial risk assessment" tools, psychological protocols that combine and weight the facts about a person and produce a numerical score associated with his risk of reoffending sexually.

MacKinnon's theories tell us that if we want to do something about sexual violence, we should look around at social structures and attitudes to understand the extent and social characteristics of sexual violence. In contrast, psychological and biological theorists like Hanson prompt us to seek understanding of sexual violence by looking at—and within—the individual.

There is nothing inherently incompatible between broader societal and narrower individual approaches to explaining and understanding sexual violence. They can coexist. Occupying parallel conceptual worlds, they provide different lenses for understanding and trying to prevent the same social evil. We ought to embrace the truths of both if we want an effective program for addressing sexual abuse.

But if we are not careful, we can allow one approach or the other to occupy our field of vision, obscuring the truths of the other framework. Hanson's work, for example, has certain features that seem to pull us in a direction at odds with the socially conscious view of feminists like MacKinnon. Hanson's scientific techniques allow us—with reasonable accuracy and at reasonable expense—to classify people according to their risk. But these tools are likely to draw our attention disproportionately to identifying and neutralizing the "most dangerous." When we look too much at individual risk, societal patterns and root causes of sexual violence are obscured.

A major thesis of this book is that such a shift is occurring, and that the predator laws result from, and in turn strengthen, an important imbalance in the approach to sexual violence. We give inordinate attention to the question made possible by Hanson's work—who are the most dangerous and how can we protect ourselves from them—and give much less to the questions posed by MacKinnon—what are the patterns of sexual violence, and how do our social structures allow them to flourish.

How is this shift occurring? Consider the following story. In 1995, responding to the imminent release, after decades in prison, of an infamous rapist who had killed a fourteen year old, the governor of Minnesota called a special session of the legislature to pass a new predator commitment law. The media attention on the matter was persistent and intense. At a legislative hearing to consider the bill, critics pointed to the serious questions of constitutionality that such preventive detention raises. In response, one of the most thoughtful (and politically liberal) members of the state senate posed the question: "How could any politician vote against this law? If we defeat this law what could I say to the family of the next victim, killed or raped by a person who would have been committed under this law?"

This powerful question has captured the American public's imagination. It seems so intuitively obvious that we ought to do all in our power to save the "next victim" from harm. Our failure to take available precautions seems clearly to implicate us in the tragedies that (looking backward) seem so preventable. We ought to spare no expense to stop the next murderer and save his next innocent victim.

But what underlies this question? We picture in our heads the deranged rapist-murderer who will surely strike again if released from prison. We conceptualize the predator laws as zeroing in on this man, picking him out of the thousands of "ordinary" criminals who pass every year through the criminal justice system and back into society. Just as the benefits of locking this "monster" away seem clear and indisputable, the alternative seems patently unacceptable. As the late U.S. Supreme Court chief justice William H. Rehnquist put it during the oral argument on the Kansas predator law: "So what's the State supposed to do, just wait till he goes out and does it again?"

The attraction of this paradigm is magnetic, but ultimately it is illusory. It is not just that the prospects of picking out the next rapist-murderer are vanishingly small. It is not simply that, once begun, this quest for safety from the "worst of the worst" will demand ever increasing resources in a spiral fueled by the politics of sexual violence. The real problem is that the vividness of this goal will blanch the larger threat from sexual violence. The real tragedy of deaths like Dru Sjodin's will be amplified because our moral fervor to prevent the next rape-murder will blind us to the concrete steps we can take to increase safety for the tens of thousands of children and women whose sexual victimization falls outside that narrow spotlight.

In this book I seek to help us find our way out of the magnetic attraction of this predator template. We need to turn from asking, how can we identify and lock up the most dangerous? to the more comprehensive, how can we design a system that will prevent the most sexual violence? We need to transfer our willingness to spare no expense from the highly visible but ultimately fruitless quest for perfect safety to the less flashy but broader efforts to get at the root causes of sexual violence and to take sensible safety precautions in regard to the vast majority of sex offenders who are released into the community. And, finally, we need to make sure that we do not sacrifice our basic democratic principles in our quest for security.

The book is divided into three parts. Part 1 sets the groundwork. In chapter 1, I describe the new legal approaches that are at the center of the problem—what this book calls the "predator laws." In chapter 2, the constitutional litigation generated by the sex predator commitment laws is examined. Chapter 3 is a primer on what we know about sexual violence. In chapter 4, I demonstrate that the new laws, by focusing disproportionately on the rare "predator," probably fail in their implicit promise to offer us the best protection from sexual violence.

Part 2 discusses the more abstract, but no less worrisome, consequences of the predator template. In chapter 5, I argue that the predator laws support a retrenchment from the more comprehensive understanding of sexual violence achieved with the leadership of feminist reformers. Chapter 6 shows that the predator template may be the harbinger of a virulent "preventive state."

In part 3, I look to a more positive future. In chapter 7, I examine some promising alternative approaches to sexual violence and pose the question whether they would be substantially more effective than the predator approach. Chapter 8 examines the politics of sexual violence that impede moving toward a more rational and effective approach to prevention. Chapter 9 ends with a prescription for getting our policy on sexual violence on the right track.

I do not advocate going easy on sexual violence or sex offenders. Rather, I present a brief for being hard on sexual violence by being smart about it.[4] Sexual assaults and rapes are crimes of violence. Perpetrators deserve punishment, sometimes severe. Society has the right and the duty to impose penal control over offenders. Some offenders are truly psychopaths with deviant sexual appetites, who pose high risk of reoffending. The criminal justice system is an important forum to express our condemnation of sexual violence and to seek to incapacitate dangerous offenders.

But one of the disabling features of the current approach to sexual violence is that it has the power to stifle or even silence open discussion about how best to really reduce sexual violence. In the struggle to reach and hold the moral—and political—high ground, politicians and others use toughness, the idea of "zero tolerance," as a club to beat down those concerned with civil liberties or alternative approaches. But zero tolerance is a chimera, a hoax. The bluster about toughness often hides a failure to address the huge part of sexual violence that is not in the news, that is not flashy, and that is appallingly common.

People who are truly serious about addressing sexual violence will look carefully and empirically at the effectiveness of their policies in accomplishing that purpose.

Finally, although a central concern ought to be what works, we should not ignore what's right. Justice and truth matter. The predator laws create a reduced-rights zone, an alternate system of justice, for a group of degraded outsiders. To justify these efforts, courts have stretched the law and distorted the nature of sexual violence. We should be chary of building our fight against sexual violence on such questionable and shaky foundations.

Part I

FATEFUL CHOICES

CHAPTER ONE

New Legislative Approaches

"There's the King's Messenger. He's in prison now, being punished:
and the trial doesn't even begin till next Wednesday: and of course the
crime comes last of all."

"Suppose he never commits the crime?" said Alice.

"That would be all the better, wouldn't it?" the Queen said.

Alice felt there was no denying that. "Of course it would be all the
better," she said, "but it wouldn't be all the better his being punished."

"You're wrong there, at any rate," said the Queen. "Were you ever
punished?"

"Only for faults," said Alice.

"And you were all the better for it, I know!" the Queen said
triumphantly.

"Yes, but then I had done the things I was punished for," said Alice,
"that makes all the difference."

"But if you hadn't done them," the Queen said, "that would be better still; better, and better, and better!"

—LEWIS CARROLL, *The Annotated Alice*

There have always been horrific, sexually motivated crimes against
children and women. But in the last years of the 1980s and first of the 1990s a
set of forces coalesced to produce two aggressively innovative legislative responses: sexually violent predator commitment laws and community notification laws. They were designed to plug a "prevention gap," produced, and then

Portions of this chapter are based on Eric S. Janus, "Civil Commitment as Social Control:
Managing the Risk of Sexual Violence," in *Dangerous Offenders: Punishment and Social Order,*
ed. Mark Brown and John Pratt (New York: Routledge, 2000).

Epigraph is from Lewis Carroll, *The Annotated Alice* (New York: W. W. Norton, 2000), 248,
quoted in Susan Granucci and Anthony Granucci, "Indiana's Sexual Psychopath Act in Operation," *Indiana Law Journal* 44 (1969): 555.

13

made highly visible, by shifts in the criminal law and a heightened awareness of sexual violence. The new laws pushed hard against established limits of constitutional law and against conventional notions of the state's role in assuring public safety. They heralded the ominous expansion of a new paradigm of state intervention: surveillance of risk rather than detection of crime, and preventive, rather than punitive, deprivation of liberty. To accomplish their preventive agenda, these new laws constructed a new legal category, the "sexual predator."

The "predator laws" represent an important turn in the way we deploy the power of the state to combat serious interpersonal violence. The legislation communicates a particular set of assumptions both by its structure and by its rhetoric. By focusing on the worst of the worst—the sexual predator—the laws depict an "architecture" of sexual violence: a model for its causes and cures, a picture of its incidence and significance, a theory of how it fits into the fabric of our society. To reveal this architecture, we have to understand the circumstances that produced the new laws and the legal rhetoric that the courts have articulated as they attempt to justify the aggressive innovations, squeezing them to fit the fundamental norms of our constitutional and democratic system.

The genesis of this movement for reform is unremarkable. As they have in other circumstances, heinous and notorious crimes against women and children provided the motive force for change. The uniqueness of this story lies in the confluence of societal forces that produced a novel, aggressively preventive approach to controlling the "sexual predator" before he can strike again.

The beginning of the movement is often traced to events in the state of Washington in the late 1980s. A parallel thread began simultaneously—though more quietly—in Minnesota. Both states turned to civil commitment as a means to prevent the recurrence of sexual violence. Half a decade later, in New Jersey, a similar story unfolded, spawning the nationwide adoption of community notification and registration laws.

In 1988 and 1989, Washington saw two horrible sex crimes. Both were committed by recently released sex offenders. In Seattle, Diane Ballasiotes, an office worker, was abducted, raped, and murdered by parolee Gene Raymond Kane. About eight months later, Earl Shriner raped, strangled, and mutilated a seven-year-old boy. The second crime was particularly horrifying, not only because it was committed against a small child and consisted of brutal mutilation but also because the offender had explicitly threatened, in his prison diaries, to commit just such brutality.[1]

The public response to the second crime was swift and loud. In it we can trace the genesis of a new category of offender, the sexual predator, who is both outside the human community and beyond the reach of normal criminal laws. The stories were repeated in the local media for weeks. Rallies attended by hundreds of citizens blamed the "legal system" and demanded action. Thousands of calls and letters flooded the governor's office.[2] In its anger, fear, and outrage, the populace of the state sought to preserve the "very sense of its own identity and morality. It defined an act that struck the community as way beyond the bounds of normal behavior."[3] In response, the governor appointed a task force to study the issue. During the public hearings held to develop a legislative response, the individual accused of assaulting the boy was "repeatedly referred to as if he were an animal, an outsider, a man who had forfeited all rights."[4] The task force proposed a legislative solution that was promptly enacted as the Community Protection Act.

At about the same time as the events in Washington were unfolding, two rape-murders occurred in Minneapolis outdoor parking facilities or ramps. Recently released from serving their prison terms for sexual offenses, David Anthony Thomas raped and murdered Mary Foley, and Thomas Schwartz raped and murdered Carrie Coonrod.[5] As in Washington, a task force was appointed to study the problem. Though they were apparently not in contact with each other, the two state task forces reached the same conclusion. Only one legal tool was available to prevent the recidivist violence of sex offenders who had completed their prison terms. This tool was civil commitment.

Five years later and a thousand miles to the east, a similar set of events occurred. It was the heinous rape and murder of Megan Kanka, a seven-year-old girl living in a small town in New Jersey. As recounted later by a member of the U.S. Congress: "On July 29, 1994, a beautiful little girl named Megan Kanka was lured into the home of a man who literally lived across the street from her. He said that he had a puppy he wanted to show her. He then proceeded to brutally rape and murder this little girl."[6] Though the brutality of the crime was manifest, two particular facets of the narrative ignited a wildfire of public outrage and demand for law reform. First, the perpetrator, Jesse Timmendequas, was a "twice-convicted pedophile." Second, despite the fact that Timmendequas lived in a house with two other sex offenders "literally across the street" from Megan, local authorities had not informed the neighbors of his presence. Underlying the narrative was the assumption that Megan's parents simply did not know of the lurking threat to their child.[7]

Community reaction in New Jersey was swift, by-passing even the pretense of deliberative study. The legislative solution seemed self-evident: give parents the tools to protect their children by notifying them when sex offenders move into their neighborhoods. Though this solution was not original (it had been included in the Washington Community Protection Act), Megan's story thrust the idea onto the national stage. From Megan's death in July, it took the New Jersey legislature less than three months to enact Megan's law (New Jersey Statute §§2C:7-1-7-11), which required sex offenders to register and public officials to notify communities of offenders in their midst. Later the same year, Congress passed the Jacob Wetterling Crimes against Children and Sexually Violent Offenders Registration Act ("Wetterling Act"), which required states (as a condition of receiving certain federal funds) to adopt sex offender registration laws. Two years later, Congress adopted its own version of Megan's law, requiring states to adopt some form of community notification about sex offenders.

Soon all fifty states had adopted sex offender registration and community notification laws. In many states, these laws passed without a dissenting vote,[8] yet, as in New Jersey, there was little if any research or forethought preceding the adoption of this legislation. Laurie Robinson, a former U.S. Department of Justice official, characterizes the legislative process as "the familiar Washington race to see who can be tougher on crime."[9] Robert Longo, a national expert and innovator on sex offender treatment and prevention, laments that "necessary, detailed research was not conducted into the cost involved, the resources necessary to implement the laws, and the potential impact on law-abiding citizens." He reports that "professionals working with and treating sexual abusers and the national organizations that focus on sexual aggression (i.e., The Association for the Treatment of Sexual Abusers, The National Adolescent Perpetrator Network, The American Professional Society on the Abuse of Children) were not contacted or asked for input into these laws."[10]

These pathways leading to the emergence of the new laws are not, in themselves, unique or surprising. They represent a well-known pattern: "a single sensational incident . . . outraged the community and led to the mobilization of community action groups and special interest groups which have placed pressure on politicians to carry out reforms of legislation and practice."[11] Nor is it unusual that it was comparatively rare and atypical crimes that provoked, and shaped, the responding legislation. As criminologist Michael Petrunik observes, "Societies act more to assuage their sense of primal fear than to address the most frequent and substantial harms. They respond to the atypical, highly visible case, as opposed to less salient, less sensational higher volume types of offences."[12]

Rather, what is notable about these stories is the particular turn that the public outrage and responsive legislation took. Examining the two most prominent stories—those of the child victims in Washington and New Jersey—what stands out most vividly is the *preventability* of the crimes. In both cases, the horrible future was in plain view. Before his release from prison, Earl Shriner had laid out in some detail "his fantasies of how he would kidnap, confine, and torture his victims."[13] Yet despite the discovery of these plans, officials were powerless to stop his release from prison. In New Jersey, the presence of Jesse Timmendequas in Megan's neighborhood was known to officials but unknown to Megan's parents. Again, it seemed that all that was missing was the ability of state officials to act on their existing knowledge of impending violence. To Lucy Berliner, a nationally prominent victims advocate from the state of Washington, it was the preventability of the crimes that was particularly important: "The community was understandably outraged that the government could know such important information and be unable to share it with citizens."[14] These stories, thus, seemed to point to *prevention* rather than (merely) punishment as the key factor that needed fixing.

A number of historical factors combined to create this perception of a prevention gap and turned public attention to legal tools that permit intervention in anticipation of crime, not just after it is committed. A widely held tenet of contemporary Western society holds that it is a duty of the state to control violence against its members.[15] On this base were overlaid two additional trends. The first was the transformation of the penal sentencing systems in many states during the 1970s and 1980s from indeterminate to determinate sentencing based on standardized guidelines.[16] The second was associated with the feminist agenda to change societal attitudes and behavior about sexual violence against women.[17]

In the early 1980s both Washington and Minnesota (along with most other states) had replaced "indeterminate" with "determinate" sentencing schemes. In the former, criminal sentences, as imposed by the court, were of indeterminate length. Parole boards, examining the inmate's response to rehabilitation in prison, determined when the inmate was "ready" for release on parole. Under determinate sentencing schemes, the terms of incarceration are set by the court at sentencing.[18] The shift from indeterminate to determinate sentencing coincided with a conservative turn in the country that replaced the rehabilitative ideal of earlier criminology (in which imprisonment was for "treatment" and was to be individualized to fit the needs of the criminal) with the "principle of just deserts," under which imprisonment was seen as punishment that should be proportionate to the severity of the crime.

The change to determinate sentencing had dual effects. In keeping with the conservative law-and-order agenda, it put an end to early releases of prisoners who had convinced parole boards that they had been quickly rehabilitated. But the law-and-order agenda produced an unforeseen consequence. By eliminating the discretion inherent in indeterminate sentences, the change deprived the states of their power to exercise long-term, flexible control over offenders deemed "too dangerous" to release from prison.[19] Under determinate sentencing, when a sentence is served, the inmate must be released. Dangerousness drops from the equation.

By the late 1980s and early 1990s, individuals imprisoned under the new sentencing guidelines became eligible for release. Since by definition "determinate sentencing" was tied to the heinousness of the crime rather than the characteristics of the defendant, even an inmate's manifest dangerousness did not provide a basis for extending his penal incarceration. This created a gap in the states' ability to protect against recidivist sexual violence.

In addition, by the late 1980s, "society's increased attention to sexual assault" had produced a "change in its perceived seriousness."[20] Feminist-inspired views of sexual violence had transformed social judgments about punishing sex offenders. Existing penal sentences for violent, recidivist sex offenders were judged to be "inadequate punishment," "too short to permit meaningful treatment of sex offenders in prison," and inconsistent with "supervised release after the prison doors are opened."[21]

As the 1980s saw a public mood that was "fearful and punitive," tolerating "zero risk to public safety," the imperative for the state to protect its citizens manifested itself in the principle of incapacitation, the notion that public protection against violence is best accomplished by locking up criminals in prisons.[22] But as Zimring and Hawkins point out, the principle of incapacitation has no internal point of balance. By its own logic, it tends to be expansive rather than limited: more protection is better.[23] Thus, the emergence of the sexual-violence prevention gap produced a strong push to extend the systems for controlling sex offenders.

Key constitutional constraints prevented states from addressing this incapacitation imperative by simply increasing criminal punishments for sexual violence. Retroactive increases would have run afoul of prohibitions on ex post facto laws and double jeopardy. Prospectively, the states could—and did—increase sentence lengths for sex offenders.[24] But both Washington and Minnesota rejected a return to "long indeterminate sentences for sex offenders,"[25] at least in part because such a scheme would be inconsistent with the principle of just deserts under which sentences are to be proportionate to the severity of the crime rather than the characteristics of the criminal.[26]

Finally, the Constitution prohibited the states from imposing criminal punishment based simply on the "status" of being dangerous, or for the punishment of future predicted crimes. This limitation on the power of government is so basic that to many of us it seems as unremarkable as the furniture in our living rooms. Yet this norm and other strict constitutional constraints relating to criminal law constitute the careful balance we, as a free society, have struck to protect our security while preserving our liberty. With very limited exceptions, before the government can lock any of us up, it must prove, beyond a reasonable doubt, that we actually committed a specific crime. This strict discipline goes a long way to assure that the awesome power of the government does not get abused.

But these basic constitutional norms stood squarely in the way of the loud, public demand for government action to *prevent* crime. Even though the crime against Megan and the crimes of Earl Shriner seemed manifestly inevitable and predictable, the public's demand remained stubbornly in the forbidden zone: the Constitution says clearly that the state cannot punish people for their dangerousness, cannot convict on a crime that has not yet been committed.

The states had only one place to turn—to the civil system of regulation. The exact border between laws that are civil and those that are criminal is, perhaps surprisingly to nonlawyers, a matter of high contention. But the basic distinction between the two categories is clear and rather intuitive. Criminal laws are those that are designed to "punish" a "crime." Civil laws are designed to "regulate" behavior to prevent some form of (future) harm. Most important for our purposes, both types of laws can diminish a person's freedom of action or "liberty," and, for that reason, both types can appear to the individual affected as a burden akin to punishment. At bottom, the distinction turns significantly on whether the "intent" of the state is to "punish" or to "regulate."

Even though the exact boundary between the criminal and civil systems is uncertain, labeling an intervention as one or the other is consequential. Criminal law is tightly constrained by a system of constitutionally mandated rules. Criminal punishment may be imposed only after "conviction" of a specifically charged, predefined "crime." The charge must allege particular acts that took place at a specified place and time (*actus reas*). Conviction requires proof of "criminal intent" (*mens rea*). Defendants have the right to a jury of their peers, and a verdict of guilty must be proved "beyond a reasonable doubt." People cannot be charged with actions that were not "crimes" when committed. Sentences, once imposed, may not be increased (ex post facto laws prohibited). A person, once convicted or acquitted of a given crime, may not be retried, even if the state is dissatisfied with the punishment imposed (prohibition against double jeopardy). A person's "status"—for example, being a "vagrant" or being an "addict" or even being "dangerous"—may not be made into a crime. Defendants may not be forced to give evidence against themselves, and they have a right to confront adverse witnesses. Finally, only crimes that have been committed may form the basis of a conviction; crimes that have not yet been committed (that is, predicted crimes) may not be punished.

None of these constitutional protections applies to "civil" or regulatory laws. Most significantly, a *civil* label frees the states from three troublesome constitutional restrictions. First, the prevention gap. Unlike criminal conviction, civil regulation could constitutionally target crimes that are predicted in the future. Second, the prohibition on ex post facto laws does not apply to civil regulation. And finally, bringing a civil proceeding after a criminal punishment poses no problem of double jeopardy.

The fact that civil regulatory measures allowed the states to circumvent constitutional limitations that would otherwise limit their powers was the central driving force behind the new laws. For example, a Minnesota task force studying the use of civil commitment for sex offenders in 1988 noted that the criminal justice system requires in-court testimony to prove a crime, whereas civil proceedings make liberal use of hearsay evidence embedded in the expert testimony. Thus, the task force surmised, sex offender commitment laws can protect society against "individuals . . . who may not have been convicted of a sex offense, because of the reluctance of young and/or scared victims to testify against perpetrators of sexual abuse." Civil commitment also allows the confinement of individuals who "may be dangerous but evade conviction due to the high burden of proof required in criminal cases." Finally, civil confinement, not being limited by the prohibition of double jeopardy and ex post facto laws, can compensate for the "comparatively short correctional sentences" for sex offenders by confining individuals after they have completed their criminal sentences.[27]

To escape from the constraints of the Constitution, the states began turning to civil legal forms to address the prevention gap that had been so violently exposed. This choice, born of intense public pressure rather than careful study or theoretical preferences, has proven both highly controversial and highly consequential.

Megan's law is the now-familiar shorthand for legislation that requires sex offenders in the community to register with law enforcement and mandates officials to warn the public of the presence of sex offenders in the community. These laws take a familiar form of legal regulation and move it to a radically new use. State regulation of dangerous activities and things is commonplace. We require the registration of firearms so that law enforcement can have ready information when a crime is committed. We require a warning on toxic chemicals so that citizens can protect themselves from harmful exposure. Megan's law takes the simple but radical step of applying these types of regulation to protect against the risks posed not by dangerous things but by dangerous people.

Legal challenges to registration and notification laws have proved largely unsuccessful. The core challenge has been that the obligations imposed are so onerous, and the public dissemination of information so embarrassing, that the laws are really "punishment," despite their "civil" label. In part, the courts have rejected this claim because the state's purpose is proper: "The purpose and the principal effect of notification are to inform the public for its own safety, not to humiliate the offender. Widespread public access is necessary for the efficacy of the scheme, and the attendant humiliation is but a collateral consequence of a valid regulation."[28] In other words, so long as the state's intention is not "punishment" but rather warning of future risk, the fact that the public humiliation of community notification feels like punishment to the offender is of no legal consequence. Uncertain at this point is whether all states must follow the lead of the majority of states and base the imposition of registration and notification burdens on some sort of individualized risk assessment.

It is worthwhile pausing here for a moment to understand the significance of the conceptual shift that has enabled the logic of regulation to transfer from risky things to risky people. At one level, if we focus on "risk," the analogy between, say, warnings on cigarettes and warnings about rapists seems strong. The harm from people can be as severe as the harm from things. But there is an important way in which the analogy is very problematic, for it suggests that it is acceptable to treat people—or some people—like objects, examining them, assessing them, and then grading and labeling them in the same way that we might grade and label various types of nuclear waste. This kind of treatment might be justified as a form of punishment, because we can certainly agree that rapists might be thought to *deserve* the humiliation of public notification. This kind of reasoning treats offenders as fully human and provides a good distinction from nuclear waste. But Megan's laws disclaim any punitive intent, basing their regulation simply on the risk posed by individuals, so distinguishing the sex offender laws from laws that regulate dangerous objects is much more problematic. As I will argue more fully in chapter 6, the underlying rationale justifying the expansion of regulatory laws is that sexual predators have been made into a new "outsider" group who inhabit an alternate justice system with much-degraded legal protections.

Sexual predator commitment laws also take a standard form of civil law and move it into an area that normally would be the subject of criminal law. Standard civil commitment laws have been universally used to confine and treat members of society whose severe mental impairments render them unable to care for themselves and who may be dangerous. At a superficial level, sex offender commitment laws simply adopt this legal form. They incarcerate "mentally disordered" sex offenders who are judged to pose a particularly severe danger of future sexual violence. Like standard mental illness commitment laws, the sex offender laws use civil, rather than criminal, procedures. Confinement is not in prisons but in secure treatment facilities. Treatment must be provided, and the conditions may not be punitive. Commitments are for an indeterminate period, ending only when the individual is no longer dangerous, or no longer mentally disordered.

The Washington and Minnesota sex offender commitment laws were not the first to use civil commitment to address sexual offending. A "first wave" of sex offender commitment laws was enacted in the late 1930s. Taking a variety of forms, their espoused purpose was to create an alternative to punishment for a certain subclass of sex offenders, those "too sick to deserve punishment."[29] Known as "sex psychopath laws," this legislation was part of a more "general social movement towards treatment of criminals as patients . . . a socially sick person."[30] Twenty-seven states and the District of Columbia enacted some form of sex psychopath law.[31]

In 1977, the Group for the Advancement of Psychiatry issued an influential report entitled "Psychiatry and Sex Psychopath Legislation: The '30s to the '80s" (the "GAP Report"). This report, along with reports by the President's Commission on Mental Health, submitted to President Carter in 1978, and the American Bar Association's Committee on Criminal Justice Mental Health Standards Project, recommended the repeal of sex psychopath legislation.[32] The GAP Report characterized sex psychopath statutes as an "experiment [that] has failed," providing neither effective treatment nor the incarceration of truly dangerous individuals.[33] By the 1980s, most of the states with sex psychopath laws had either repealed or had ceased using them.[34]

Despite the acknowledged failure of the earlier sex offender commitment laws, Washington and Minnesota returned to this legal form in the early 1990s to address the "gap" in social control. A few other states—Kansas, California, Illinois—quickly followed suit. The reborn sex offender commitment laws were a mutated version of the earlier laws. While the early sex psychopath laws were consistent with the "clinical ideal," seeking, at least in form, to care for those too sick to punish, the primary justification for the later versions was explicitly public safety. The second-wave laws sought to continue the incarceration of offenders considered "too dangerous" to release from prison. The earlier laws were, at least originally, diversions from the criminal justice system, hospitalizing offenders instead of imprisoning them. The current laws impose hospitalization only after imprisonment has run its course.

A comparison of the first- and second-wave nomenclature underlines this evolution. The first-generation laws claimed to identify and hospitalize "sexual psychopaths," using a term with a distinctively psychiatric provenance that emphasized the "too sick to punish" rationale. Almost all of the second-wave laws claim to address "sexual predators," a term that invokes images of nonhuman beasts, and places the role of psychiatric disorder more in the background.

While mental health professions were somewhat ambivalent about the first-wave sex psychopath laws,[35] those first-wave laws clearly arose from a notion that psychiatrists had some expertise that could appropriately address sexual violence. The second generation of sex offender commitment laws had a distinctly different origin. In the 1990s, states turned to civil commitment not because they believed that mental health professionals were better at addressing the problems of sexual violence but simply out of necessity. States wanting to address the "prevention gap" saw no other way to do so than in the form and language inherent in civil commitment laws.

In fact, organized psychiatry staunchly opposed the second wave of sex offender commitment laws. In 1992, the Minnesota Psychiatric Society opposed the use of civil commitment for sex offenders, warning that for the great majority of those committed "there is no form of treatment that has a reasonable expectation of success."[36] A 1996 draft report of a task force of the American Psychiatric Association (APA) condemned sex offender commitment laws because they "distort the traditional meanings of civil commitment, misallocate psychiatric facilities and resources, and constitute an abuse of psychiatry."[37] The final version of the report, issued in 1999, toned down the language but retained the condemnation, characterizing sex offender commitment laws as "bending civil commitment to serve essentially nonmedical purposes" and constituting "an unacceptable misuse of psychiatry."[38] The National Association of State Mental Health Program Directors, in their 1997 "Position Statement on Laws Providing for the Civil Commitment of Sexually Violent Criminal Offenders," warned that sex offender commitment programs "undermine the mission and integrity of the public mental health system, . . . divert[ing] scarce resources away from people who both need and desire treatment."[39]

As of 2005, fifteen states and the District of Columbia had sex offender commitment laws on their books. A number of states considered and rejected sex offender commitment laws, in large measure because of opposition by professional groups concerned, among other things, with the expense of carrying out these laws.[40] But the momentum for predator commitment laws is not dead. There are active lobbies for passage of new commitment laws in New York (where it has the support of the state's attorney general),[41] Delaware, New Mexico,[42] Ohio,[43] and Vermont.[44] Pennsylvania has a law that allows the state to retain juveniles in confinement indefinitely, even after they reach adulthood, if they are considered "dangerous."[45] At least one advocacy group, Parents for

Megan's Law, urges states to pass civil commitment laws as a means to "pro-tect children from [sexual] predators."[46]

In some ways, the predator laws exemplify good public policy. They can be characterized as outside the box thinking, creatively borrowing legal forms from one area to solve problems in another. In passing these laws, government responded quickly to the expressed needs of the populace. And, by addressing the protection of women and children from sexual assault, these laws could be seen as contributing to the correction of longstanding male biases that mar-ginalized this kind of criminality.

But overall these new laws are not good policy at all. They distort our un-derstanding of the real nature of sexual violence; they lead us to misallocate our prevention efforts; and they introduce dangerous principles into the sen-sitive balance between liberty and security. These problems make a poor foun-dation on which to build a program to reduce sexual violence.

CHAPTER TWO

Judicial Promises and Betrayals

Substantive due process forecloses the substitution of preventive detention schemes for the criminal justice system, and the judiciary has a
constitutional duty to intervene before civil commitment becomes the
norm and criminal prosecution the exception.

—CHIEF JUSTICE A. M. "SANDY" KEITH, *In re Linehan*,
Minnesota Supreme Court (1996)

[Civil commitment of sex offenders] is not an unusual thing anymore.

—KEVIN GOODNO, Minnesota commissioner
of Human Services (2006)

From the state's perspective, predator commitment laws provide a
welcome bypass around constitutional constraints on its social-control powers. Looked at from the perspective of the citizen who is targeted, however,
these laws create a realm in which key protections of the Constitution do not
apply—a reduced-rights zone. Either way, the laws amount to a special dis-
pensation from the "great safeguards which the law adopts in the punishment
of crime and the upholding of justice."[1]

Two questions have characterized the litigation challenging the predator
commitment laws. The first is whether, in principle, a state can excuse itself
from compliance with the standard norms of the Constitution when it locks
people up. This is not a question of only academic or transitory interest. Protecting the citizen from the unconstrained power of the state, especially its
power to curtail liberty, has been an enduring struggle central to American

Goodno epigraph is from an article reporting on "plans to increase capacity fivefold at a
prison-like treatment center" for postprison detention of sex offenders. Conrad deFiebre,
"Non-sex Offenders Face Lockup for Decades," *Minneapolis–St. Paul Star Tribune*, Jan. 15,
2006, A1.

democracy. Among the causes listed in the Declaration of Independence for breaking away from the "tyranny" of George III were "depriving us in many cases, of the benefits of Trial by Jury" and "transporting us beyond Seas to be tried for pretended offences."

Nonetheless, the courts have answered the first question in the affirmative, no doubt in large measure because of the compelling narratives of sexual violence that led to the adoption of the predator commitment laws. This approval required an answer to the second question: What are the limits of this power to create a reduced-rights zone that bypasses the normal constitutional constraints?

We can think of the rhetorical function of court decisions as a form of moral narrative—showing how an important societal conflict is resolved in a just and legitimate way. In the predator cases, the conflict requires courts to explain how it is possible, in our democratic system, to pick out some people and subject them to a form of government intervention—preventive detention—that is considered otherwise totally inconsistent with our basic principles. The real reason for selecting the disadvantaged group—sexual predators—is that we are very scared of the risk posed by "these people." But this does not provide a sufficient rationale, because it does not explain why the same treatment could not be turned on other groups whom we fear, be they "terrorists" or simply people whose race, national origin, or sexual orientation are different from the norm. Fear of danger provides no logical stopping point, no principled limitation on governmental power.

Thus, the central task for the courts has been to show that there is some *principled* limitation that will prevent uncontrolled spread of what is otherwise an unconstitutional application of government power. In order for this judicial narrative to be successful, it must articulate some *fundamental difference*— some difference in kind—between those who are entitled to the normal protections of the Constitution and those who are not.

In struggling to explain how there can be a group of people whose rights are substantially diminished from the norm, the courts have been at pains to reassure us—and themselves—that they were not approving an elastic alternative system of social control that could expand at will, swallowing the criminal justice system and all of its carefully calibrated protections. As the guardians of our constitutional order, the courts have promised that they will "intervene before civil commitment becomes the norm and criminal prosecution the exception."[2] The courts have assured us that they will impose strict limits on civil commitment: allowing its use only for the most dangerous and, among those, only for those who are so mentally disordered that their impaired ability to control their behavior somehow distinguishes them from ordinary dangerous recidivists.

But looking back on more than a decade of judicial experience with the predator laws, these judicial promises of principled limitations are belied in application. The principled limitations of inability to control, of mental disorder, and of dangerousness have proved to be so permeable that they are no boundary at all.

The Case of Dennis Darol Linehan

In many ways, the story of Dennis Darol Linehan is the story of the predator commitment laws. In his violent history, one can understand the compelling pressure on the states to enact the predator laws. The litigation of his case reflects the ambivalence of the courts as they are confronted with aggressive state laws that seem to bypass the Constitution, their promises to impose and enforce strict limits on the use of predator commitment laws, and, in the end, the betrayal of those promises.

In 1965, Linehan, age twenty-four, killed a fourteen-year-old girl in the course of a sexual assault. As a raging, drunken, and often out-of-control adolescent and young adult, he sexually assaulted (or attempted to) at least seven girls and young women. He caused untold fear, sorrow, heartache, and pain, disrupting and destroying the lives of his young victims, their families, friends, and others who grieved and feared at a distance. After Linehan killed the girl, he hid her body, putting her family through the agony of an extended search. Eventually, he was arrested and pleaded guilty to kidnapping. He was sentenced to serve up to forty years in prison. After serving ten years, he escaped from minimum security custody; he was arrested days later and two states away for attempting to sexually assault a twelve-year-old girl.

With credit for good behavior in prison, he was legally required to be released on parole in 1992. Having served twenty-seven years in prison, he became one of the first candidates for predator commitment in Minnesota.

Lisbeth Nudell, a lawyer with expertise in civil commitment law, was appointed by the court to defend Linehan in the commitment proceedings. Nudell called me at my office at William Mitchell College of Law where I teach, with a particular focus on the boundaries of the state's ability to use civil commitment to protect public safety. She asked me if I would consult from time to time on the case. I agreed, and eventually I was appointed to work with her as co-counsel for Linehan. Some ten years later, in 2002, after three arguments before the Minnesota Supreme Court, an appeal to the United States Court of Appeals for the Eighth Circuit, and two petitions to the U.S. Supreme Court, we closed the file on the constitutionality of his commitment. Some fourteen years after the lawful expiration of his criminal confinement, Linehan remains in maximum-security confinement at the facility of the Minnesota Sex Offender Program. He has slowly worked his way to the final stages of that program. In 2006 he was sixty-five years old.

Dennis Linehan is precisely the kind of person many people have in mind when they justify the Constitution-stretching predator laws. As a young man, he was apparently bereft of the normal controls necessary for civilized society. The fact that his crimes were decades in the past, that he had served twenty-seven years in prison, that he successfully completed chemical dependency and sex offender treatment, and that on his release he would have been fifty-one years old—none of this changed the perception of him as a monster who killed an innocent fourteen-year-old girl. In this sense, his is the paradigm case for sex predator commitment. Tracing his case through the courts paints a picture of the promises made by the courts to justify predator commitments, and the betrayals of those promises that followed promptly as these laws were applied to real people.

When I first met him, Dennis Linehan was in his early fifties. Six feet tall, with a full head of graying hair, he looked like many men who had spent their prime years in prison—he had a muscular frame in decline and an impassive face that was prematurely aged. As a client, he was attentive, interested in getting advice and helping with his defense. Though one could see in his visage the young adult with slicked back black hair who stared sullenly from the newspaper photos following his arrest in the 1960s, he seemed to have developed some insight and control of the rage that must have driven him as a teen. He was able to talk about the sexual and physical abuse he had suffered as a child at the hands of his sister and father, and he seemed to understand how the shame and rage associated with his chaotic and abusive childhood contributed to his own destructive and criminal actions.

The main prosecutor in the commitment case was a career lawyer in the criminal division of the Ramsey County Attorney's office. The prosecutor's theory of the case was that Linehan was, and continued to be, a bad man with a long criminal record, unrepentant and dangerous. A key witness, licensed psychologist Nancy Steele, was an experienced state psychologist who had designed and run the prison sex offender treatment program. In her judgment, Linehan's successful completion of the sex offender and residential chemical dependency treatment indicated that he could appropriately be placed in the community for continuing treatment. The state's theory was that Steele had been duped by Linehan.

The law under which the state sought Linehan's commitment, the Minnesota "psychopathic personality" commitment law, had been adopted in 1939; it was resurrected from near abandonment in the early 1990s. It was vague and broad, allowing for the civil commitment of anyone whose

> conditions of emotional instability, or impulsiveness of behavior, or lack of customary standards of good judgment, or failure to appreciate the consequences of personal acts, or a combination of any such conditions, . . . render such person irresponsible for personal conduct with respect to sexual matters and thereby dangerous to other persons.

After it was enacted it was immediately challenged as unconstitutionally vague by one of the first candidates for commitment, one Charles Edwin Pearson. This was in 1939, well before the civil rights revolution and the rights-expanding Warren Court of the 1960s. Yet the Minnesota Supreme Court balked at the breadth of the law, noting that a literal application "would . . . make the act impracticable of enforcement, and perhaps, unconstitutional in its application." Instead of striking the law down, the court followed standard practice, narrowing its meaning as necessary to comply with constitutional standards. Thus, the *Pearson* test allowed commitment only of

> those persons who, by a habitual course of misconduct in sexual matters, have evidenced an *utter lack of power to control* their sexual impulses and who, as a result, are likely to attack or otherwise inflict injury, loss, pain or other evil on the objects of their uncontrolled and uncontrollable desire. (Emphasis added)

The case then went to the United States Supreme Court, which upheld the statute as narrowed by the Minnesota Supreme Court, warning that a broader application "might render it of doubtful validity."

By 1992, at the time of Linehan's trial, the *Pearson* "utter lack of power to control" standard had been virtually forgotten, more or less hidden in forty-year-old law books. The state's case against Linehan ignored it altogether. This was understandable, because no one really understood what it might mean to "utterly" lack "power to control" one's behavior. Further, if those words meant anything, they seemed to suggest some sort of diminished criminal responsibility. While this meaning was consistent with the original purpose of the law, aimed at offenders who were "too sick to deserve punishment," time had transformed that purpose, so that in 1992 the idea was to continue the confinement of those who had been held to be criminally responsible for their crimes. The state's case focused not on showing that Linehan was so "sick" that his power of control was disabled but rather on how bad he had been, and continued to be. Instead of diagnosing and explaining his behavior, the state sought to judge it once again.

Key expert witnesses, called by the state to opine that Linehan should be committed, admitted that they had not heard of the *Pearson* standard. For example, a psychologist named Richard Friberg testified that Linehan's crimes "reflected a much more planful, controlled, goal directed kind of a situation than he would like us to believe." He described Linehan as being a "stable, intact and fairly controlled personality." Another doctor who supported the commitment testified under my questioning:

> Q. Do you understand the difference between uncontrolled desire and uncontrollable desire?
> A. The definition of uncontrolled desire and uncontrollable desire?
> Q. Yes, the distinction between the two? Do you understand that distinction?
> A. No, I don't.

These doctors acknowledged that Linehan had had no "out of control" behaviors during his decades in prison and that he had the *capacity* to take responsibility for his actions.

As it turned out, these statements by the expert witnesses were a critical mistake for the state. Though the trial court committed Linehan and the court of appeals affirmed, in 1994 the Minnesota Supreme Court reversed Linehan's commitment precisely because the state had not met the *Pearson* standard. It had not proved that he lacked the "power to control" his sexual impulses.

There is great and tragic irony in the fact that the fight over Linehan's freedom in 1992 depended on a tug of war over this idea of his "power" to control his behavior. In fact, when he was a late adolescent and young adult—when he was at his most destructive—a good case could have been made that he was "unable" to control himself. Years of sexual and physical abuse in a chaotic and unstable family situation left him full of shame and rage, alcoholic, and without boundaries. If anyone could have claimed that his bad behavior was powerfully determined by a rotten childhood, Linehan could have. His past could not excuse his crimes, but early and effective social services intervention might have prevented them. Ironically, decades later, after the abuse and the crimes, after the time in prison, when his maturation had dampened his violence and increased his control, the state sought to lock him up for treatment.

In the early 1990s Linehan's case was among a handful of psychopathic personality cases working their way through the Minnesota courts. Ahead of Linehan's, the Minnesota Supreme Court heard the case of Phillip Blodgett. Blodgett did not challenge the finding that he fit the *Pearson* standard—rather, he mounted a head-on attack on the idea of predator commitments, claiming that, even as narrowed in *Pearson,* the statute was unconstitutional. The court rejected his challenge, noting that the state had the power to use civil commitment to lock up individuals who had such severe mental disorders that they exhibited an "utter lack of power to control." The Court upheld the statute, but three of the seven justices dissented, reasoning that the application of civil commitment in the absence of a true "mental illness" was unconstitutional.

Along with the dissenters, the majority opinion in *Blodgett* warned against an overly broad, and therefore abusive, use of the predator commitment laws. But the *potential* for abuse was not enough to strike down the statute: "The remedy for misapplication is not to declare the statute unconstitutional but to appeal erroneous decisions and get them reversed." Appellate courts, in other words, had the responsibility to enforce the constitutional limits on predator commitments.

As if to show that it was serious about applying strict constraints on civil commitment of sex offenders, the court promptly reversed the commitments in the next two cases to come before it. Peter Rickmyer was a "non-violent pedophile" who had been convicted of indecent exposure and "spanking" young boys over their clothes on the buttocks. Predator commitments should be limited to the "most dangerous," and the court found that his case did not involve the kind of danger necessary to invoke civil commitment. The other case was Linehan's. The court reversed his commitment because the state had not proved the "lack of power to control" element.

Thus, the first chapter of the *Linehan* case ended with a clear message from the Minnesota Supreme Court. Real limits bounded the state's ability to use civil commitment to bypass the constitutional protections of the criminal law, and the court would enforce those limitations.

The message may have been clear, but it was not welcome. Almost immediately, intense criticism erupted. The court's ruling quickly hit the headlines: In a *Minneapolis–St. Paul Star Tribune* article headlined "Specter of Freed Sex Predators Worries Officials," Mike Hatch, then a candidate for state attorney general, was quoted as urging the governor to call a special session of the legislature to "tighten" (more accurately, "loosen") the civil commitment law. Attacking the core limit articulated by the court (the "utter lack of power to control" standard) Hatch advocated focusing on the risk posed by offenders, rather than on their "psychological condition." A week later the same newspaper's headline blared: "Panel Blasts Court Decision to Free Sex Offenders." The article quoted State Representative David Bishop, who called Chief Justice A. M. Keith "the chief zookeeper of the zoo. . . . Now he's proposing to let the tigers out one by one to see if they're dangerous."

Despite the firestorm, the court stood by its decision, and Linehan was released from the state treatment facility and placed on "supervised release" status, under the control of the Department of Corrections. The state converted an old house on the grounds of the state prison to a single-person halfway house for Linehan. Two guards stayed with Linehan in the house around the clock. Although neither Linehan nor his lawyers knew it at the time, the residence contained four hidden closed-circuit TV cameras so that officers stationed outside of the house in a trailer could observe Linehan as he moved through the house, even out of the sightlines of the two guards. Those cameras observed him even when he went into the bathroom.

Within two months after the Minnesota Supreme Court's decision, the governor convened a special one-day session of the legislature, which unanimously passed a new predator law. The new law allowed commitment upon a finding that the individual had a past pattern of harmful sexual behavior, currently has a "sexual, personality, or other mental disorder or dysfunction," and, "as a result, is likely to engage in acts of harmful sexual conduct." Clearly aimed directly at Linehan, the new law specifically stated that no proof of lack of control was necessary.

Three days later, the state petitioned to have Linehan committed under the new Sexually Dangerous Persons law. As the trial began, the media headlined the story. The state brought in several of Linehan's sexual assault victims to be witnesses against him—even though the assaults had taken place decades before and the real issue in the trial supposedly concerned Linehan's mental condition at the time of the trial. The gallery in the courtroom was filled with reporters. The prosecutors and defense attorneys faced phalanxes of TV cameras as they left the courthouse each day. When the testimony from the victims finished, the trial turned to the subject matter ostensibly made relevant by the law, expert opinion about whether Linehan had the legally required "mental or personality disorder" and whether this, together with his past behavior, made him "likely" to reoffend. Unsurprisingly, the media coverage evaporated during the dry recitation of this expert evidence.

An Alternate Legal Universe

Sex predator commitment cases and criminal cases about sexual violence share one key feature: they both can result in long-term loss of liberty. Beyond that, they have little in common. Predator cases differ from criminal cases precisely because commitment cases bypass the constitutional protections that constrain the criminal law.

In essential detail, the Constitution dictates the shape of criminal procedure. Criminal prosecutions focus sharply on a well-defined question: Did the defendant commit the specific crime alleged, at the time and place specified, with criminal intent. Testimony is, for the most part, about facts in the real world. It is given by witnesses who personally observed those facts and who are in court, properly sworn, and available for cross-examination. Defendants have a right to silence; the secrets they reveal during psychiatric or medical treatment generally have no place in criminal trials. Criminal cases punish a person for an act freely chosen. With few exceptions, these cases exclude evidence about who a person is and what his character is like, both because that kind of evidence is considered irrelevant to determining whether he committed the crime charged and because the Constitution prohibits punishing a "status." We are supposed to punish people for what they have done in the past, not because of who they are.

In almost every way, predator commitment cases inhabit an alternate universe, an Alice-in-Wonderland world in which these normal rules are turned on their heads. Most fundamentally, they take away a person's liberty not as punishment for a past act but to protect against a feared, but uncertain, future act. Where criminal prosecution requires specific allegations of a particular act that violates a specific law, predator cases allege vague future harm, at some unspecified place, under unstated circumstances, and at indefinite times. Predator cases are unambiguously about "who" a person is—what his character is, what his "propensities" are, what "risk" he poses. Predator cases incarcerate people for the status of being a dangerous mentally disordered person, so the relevant "facts" are psychological constructs, whose only reality is in the expert judgment of mental health professionals.

Once a person is caught in the spotlight of a predator commitment, everything the individual says or does is subject to interpretation, woven into the professional's diagnosis and prediction. Much of the foundation for the expert opinions comes from the voluminous records of prisons and treatment facilities. Key information is based on the unsworn handwritten notes of institutional guards and attendants, whose propensity for accurate and unbiased observation is unknown, and whose absence from the courtroom shields them from cross-examination. Much of the rest of the information comes from the mouth of the person subject to loss of liberty, because in predator commitments, the Fifth Amendment right of silence and the confidentiality of psychological treatment are nullified.

Some aspects of these trials are Kafkaesque. If a person acknowledges that

there is a risk that he will reoffend, this is taken as an admission of his dangerous propensities. But if he states that he will not reoffend, this is taken as a lack
of insight and is counted as a risk factor. A person's misbehaviors and infrac-
tions, accumulated over decades in prisons and treatment institutions, are me-
thodically recorded, listed, and recited. Good behavior is rarely documented
and is, in any event, deemed irrelevant, given the total control of these institutions. Worse, good behavior can actually count as a risk factor. Reflecting on
Linehan's years of incident-free prison life, one of the psychologists at Linehan's trial opined that Linehan could "make himself look good," finding in this
further evidence of Linehan's sophisticated ability to manipulate and cover up
his inherent dangerousness.

Unsurprisingly, predator trials devolve into a battle of the experts, in which
opposing attorneys each deploy their chosen psychologists in a game of chess,
moving abstract diagnoses and risk assessments to gain advantage. The connection between these abstractions and the real world is hard to discern, except that the stakes—the liberty and safety of real persons—are high.

"Subtler Acts Take on Larger Meanings"

The expert judgments offered at Linehan's 1995 trial under the new predator
law were roughly equally balanced. All of the mental health professionals who
testified agreed that Linehan could be diagnosed as having an "antisocial personality disorder," a diagnosis shared by a large majority of incarcerated criminals. But there was no consensus that he had any sort of disorder of sexual
deviancy (known as a "paraphilia"). All of the mental health professionals who
had worked with or treated Linehan either testified that his risk was manage-
able in the community or that they were unable to assess the risk. The state's
experts thought the risk was too great.

The trial judge's assessment was that the battle of the experts was a draw.
He was convinced Linehan had an "antisocial personality disorder" but made
no findings as to any other type of mental disorder. On the question of risk, he
thought that neither side's experts had the clear advantage.

The judge's conundrum is not surprising. How does one predict what a
fifty-two-year-old will do based on his behavior when he was in his twenties
and thirties? What weight should one give to good behavior in prison, to the
completion of chemical dependency and sex offender treatment, to the maturation that comes with age? The trial judge, a seasoned and highly competent
jurist, displayed his honesty and wisdom as he described how he found his way
to a conclusion: "In assessing whether his current conduct bodes well for the

future, one has to look for more subtle signs than rape and killing. For this reason, [Linehan's] subtler acts take on larger meanings."

In the end, the trial court seemed to discard the abstractions of the psychologists, finding three "subtle signs" to be persuasive. A psychologist testified that Linehan had said in the course of their interview that he "has only caused a total of twelve hours of misery to others." A correctional officer testified that he had overhead Linehan say in a telephone conversation in reference to one of his victims: "Any girl who placed herself in the same position that [she] did deserved what she got."

The third subtle sign requires a bit of background but deserves mention because of what it says about predator commitments. Though Linehan had been in prison for almost three decades, he had struck up a relationship with a woman on the outside, and they eventually married. She had a daughter from a previous relationship, and the girl became Linehan's stepdaughter. During the time that Linehan was in the halfway house, his wife often came to visit Linehan and sometimes brought her daughter, who was then nine years old. Present in the house at all times were two correctional guards, who kept Linehan (and his visitors) under observation. These guards had permitted Linehan and his wife to sit or lie together, fully clothed, on Linehan's bed—which was no more than a dozen feet from one of the guards who sat at a desk to observe. The guards permitted Linehan and his wife to have some physical contact, what might be described as light "making out," but not "heavy necking" and nothing approaching sexual intercourse. Meanwhile, the nine year old, growing bored, would zoom around the small house, jump up on the bed and pester the adults to pay attention to her. The girl sometimes momentarily came into physical contact with Linehan, and at least once she sat on his lap or thigh and he bounced her up and down. During several visits, Linehan got up from the bed and went upstairs to the bathroom, returning several minutes later.

Linehan and his wife did not know that they were being observed not only by the two guards who were physically present in the house but also by an officer in the trailer outside of the house, who was watching the feed from the four hidden cameras in the house. This officer could observe Linehan in the bathroom—from the chest up—and concluded that Linehan was masturbating in the bathroom (out of sight of the wife and the girl). In the guard's mind, the masturbation was associated with Linehan's "intense play" with the stepdaughter (and not Linehan's concurrent physical contact with his wife). The juxtaposition of the masturbation and the contact with the girl sickened the officer. He reported it up the line.

These events took place just as Linehan's trial was beginning, and they assumed some importance at the trial. The judge found the masturbation "significant." Despite the fact that a guard in the house had directly observed Line-han's contact with the girl and had found nothing untoward about it, the judge concluded that Linehan's masturbation showed that Linehan had "a continu-ing sexual attraction to young females" and "suggest[ed] a degree of impul-sivity and lack of control in connection with sexual impulses." Putting these "subtle signs" together with Linehan's history of violence, the judge found that it was "highly probable" that Linehan would commit further acts of harm-ful sexual behavior. The judge committed Linehan as a "sexually dangerous person," and he was transferred from the halfway house to the secure treat-ment facility housing the Minnesota Sex Offender Program.

On appeal, this decision reached the Minnesota Supreme Court in 1996, where Nudell and I, as Linehan's lawyers, argued that the new law—omitting all reference to inability to control—was too broad. Linehan's "antisocial per-sonality disorder" was not sufficient to justify civil commitment. We argued that the *Pearson* standard—"utter lack of power to control"—expressed the constitutional standard. Under the Constitution, we argued, civil commitment had to be the exception, not the rule. If Linehan's "antisocial personality dis-order" was a constitutionally sufficient mental condition, then the state's ability to use civil commitment would be boundless. As one author put it, "Applying the diagnosis antisocial personality to imprisoned offenders [is like] looking for hay in a haystack."[3]

The court's decision accepted the major premise of our argument but not its conclusion:

> Linehan raises important issues and valid concerns in a difficult field of consti-
> tutional law. Substantive due process forecloses the substitution of preventive
> detention schemes for the criminal justice system, and the judiciary has a consti-
> tutional duty to intervene before civil commitment becomes the norm and crimi-
> nal prosecution the exception. . . . But that is not this case.

Linehan's antisocial personality disorder and the risk he posed were sufficient, according to the court, to support his commitment. Thus, in the second chap-ter of the *Linehan* case, the Minnesota Supreme Court abandoned its clear promise to enforce narrow boundaries on predator commitments. Even the ubiquitous "antisocial personality disorder" would suffice for commitment, and predictions of dangerousness could be founded on "subtle signs."

In the Highest Courts

Meanwhile, litigation challenging predator commitment laws was proceeding in other states. A trial court in Wisconsin and a federal court in Washington found those commitment laws unconstitutional, while the supreme courts of Wisconsin and Washington joined the Minnesota Supreme Court in upholding the laws. In 1996, the Kansas Supreme Court became the fourth state supreme court to rule on the constitutionality of a new predator commitment law and the first state supreme court to find the newly crafted law unconstitutional. Having denied review on the prior three cases, the U.S. Supreme Court agreed to hear Kansas's appeal in the *Hendricks* case.

Hendricks presented the Supreme Court with a question that it had rarely faced so squarely before: What are the *substantive* boundaries on the state's power to use civil commitment to deprive a person of liberty? In 1975, the Supreme Court had held in *Donaldson* that states could not confine people in mental hospitals who were not in some sense dangerous. Then, a series of cases had led some observers to believe that dangerousness was not only necessary but also sufficient to support civil commitment. Under this approach, as long as the state's purpose was not to punish, it could deprive "dangerous" people of their liberty (preventively detain them) even if they were not mentally ill. But the Court dealt this broad theory a serious setback in its 1992 *Foucha* case, in which it said that dangerousness alone was not enough to support commitment. "Mental illness"—along with dangerousness—were the necessary constitutional predicates for civil commitment.

The arguments in the *Hendricks* case approached this important task of setting boundaries by two conceptually separate, but clearly related, routes. The legal theory favored by most of the challengers to state predator commitment laws was that they were not really "civil" commitment laws but actually criminal laws masquerading as civil laws. Critics argued that the states adopted these laws in order to continue the punishment of sex offenders who otherwise would be released from prison. If true, the predator laws would violate two provisions of the Constitution. The clause relating to double jeopardy prevents a state from lengthening a criminal sentence after it has been imposed. The ex post facto clause prevents a state from increasing the punishment for a crime after the crime has been committed. In support of these arguments, critics pointed to the origins of the laws, which arose precisely because criminal sentences were too short and too inflexible to deal with the perceived danger of certain offenders. Civil commitment was intended to do what the Constitution prohibited: lengthen the incarceration of offenders who were considered too dangerous to release from prison.

The Supreme Court quickly identified the fundamental weakness in this argument. States routinely use civil commitment to protect against harm (to self or others) by severely mentally ill and mentally retarded persons. These traditional civil commitment laws are constitutionally valid even though they have public protection as a purpose. Thus, the bare fact that predator laws had public protection as their avowed purpose did not suffice to paint them as punitive and thus unconstitutional.

The better argument acknowledged that predator laws are not really criminal laws and, instead, claimed that they exceed the constitutionally allowable scope of *civil* laws. This argument is known as the "substantive due process" argument. Beginning with the principle from the *Foucha* case that civil commitment is not constitutional unless the individual is both dangerous and "mentally ill," it argues that predator laws confine people who do not exhibit the kind or severity of "mentally illness" required under the *Foucha* standard.

This issue of what kind of "mental illness" is constitutionally required became the center of the legal debate. What is it that marks a person as appropriate for the reduced-rights zone of civil commitment? In what way does a person's "mental or personality disorder" give the state the green light to bypass the normal protections of the criminal law? These questions, hard enough on their face, are made more difficult by the fundamental disagreements even among psychiatrists about what constitutes a "mental disorder." Psychiatry, acknowledging that the "concept of mental disorder . . . lacks a consistent operational definition,"[4] debates whether particular patterns of personality or behavior—such as rape—qualify for the category.

The Supreme Court's 1997 decision in *Hendricks* upheld the constitutionality of the Kansas law and in doing so gave somewhat mixed messages on this central question. The Court affirmed that some form of mental impairment was constitutionally required for civil commitment, but it rejected a narrow or technical definition of "mental illness," suggesting instead that states retain great latitude in defining the conditions sufficient for civil commitment. Then, in a move that echoed the sixty-year-old *Pearson* standard, the Court seemed to embrace a much more restrictive constitutional boundary for predator commitments. The Court's opinion focused considerable attention on the notion—first raised in *Pearson* in 1939—that a mental disorder becomes sufficient to justify predator commitments only if it impairs the person's ability to control his behavior: "States have in certain narrow circumstances provided for the forcible civil detainment of people who are unable to control their behavior and who thereby pose a danger to the public health and safety." The Court emphasized that the scope of civil commitment is narrowed by focusing only on a "small but extremely dangerous group of sexually violent predators," "a limited subclass of dangerous persons," "only a narrow class of particularly dangerous individuals."

Five years after *Hendricks*, the Supreme Court decided a second sexual predator commitment case. In *Crane*, the Court resolved much of this ambiguity, holding that states did not have unlimited discretion to define the "mental disorder" that is a prerequisite for predator commitments. Emphasizing the need to place narrow bounds around civil commitment, the Court held that a "mental disorder" is constitutionally adequate only if it "*distinguish[es]* a dangerous sexual offender subject to civil commitment from other dangerous persons who are perhaps more properly dealt with exclusively through criminal proceedings." (Emphasis added.) The Court pointed to two factors that support this constitutional distinction. First, the individual must suffer from a condition the "psychiatric profession itself classifie[s] . . . as a serious mental disorder." Second,

> there must be proof of serious difficulty in controlling behavior . . . [that] must be *sufficient to distinguish* the dangerous sexual offender whose serious mental illness, abnormality, or disorder subjects him to civil commitment from the *dangerous but typical recidivist* convicted in an ordinary criminal case. (Emphasis added)

The bottom line of the message from the Court is that people subject to civil commitment must in some sense be *different* from ordinary recidivist criminals. The difference does not reside simply in their dangerousness (though it must be serious) but in their "special and serious lack of ability to control behavior." It is this condition, the Court said, that will "distinguish" committable people from the "dangerous but typical [criminal] recidivist."

After its decision in *Hendricks* (but before its decision in *Crane*), the U.S. Supreme Court addressed the petition for review in the *Linehan* case. The Court vacated the judgment and remanded the case to the Minnesota Supreme Court with instructions to reexamine its decision. This remand placed the Minnesota court in a dilemma. In 1939 it had held that "inability to control" was the defining feature of predator commitments. Its 1994 decisions in *Blodgett* and *Linehan* had relied on that standard. But the legislature had challenged the state court by stating in the new predator law that "it is not necessary to prove that the person has an inability to control the person's sexual impulses," and the court had bowed to the legislative command to cast the commitment net broadly. Now, the U.S. Supreme Court seemed to say, in *Hendricks*, that "inability to control" was indeed the standard for commitment, a principle that was later confirmed in *Crane*.

Reversing itself for a second time, the Minnesota Supreme Court reinterpreted the "not necessary to prove" language of the new predator law. Engaging in legalistic hairsplitting, the court said that the new law simply meant that the state need not prove the *Pearson* standard—"utter lack of power to control"—but did require the state to prove that the individual has a mental "disorder or dysfunction [that] does not allow the person to *adequately* control his or her behavior." This requirement, the court asserted, satisfied the standard articulated by the United States Supreme Court. Applying this standard to the facts in the *Linehan* case, the Minnesota Supreme Court held that the "subtle" signs pointed to by the trial court—the masturbation in particular—demonstrated that Linehan lacked "adequate" control over his sexual behavior and that this proof was constitutionally sufficient to support indefinite commitment.

So ended the third and final chapter of the *Linehan* litigation. From this story, we can pick out the broad contours of the judicial struggle to deal with the Constitution-challenging predator laws. The vacillation of the Minnesota Supreme Court—first promising strict limits, then bowing to intense popular and legislative pressure for expansive powers, then adopting a minimalist version of its initial limits—is a clear manifestation of two powerful but contrary forces: on the one hand, the compelling narratives of sexual violence and the popular mandate for protection; on the other, the centrality of the "great safeguards" of the Constitution and the need to confine their breach to a narrow and extraordinary zone.

This same tension appears in the U.S. Supreme Court cases. On the one hand, the Court approved the use of predator commitments in the face of clear evidence that their central purpose was to bypass the limits of the criminal law. On the other, the Court insisted that the bypass was to be narrowly limited to those who are "different" from ordinary criminals. Volitional control—the ability to *freely control* one's own actions—is a hallmark of what it means to be fully human. By focusing on an impairment of self-control, the Court was reassuring us that the normal protections of the Constitution are preserved for those who are fully human and that they may be denied only to those who lack the capacity that characterizes human beings—self-determination. This is a promise to us that the encroachment on constitutional rights has a principled limitation that will protect us from its expansion.

The Linehan litigation adds an ominous end to this story. There is an abyss between the judicial rhetoric of constitutional limitations and their practical application to individual targets of state intervention. The fact that the Minnesota courts found the "subtle signs" sufficient to impose a profound deprivation of liberty suggests that the lofty constitutional promises are hollow. The legal standards set by the courts for risk, mental disorder, and volitional impairment are exceedingly vague, offering little guidance to courts or experts in selecting people for the extraordinary deprivation of liberty.

Studies of committed populations show wide variation on several measures that are closely associated with the likelihood of future offending and the severity of the past offenses exhibited by these individuals.[5] Though it seems probable that committed offenders are, as a group, more dangerous than those who are not committed,[6] some experts in a position to know conclude that a substantial percentage of the men held in predator programs would not present an unmanageable risk in the community.[7] In one of the few studies of the ability of forensic psychologists to accurately apply the legal criteria for predator commitments, the researchers found that experts were "accurate in their predictions of future sexual violence approximately one-half of the time."[8]

"Difficulty controlling" behavior is ubiquitous among "normal" human beings. Many people have difficulty—serious difficulty—controlling their eating, smoking, gambling, alcohol or drug use, computer gaming, or work hours. Of course, none of these is as dangerous to others as sexual violence—but the point of the "volitional dysfunction" requirement is to identify some mental characteristic of commitment candidates that distinguishes them from others. Impaired self-control does not accomplish this. The legal standards for volitional impairment are so vague that they are unlikely to provide any kind of guidance or limitation on commitment decisions.

The courts would have us believe that predator commitments are safely contained, that our constitutional rights are preserved, because commitments address people who are different in kind from the rest of us. But in the technical details of the legal system, as the broad principles of limitation are interpreted and applied in individual cases, these hopeful principles of constitutional limitation are largely eviscerated. The rhetoric is preserved; the evisceration is nearly invisible, announced not in the forceful language of appellate courts but in the silent findings of fact of hundreds of local courts.

But those who work with predator commitments understand that the constitutional assurances are mere window dressing. Stephen Huot, then the clinical director of Minnesota's predator program, stated the truth plainly when he said, "They are not a totally different breed of human beings [from those who are not committed]. The difference is that there is a little more [criminal] history for those committed, or a little more violence."[9] But not, apparently, a little more "inability to control." And they are certainly not "different in kind."

If we are honest, we know that the constitutional pronouncements are a fig leaf, designed to cover the embarrassment of a law that plainly breaks from fundamental American principles of freedom.

CHAPTER THREE

A Factual Primer on Sexual Violence

They're everywhere.

From the low-rent district of Suncoast Estates in North Fort Myers to the wealthy, gated enclave of Bonita Bay. On the sandy beaches of Sanibel and Fort Myers Beach and in the family neighborhoods of Cape Coral and Lehigh Acres.

About 400 registered sex offenders saunter about Lee County each day. They live near schools and playgrounds, nursing homes and parks.

"We don't like it, but we know it," said Mary Miller, 81, a 22-year resident of Suncoast Estates who lives about a half-mile from a sex offender. "I'm concerned for the young people, because, well, once a thief always a thief."

—*Lee County* (Florida) *News Press*

Public's Overriding Fear: Will They Do It Again? Anxiety Remains Despite Low Recidivism among Many [Sex] Offenders.

—*San Francisco Chronicle* headline

Suppose a policymaker, seeking to design a rational program to combat sexual violence, wanted to know which of the following groups posed the greatest risk: (a) people with a prior conviction for a sex crime; (b) people with a prior conviction for a crime of violence; (c) people without either a prior

Portions of this chapter are based on Eric S. Janus, "Treatment and the Civil Commitment of Sex Offenders," in *Protecting Society from Dangerous Offenders: Law, Justice, and Therapy*, ed. Bruce J. Winick and John Q. LaFond (Washington, D.C.: American Psychiatric Association, 2003), 119–30, and on Eric S. Janus and Robert A. Prentky, "The Forensic Use of Actuarial Risk Assessment with Sex Offenders: Accuracy, Admissibility and Accountability," *American Criminal Law Review* 40 (2003): 1443.

Epigraph sources are Wendy Fullerton, "Tracking Sexual Offenders: Lee Sheriff's Program Provides 24/7 Monitoring," *News-press.com*, April 18, 2004, http://www.news-press.com; and Jim Doyle, *San Francisco Chronicle*, July 12, 2004.

Table 1. Risks of sex crime relative to prior conviction

Offense history	Individual risk	Group risk
(a) Prior conviction for a sex offense	Highest	Lowest
(b) At least one prior conviction for a violent offense	Middle	Middle
(c) No prior conviction for a violent offense	Lowest	Highest

conviction for a crime of violence or a sex crime. Most of us would have some intuitions about the answer. But careful attention to scientific data might provide some surprising—and useful—insights.

First, empirical studies would confirm what most of us would probably guess—that people convicted of a sex crime are more likely than people convicted of nonsex crimes to commit a sex crime after release from prison. So, if we looked at the risk posed by any particular individual, the risk that that person would commit a sex crime would be (in decreasing order): (a), (b), (c).

But, if we consider each of these categories as a group, and ask how much risk the group poses, the order is reversed (summarized in table 1). It turns out that most sex crimes—at least those that result in a prison sentence—are committed by people who have never before been convicted of a violent offense. Group (c) produces 75 percent of the people imprisoned for sex crimes. Group (b), those with a history of a violent offense, comprises about 25 percent of imprisoned sex offenders. People with prior sex offender convictions, group (a), pose the smallest risk of all—they produce only about 14 percent of the sex convicts in prison.[1]

It is not immediately apparent what the implications of these rankings are in the design of a public policy to combat sexual violence. Should we concentrate on the highest-risk individuals or the highest-risk group? This is the issue that is addressed in part 3 of this book. The point made here is that we do not even begin to ask this question, and we do not have the tools to attempt to answer it, unless we pay attention to empirical research findings about sexual violence.

Scientific knowledge about sexual violence and abuse is incomplete but growing. If we are serious about preventing as much sexual violence as possible, our public policy ought to be fully informed by what we do know, and to support research into what we do not. Science can help us understand the root causes of sexual violence so that we can seek to change those conditions in our society. Empirical research is critical for giving us a clear vision of the scope of sexual violence and the circumstances in which it is manifested. Without careful research findings, our ability to identify and assess the risk of sexual violence will be limited. Our notions of what works to reduce the risk will be mere guesses.

Our policy ought to respect science in two ways. First, the findings of science ought to be directly reflected in the underlying assumptions that shape our public policy. Do most sex offenders reoffend, or do only a few? Are most sexual offenses directed against strangers, or against acquaintances? Can we meaningfully assess the risk posed by particular individuals? Are there any interventions, such as treatment or supervision, that reduce the risk? The answers to these and similar questions should affect how we construct our laws.

Second, we ought to be identifying the gaps in our knowledge. Our government should support research designed to fill those gaps and reduce the uncertainty under which we are operating. Research into the patterns and rates of recidivism has burgeoned in the past decade. But our empirical knowledge about what kinds of interventions might work to address the root causes of sexual violence, or reduce an offender's risk of reoffending, is still in preliminary stages.

This book is about policy and law and is not a scientific or technical manual about the nature of sexual violence or how best to manage it. Still, it is important to touch on the state of our scientific knowledge. One reason is that, as noted, scientific knowledge should shape our public policy by helping us understand how best to prevent sexual violence. Failure to use science in this way is a missed opportunity to be as effective as we can be in prevention. A major thesis of this book is that our current policies do not match very well with what we know empirically, that science has been in large measure ignored. If this is correct, then every day there are people who are needlessly becoming victims of sexual violence that could be prevented by a more informed public policy.

There should be a strong link between science and public policy. But there can be a danger if the link becomes too strong. Science cannot—indeed should not—determine public policy on sexual violence in any kind of automatic way. Empirical knowledge must be disseminated to, and understood by, policymakers. It must be interpreted and used properly. And it must be filtered through the values (moral, political), fears, and aspirations of our democratic society.

We can identify three ways that science and law might be connected too closely. First, the law might claim undeserved legitimacy from its link with science. The fact that predator commitment laws rely extensively on behavioral science experts does not remedy the essential standardlessness of these schemes. Second, there is a danger that what is scientifically possible will become politically necessary. There is a real worry that as increasing knowledge of the nature of violence gives rise to an enhanced ability to predict who will become violent, pressure will grow for the law to use that new knowledge in ways that challenge our basic democratic principles. Finally, the ways in which the law and public policy influence science need to be carefully monitored and managed. The introduction of the predator laws has provided strong encouragement for research into recidivism and risk assessment. This is a positive connection. On the negative side, focus in sex predator commitment proceedings on the "mental disorder" of the offender has clearly put pressure on behavioral science experts to develop new definitions of mental disorder to describe criminal sexual behavior. This is a negative result, a distortion of science in service to the law. It is a result that can only weaken the foundations both of science and of our public agenda against sexual violence.

Science can contribute to the sound design of public policy on sexual violence in four major areas. First, what is the scope of sexual violence in our society? What is the nature and scope of the risk viewed from the perspective of the society as a whole? Second, what can we say about the risk posed by particular individuals? Do sex offenders frequently repeat their crimes? Can we differentiate high-risk from low-risk individuals? Third, what are the root causes of sexual violence? Lastly, what interventions are effective in reducing sexual violence, either on a societal or an individual basis?

The Scope of Sexual Violence

At the center of many of the public policy debates lies the deceptively simple question of describing and measuring sexually abusive behavior. Obtaining an accurate picture of sex offending in the United States is complicated by the variety of measures used, as well as changing definitions of sexual offending. Traditionally, offending has been measured by collecting statistics from law enforcement authorities about the number and disposition of crimes reported to them. But this undercounts crime, because many crimes are not reported to authorities. This problem is particularly severe for sexual crimes. The National Crime Victimization Survey (NCVS) attempts to address this issue by going directly to the public—actually a representative sample—and asking them about the crimes they have experienced.[2]

Another complication in the measurement of sexual violence is that the definition of the phenomenon has been highly contested. A major thrust of the feminist-inspired reforms of recent decades has been to reconceptualize sexual violence, expanding the concept so that it more clearly includes unwanted sex between acquaintances and intimates and sex between adults and children. In the early 1990s the National Crime Victimization Survey was reworded to inquire more inclusively about sexual assaults and other unwanted sexual contacts. The modified survey was estimated to have measured rates of sexual violence four times higher than previously measured.[3]

Sexual violence is widespread. The National Crime Victimization Survey estimated that there were 198,850 rapes and sexual assaults of persons over twelve in 2003, with a rate of 0.8 per thousand individuals. Based on law enforcement reports (rather than direct questioning of crime victims), the Uniform Crime Reports estimate 93,433 forcible rapes in 2003. In a 1995–96 National Violence against Women Survey by the National Institute of Justice and the Centers for Disease Control and Prevention, 17.6 percent of women, and 3 percent of men, reported having been raped at some time in their life.[4]

Sexual violence is mainly directed at the young. The rate of sexual assault varies dramatically with the age of the victim. Persons under age twenty-five experienced 4.4 sexual assaults per thousand; the rate for those ages twenty-five to forty-nine was 2.1, and for those age fifty and older, 0.1.[5] Two-thirds of sex offenders in state prisons in 1991 committed their crimes against children under age eighteen.[6] Most victims of rape (forced sexual intercourse) are adults (63%), while most victims of sexual assaults (other forms of unwanted sex) are eighteen or younger (78%).[7]

Sexual violence is predominantly committed by relatives or acquaintances. About 69 percent of female victims of rape were victimized by someone known to them.[8] When rape and sexual assault are combined, nearly 60 percent of such crimes were reported by victims to have occurred in their own home or at the home of a friend, relative, or neighbor. In the National Violence against Women Survey, 7.7 percent of the surveyed women reported that they had been sexually assaulted by an intimate partner at some time in their lives.[9] About 30 percent of imprisoned rapists, and less than 15 percent of imprisoned sexual assaulters, reported that their victim had been a stranger to them. Fewer than 10 percent of the inmates incarcerated for sexual assault of children reported that their victims had been strangers to them. Sixty-eight percent of child molesters molest someone in their own family, and 40 percent molest children in their "social circle."[10] Victims of rape and sexual assault report that in nearly three out of four incidents the offender was not a stranger. Based on police-recorded incident data, in 90 percent of the rapes of children younger than twelve, the child knew the offender; two-thirds of the victims eighteen to twenty-nine years old had a prior relationship with the rapist.[11]

Many sexual assaults are "hidden." Despite the ubiquity of sexual assault, a substantial proportion of sexual abuse is never reported to law enforcement authorities and never enters the criminal justice system. The National Crime Victimization Survey indicated that only 53 percent of female victims of rape reported the crime to police. The proportion of victims who made official reports increased to 61 percent when the crime was completed rather than attempted, 65 percent when additional physical injuries were sustained by the victim, and 75 percent when the victim received medical care.[12] The rate of reporting when the offender was a stranger was dramatically higher than when the offender was a nonstranger (in one study, "disclosure was 3.69 times more likely to occur when the perpetrator was a stranger").[13] In 2003, 44 percent of forcible rapes known to police were cleared by arrest. In larger cities, the clearance rate was 48.5 percent, while in smaller cities the rate was lower.[14]

Most sex offenders are in the community. As the preceding paragraph makes clear, many sexual offenses are never reported to authorities, or never solved by authorities. So the perpetrators of those unreported offenses remain—at least for the time being—in the community. But even most of those offenders who are apprehended will either remain in, or be returned to, the community. Of those arrested for rape, about half are released pending trial.[15] Nearly 60 percent of sex offenders who are under the control of correctional authorities are under supervision in the community, not incarcerated in jails or prisons.[16] Most sex offenders who are serving time in prison will be released to the community after their sentences are served.

Sexual homicides are extremely rare. The most visible sexual assaults are those in which the rapist kills the victim. For the most part, it is these rape-murders that generate the intense public pressure for more effective and tougher responses to sexual violence. Fortunately, rape-murders are rare. In her book *Harmful to Minors: The Perils of Protecting Children from Sex,* Judith Levine discusses estimates of the number of stranger-murders of children, only some of which involve rape:

> Studies commissioned under the Missing Children's Assistance Act of 1984 estimate that between 52 and 158 children will be abducted and murdered by nonfamily members each year. Extrapolating from other FBI statistics, those odds come out between 1 in 364,000 and fewer than 1 in 1 million. A child's risk of dying in a car accident is twenty-five to seventy-five times greater.

David Finkelhor, director of the Crimes against Children Research Center at the University of New Hampshire, estimates that forty to fifty of the sixty to seventy thousand arrests each year for sex crimes against children involve homicide.[17] Franklin Zimring reports that there were 160 sex crime–related killings in 1998–99, amounting to about 0.5 percent of the homicide arrests in the United States,[18] a finding consistent with the 0.7 percent figure cited in another study.[19] Compared to the number of sex-related arrests during the same period (27,469 rapes, 93,399 "other noncommercial sex offenses"), the rape-murders constituted about 0.1 percent of sex crime arrests.

Recidivism

The fear of sex offender recidivism is at the very core of the predator legislation. The key "legislative finding" supporting the state of Washington's predator legislation reads: "Sex offenders' likelihood of engaging in repeat acts of predatory sexual violence is high."[20] The Florida Sexual Predators Act states: "Sex offenders are extremely likely to use physical violence and to repeat their offenses."[21] And a draft bill in Minnesota that would have increased sentences for sex offenders declared that sex offenders are "particularly likely to be dangerous after their release from imprisonment."[22]

The claim is not simply that sex offenders repeatedly commit sex crimes. Recidivism has the more particular meaning that sex offenders continue to commit sex crimes even after they have been caught, convicted, and punished. Recidivists are sex criminals who have not (and perhaps cannot) learn the deterrence lesson intended by criminal punishment.

Obtaining accurate information about recidivism rates is a challenging undertaking. Researchers must specify the criterion for recidivism: Is it rearrest? Reconviction? Revocation of parole or other supervised release? It turns out that offenders continue to reoffend over a long period of time. Thus researchers must determine over how long a period offenders will be tracked. Recidivism research is necessarily conducted on a limited sample of offenders, so there is always a question about whether the sample is sufficiently representative of sex offenders in general.

Most of these concerns can be addressed through careful definition. A more intractable problem, however, concerns the inability of researchers to discover all offenses that an offender commits. The problem, at bottom, is that many sexual offenses are not reported to authorities, and, of those that are, some are never resolved through arrest or conviction. Because recidivism researchers most often must rely on official sources (such as arrest and conviction records), it follows that measured recidivism rates will be somewhat lower than actual rates of reoffense. According to one respected researcher, Karl Hanson, a "reasonable estimate would be that actual recidivism rates are at least 10% to 15% higher than the observed rates."[23]

Despite the difficulties, increasingly accurate information about sex offender recidivism has been developed, alongside the predator laws, in the past fifteen years. This information presents a more complex picture than acknowledged by the legislative findings and political pronouncements. The foundational assumption—that sex offenders have an extraordinarily high rate of recidivism—is, at best, problematic.

In a large, nationwide study, the Department of Justice tracked all 9,691 male sex offenders released from prisons in fifteen states in 1994. This group represented two-thirds of all male sex offenders released in the United States in that year. The study tracked the men for a three-year period after their release. The results were surprising to many and seemed to confound the basic assumption of the predator laws. During the three-year follow-up period, almost 95 percent of the released sex offenders were *not* arrested for a new sex offense. The rate of sexual recidivism—rearrest for a new sex crime during the follow-up period—was 5.3 percent. The rate at which convicted child molesters were rearrested for a new crime against a child was even lower—3.3 percent. Further confounding the common wisdom, the study found that sex offenders were less likely to be rearrested for any kind of crime than were non-sex offenders. In fact, an earlier similar study by the Department of Justice found that sex offenders had a same-crime reoffense rate that was, compared to other criminal groups, among the lowest.[24]

One finding in the Department of Justice study seemed to support the common stereotype. The sex offenders in the study were four times more likely to be rearrested for a new sex crime than were offenders who had not been convicted of a sex crime and had been simultaneously released from prison, a statistic cited repeatedly by courts and advocates to support the predator laws. For example, the Supreme Court's opinion upholding Alaska's Megan's law contains the following passage:

> The legislature's findings are consistent with grave concerns over the high rate of recidivism among convicted sex offenders and their dangerousness as a class. The risk of recidivism posed by sex offenders is "frightening and high." . . . When convicted sex offenders reenter society, they are much more likely than any other type of offender to be rearrested for a new rape or sexual assault.[25]

But the Justice Department study pointed out that the lower *rate* at which offenders that were not convicted of sex crimes commit such crimes after their release from prison is offset by the much larger *number* of such offenders compared to sex offenders. Thus, on the assumption that each of the criminals rearrested for a sex crime victimized no more than one victim, the Department of Justice study concluded that offenders not convicted of sex crimes account for 87 percent of the sex crimes committed by prisoners released from prisons.

As this short discussion suggests, the connection between sex offender recidivism and the design of public policy is not as straightforward as one might expect. From a policy-development perspective, there are three main insights that we can derive from the research on recidivism. First, recidivism is time dependent. Though a substantial proportion of sexual recidivism occurs relatively early in prisoners' reentry into society, the risk of reoffense continues for years. Generally accepted estimates of rates of sexual recidivism for sex offenders are 10–15 percent after five years, 20 percent after ten years, and 30–40 percent after twenty years.[26] In a large metastudy involving sixty-one different data sets and over twenty-three thousand offenders and an average follow-up period of four to five years, the recidivism rate for sexual offenses was 13.4 percent. A Minnesota study found that the recidivism rate for persons placed on *probation* after conviction of a sexual crime was 9 percent over seven and a half years.[27]

Second, the fact that most sex offenders are not rearrested for another sex crime even over extended periods of time in the community seems to highlight our intuition that *some* offenders are more dangerous than others. The construction of large databases of recidivism data has allowed researchers to attempt to subdivide sex offenders into stable subgroups that exhibit higher or lower rates of recidivism. The effort to do so is described in the section on "risk assessment."

Finally, we ought to stop to reflect on the powerful way in which our focus on recidivism as a measure for the level of sexual violence is a choice that has an important effect on the shape of the resulting public policy. Recall the table from the head of the chapter showing that we can look at the recidivism risk in two ways: as an individual measure of risk, and as a way to understand the amount of sexual crime generated by a group or population. We saw that the people who individually posed the highest risk actually posed the lowest aggregate risk, while the larger group of lower-risk individuals collectively caused the most sexual violence. Framing the problem in terms of "high" recidivism may make us miss the larger problem caused by "low" recidivism in a broader group.

But the use of recidivism exerts an even more powerful shaping influence because it directs all of our problem-solving energy to the period *after* a sex crime has been committed. By definition, recidivism is a measure of the crimes committed by released prisoners. Yet this is a small part of the problem. The vast majority of sexual violence is most likely not committed by released sex offenders. In fact, of the most serious sexual offenders (those who receive prison sentences) only one in seven had a prior conviction for a sex offense. By defining the problem in terms of recidivism and recidivists, we have automatically omitted from consideration most sexual violence. We have restricted our focus to the "downstream" part of the problem—those individuals who continue to offend even after they have gone to prison—and have rendered less visible the "upstream," but much larger, aspect of the problem.

Causes and Types of Sexual Violence

The etiology of sexual violence is not well understood. Proffered causes include political and economic forces in the society; cultural attitudes favoring aggression; social learning theory; misogynist values and attitudes; brain chemistry; evolutionary predispositions; deficient behavioral skills; anger and rage; deviant sexual preferences; impulsivity; low self-esteem; prior victimization; and bad moral choices. Most researchers agree, however, that sexual offending is complex and heterogeneous and that it has multiple independent causes.[28]

Two predominant theories of etiology are behavioral and biological. Behavioral theories suggest that deviant sexual arousal patterns develop through "conditioning" early in life. This combined with poor social skills makes appropriate relationships difficult and creates cognitive distortions that permit the individual to justify sexual offending.[29] Biological explanations for sexual violence focus on temporal lobe dysfunction, imbalanced male sex hormones, and misfiring neurotransmitters.[30]

The role of deviant sexual arousal patterns in causing sexual violence is unclear. Some studies have demonstrated that rapists are more likely to be aroused by depictions of violent sex than are nonrapists.[31] But other scholars suggest that rape is essentially a criminal rather than a sexual offense, and argue that rapists often engage in other forms of criminal activity as well.[32] Others argue that rape is essentially a misogynist act, reflecting attitudes and emotions toward women.[33] Further, although strong sexual attraction to children identifies some child molesters, others appear to attack children because they are vulnerable targets of opportunity.

In some studies, sex offenders are found to be substantially more likely than other offenders to report having experienced physical or sexual abuse while growing up. One study reports that more than 47 percent of the admitted child molesters had been sexually abused as children.[34] In another study, though, about two-thirds of sex offenders (rapists and child molesters) reported that they had never been physically or sexually abused as a child.[35]

Whatever the individual biosocial factors are that make some individuals more prone to sexually abusive behavior, many scholars—and most notably feminists—point to social and cultural overlays that "foster a rape conducive climate."[36] The precise role that these social and cultural factors play is unresolved and, indeed, forms a major undercurrent in social policy disputes about approaches to sexual violence. Nonetheless, the evidence seems clear, as noted by Robert Prentky and Ann Burgess, that "sexual aggression, in its many facets, represents institutionalized, normative behavior [and is] deeply ingrained and indelibly embedded in the social fabric."[37]

Predator commitment laws generally require, as a legal predicate for civil commitment, a finding that the individual's sexual offending behavior is linked to a "mental disorder or abnormality." Courts have been a bit coy about whether this statutory criterion is meant to require some kind of legitimate medical diagnosis or, alternatively, is strictly a legal concept, definable at the will of the legislature. As discussed earlier, the Supreme Court has explicitly said that in order to support predator commitments, the targeted individual's mental condition must evidence some impairment in the ability to control his behavior, and it must also serve to distinguish the individual from other, potentially dangerous criminals. The Court has also strongly suggested, but has not clearly held, that a valid medical diagnosis is a necessary condition for commitment.

These legal criteria are easily applied to the subset of sex offenders who repeatedly abuse young children. Many of these people are readily diagnosable with "pedophilia." This is a mental disorder defined in the *Diagnostic and Statistical Manual of Mental Disorders Fourth Edition* (DSM-IV-TR), the official diagnostic classification manual published by the American Psychiatric Association. This diagnosis applies to people who have recurrent intense sexual urges, fantasies, or behaviors involving sexual activity with a prepubescent child for at least six months. The intensity and the recurrence of the sexual urges seems to fit nicely with the legally required impairment of behavior control and also arguably provides a point of differentiation from "ordinary" criminals whose crimes seem less likely to be generated by such intense "drives."

But the definition of pedophilia does not cover people who abuse adolescents or rape adults. A small number of these people would be covered by the definition of "sadism," a disorder that, like pedophilia, falls under the broader category of disorders called "paraphilia," all of which share the quality of intense, recurrent sexual urges (in the case of sadism, involving the suffering of other people). But most sex offenders do not fall into this or any other category of paraphilia. Over the years, the question of whether the DSM should provide a diagnosis for rapists has provoked sharp controversy, but the APA has rejected such proposals.[38] Nonetheless, because some mental disorder diagnosis is required in the predator commitment context, mental health practitioners have begun to use unofficial diagnostic terms to label rapists ("paraphilia-rapism") and abusers of adolescents ("hebephilia"). Presumably, the motivation for this "definitional drift"[39] is to provide a mental disorder label that distinguishes these offenders from other sorts of recidivist criminals.

Some (perhaps a large proportion) of sex offenders can be diagnosed as having "personality disorders" such as "antisocial personality disorder." But this disorder—which essentially comprises a persistent pattern of criminal (or other antisocial) behavior and a set of attendant characteristics such as impulsivity is common among criminals of all types, and it does not in any way distinguish sex offenders or set them apart from other criminals.

Sex Offender Treatment

Sex offender treatment programs have evolved rapidly, and methods used twenty years ago are now considered inadequate and obsolete.[40] Professional and public policy views about the efficacy of treatment have changed as well. In the first half of the twentieth century, optimism about the powers of psychiatry produced a rash of sex offender commitment laws.[41] Pessimism about the efficacy of the treatment contributed to the demise of these laws in the 1970s and '80s.[42] An influential report in 1989 concluded: "There is as yet no evidence that clinical treatment reduces rates of sex offenses in general and no appropriate data for assessing whether it may be differentially effective for different types of offenders."[43]

But since that time, there has been significant work on the design and evaluation of sex offender treatment. There is no consensus about the efficacy of sex offender treatment. Some influential commentators believe that the evidence supports an "optimistic outlook" on the efficacy of treatment.[44] Others, conceding that "the jury is still out," find the evidence "encouraging."[45] Some respected commentators pessimistically conclude that "there is little evidence that high-quality, state-of-the-art treatments significantly reduce recidivism."[46] While some commentators claim that treatment of sex offenders is "successful" in 90 percent of cases, others are more conservative. A meta-analysis of sex offender treatment studies found a "small but robust treatment effect, medium sized with respect to outpatients, small with respect to inpatients."[47] A more recent meta-analytic study authored by five leading researchers, which considered a wide range of treatment studies of more than nine thousand offenders, found that sex offender treatment programs reduced recidivism rates from about 17 percent for untreated offenders to 10 percent for treated offenders, a reduction in rate of about 40 percent.[48] The Solicitor General of Canada noted that the "policy implications" of the study were that "treatment programs can contribute to public safety by reducing the risk of reoffending among sexual offenders."[49] One point seems clearly suggested and may well explain the variable assessments of the efficacy of treatment: well-designed treatment programs that follow established principles of offender treat-

ment are more likely than poorly designed programs to produce significant re-
ductions in recidivism.[50]

Treatment for sex offenders falls into several categories. Though nonbe-
havioral psychotherapy treatment was the norm until recently, researchers now
hold it to be ineffective.[51] Surgical castration shows good results in some settings, but it has not been shown to be effective for nonconsenting offenders or
sex offenders whose crimes reflect antisocial rather than sexually deviant impulses.[52]

Antiandrogen medications are used to achieve, through pharmacological
means, the same sex drive–reducing effects as surgical castration.[53] Though
some respected researchers conclude that these drugs can play an important
role in treating sex offenders,[54] others report that there is no research of efficacy among offenders who are forcibly medicated.[55] Some success has been reported with a class of drugs called selective serotonin reuptake inhibitors
(SSRIs) for sex offenders with concurrent mood or anxiety disorders. But further research on the effectiveness of these drugs is needed.[56]

The most common contemporary approach to treatment of sex offenders is
cognitive-behavioral treatment.[57] This technique seeks to change offenders'
beliefs and attitudes, and to increase their knowledge, skills, and empathy. Central to this form of therapy is "relapse prevention," which teaches strategies to
anticipate and resist deviant urges.[58] The APA Task Force on Sexually Dangerous Offenders concludes: "The treatment approach most likely to have an
effect on recidivism is a combined pharmacological, cognitive-behavioral, and
relapse prevention approach."[59]

One further point, which will be developed more in chapter 7, concerns
what happens after treatment. The best current thinking holds that treatment
must be followed up in the community with long-term, interdisciplinary, individualized supervision. A recently published, well-designed study of a sex
offender treatment program in California prisons attributed the failure to de-
tect a reduction in recidivism in part to the deficient design of the treatment
program and in part to the absence of follow-up with careful community
supervision.[60]

Risk Assessment and Prediction

From their beginnings, the sex predator laws were developed with a central feature in mind: that government can—and therefore should—protect us from
dangerous sex offenders. Who, exactly, these people are and how we would
identify them from the larger population was not immediately apparent to pol-

icymakers as issues that would need to be addressed. Once these people had committed the heinous murders and mutilations, their distinctiveness from the great mass of more harmless offenders seemed self-evident. Of course, to be at all effective these laws would need to be able to distinguish the "worst of the worst" before they commit their next offense, and this problem of prediction was much more intractable than knowing after the fact whom we wished we had locked up.

The task can be conceptualized in a couple of ways. The most common way of thinking about this problem has been to ask which offenders are "dangerous," in the sense that they would commit another crime. Since we cannot really know the future, the best we could do is predict whether each individual would reoffend. Based on these predictions, offenders would be sorted into two groups—the dangerous and the safe. Under this two-choice system, gradations of risk were difficult to ascertain. An alternate conceptualization conceives of offenders being classified by their risk of reoffense, which might vary from low to moderate to high. This risk assessment is not so much a prediction about the future as it is a statement about a certain present characteristic of the individual—his "risk."

The risk assessment model fits well with the predator laws. As mentioned, these laws require an accurate method to sort sex offenders into more than two categories. After all, the "worst of the worst" assumes that we can differentiate among the "worst," picking out for intervention a particular subgroup that poses a particularly severe risk. Accurate risk assessment is critical. The most obvious concern is a system that misses truly dangerous individuals, with the possible result of preventable sexual assaults. But the opposite problem— overestimating risk—is equally a concern. Prevention resources are expensive; accurate assessment helps policymakers ensure that the most expensive interventions—civil commitment and prison—are directed only at the most risky. Overprediction of dangerousness can result in a misallocation of resources. In the same vein, public notification schemes are effective only to the extent that they provide useful information that people can act on. Databases with tens of thousands of names, with no calibration of risk differences, provide scant guidance for action. Equally as important, the moral and legal justifications for the extraordinary deprivations of liberty in the predator laws depend on the axiom that they are truly needed; scattershot, arbitrary, or overbroad application of the laws undermines their legitimacy.

There are two basic approaches to the task of risk assessment. The *clinical* method relies on the judgment and expertise of the professional, who gathers information about the subject through interviews, records, and other sources, and transforms the information into an assessment of dangerousness or risk through the application of his or her expertise. One might say that in the clinical method, the expert's assessment is constructed in his or her head. Ideally, the clinician's judgment is informed by the latest scientific findings about sexual offending and risk assessment. But since the assessment turns, in the end, on the exercise of "judgment," an invisible process within the expert's head, there is no practical way to assess whether the expert is applying the learning correctly or consistently. Further, though theoretically possible, there is no systematic and practical way to check each expert's accuracy by following up to determine whether his or her predications turn out to be true.

The second method for assessing risk is the *actuarial* method. An actuarial approach isolates the most important factors that indicate risk of reoffense, combines them through empirical research into a formula that weights each factor optimally, and produces a score for each individual based on the combination of risk factors.[61] The formula is applied to a large sample of sex offenders whose post-release history is then followed and whose reoffenses are observed. Researchers then count, for offenders in the sample, the frequency of sexual reoffense for each score level. This frequency is then taken to be the probability of recidivism associated with the given score.[62]

There is substantial evidence that actuarial methods are generally more accurate than clinical approaches to risk assessment.[63] This seems counterintuitive to many people, because the clinical method seems able to take into account the highly variable circumstances of each individual. But it turns out that humans—even highly trained experts—have difficulty analyzing complex bodies of data. Though actuarial methods are less individualized, they gain an advantage by systematically capturing important relationships in the data.

An example of the actuarial method is the STATIC-99, an assessment instrument that combines ten factors.[64] The factors include number of prior sex offenses (charges or convictions); prior nonsexual violence; whether victims have been unrelated, strangers, or males; age; and marital status. An individual's scores on these factors are totaled, and the score is compared to a table that shows the reoffense frequencies associated with each score.[65] The table indicates, for example, that sex offenders with a score of 5 have a frequency of sexual recidivism (over a five-year follow-up period) of 33 percent.[66] The highest risk category shown on the table—scores of 6 or above—is associated with a measured frequency of sexual recidivism (over a five-year period) of 39 percent.[67]

How adequate are actuarial methods in achieving the kind of accurate risk assessment that ought to be required by the predator laws? Though the answer is a bit complex, one clear measure looks at the how dangerous the riskiest group identified by each test is. For example, the STATIC-99, just discussed, will help us identify a group of people with a 39 percent risk of reoffending in five years. This means that most of the people in that group will not be rearrested for a reoffense during that period. How do the other tests stack up?

The developers of the MnSOST-R claim that the highest risk group identified by the tool—those with MnSOST-R scores of 13 and above—has a recidivism rate of either 70 percent or 88 percent, depending on the follow-up period.[68] Though not entirely clear in the documentation, a reasonable inference is that the 70 percent figure is associated with a six-year follow-up period, while the 88 percent is associated with a twenty-year follow-up.

Other well-accepted and well-validated risk assessment instruments make claims that are less impressive than the developers' claim for the MnSOST-R. For example, the highest risk group identified by the RRASOR risk assessment method is claimed to have a 73 percent sexual recidivism rate, but only with a follow-up period of ten years.[69] The STATIC-99, intended to be an improvement on the RRASOR, claims its riskiest group shows 52 percent sexual recidivism over a fifteen-year follow-up period.[70]

The use of actuarial assessments has engendered a new set of controversies about forensic risk assessment.[71] Actuarial instruments resemble standard psychological tests that we have become accustomed to (e.g., IQ tests), so there is a strong tendency to think of the risk numbers produced by the tools as similar to the results of these other tests—as descriptive in some fundamental way of the characteristics of the subject. But the risk assessment tools are at a much earlier stage of development, and serious questions can be raised about their development. For example, the usefulness of the tests is directly tied to the similarity of the development samples to the current group of sex offenders. Recent advances in treatment and supervision, for example, may mean that current offenders behave differently on release than those in the development samples. Further, the inflexibility of the scoring methods might mean that key information about the individual is not taken into account or given sufficient weight. Similarly, actuarial methods—at least as developed to date—are not very good at measuring changes in risk. The actuarial tools, for the most part, rely on relatively static and unchanging historical information about the individual. Thus, the information they produce cannot be regarded as taking into account changes in risk brought about by treatment, aging, or improved conditions of supervision in the community. In addition, like any psychological test, the accuracy of actuarial tools is limited by errors in scoring, both in developing the tools and in applying them.

As indicated, actuarial risk assessment brings certain advantages to the risk assessment process. Because it is developed using the scientific method, it is more transparent than clinical methods, and both its flaws and benefits can be made more apparent. Actuarial tools can be evaluated and improved as new research is undertaken. Actuarial methods reveal aspects of risk assessment that are hidden or obscured by the clinical method. Most important, the actuarial method exposes the fact that risk assessment is essentially a group-based exercise. Risk assessments are, in essence, simply statements about how *groups* of people will behave, what proportion of them will commit a new crime, and what proportion will not. Clinical evaluations seem to have the advantage of being much more individualized. The clinician, after all, is focused only on *this* subject, seemingly taking into account all of his individuality. But to the extent that clinical judgment is based at all on science, it basically has the same structure as actuarial judgments—the clinician reaches into his or her own database of knowledge and attempts to align the particular subject with the characteristics and outcomes of other similar individuals. The actuarial method simply exposes this process more clearly and, according to the research, does it more accurately.

What We Know and What We Need to Know

As with many complex human behaviors, our understanding of sexual violence is at a beginning stage. Our ability to reduce sexual violence depends on increasing the sophistication of this knowledge and then designing public policy to take account of what we've learned. Both the growth of scientific knowledge and its ability to shape policy have been uneven. Driven in large measure by feminist thinkers, our knowledge about the scope and nature of sexual abuse has improved immensely. But as I argue in chapters 5 and 8, these lessons of the feminists are too often cast in the shadow of the predator model with its emphasis on the most visible, though rarest, of crimes.

Many advocates want public policy to focus more effectively on the root causes of sexual violence. But a substantial part of the research resources have gone into trying to understand phenomena that are substantially downstream from the headwaters of sexual violence. Research into recidivism and risk assessment tells us little or nothing about what causes sexual violence in the first place. The clear benefit of this knowledge—measuring repeat sexual violence at a societal and individual level—helps us deal with only a small portion of the problem, the risk posed by the relatively small proportion of sexual abusers who are reported to authorities and convicted in the criminal justice system. And even that benefit is limited because this research provides at best a foundation for learning how most effectively to deal with the risk posed by released sex offenders.

There ought to be a clarion call for an explosion of knowledge about how to prevent sexual violence before it happens. Research into the root causes of sexual violence and the design of effective programs of primary prevention (discussed in chapter 7) could have a major impact on the incidence of the problem by pushing effective interventions much farther upstream. Much of this research is still in its infancy. Our knowledge of how to design effective treatment and supervision for known sex offenders, while more advanced, still lacks the kind of rigor that can produce widespread consensus about how to reduce recidivism.

We have enough information to act. Our public policy needs to hew much more strongly to what we already know. But pouring more resources into research that will enhance prevention is a compelling imperative.

CHAPTER FOUR

Benefits and Costs

What is the price of yet another victim, the innocence stolen from another child, the sense of safety at night for another woman?

—State Representative KURT ZELLERS, R–Maple Grove, Minnesota

Sex predator laws make an attractive, even seductive, claim: by pushing a bit against the conventional boundaries of law, we can provide real protection from future sexual violence. These laws, it is assumed, prevent sex-crime tragedies.

Quibbling about the *costs* of these laws seems not only politically unwise but also unseemly. How would one put a price on freedom from fear or on an increased sense of control over the risks of modern life? What could one say to the family of a victim whose life could have been saved by such a law? No matter what one thinks about the constitutional or moral shortcomings of the predator laws, their efficacy seems unassailable: by locking up the most dangerous offenders and informing citizens about sex offenders in their midst, lives have been saved and rapes prevented.

But it is not quite so simple. Putting money into predator laws inevitably means having less money for other public purposes, including other efforts to fight sexual violence. There are tradeoffs when we make public policy regarding sexual violence and commit public resources to those policies. We ought to be concerned about these tradeoffs, not simply out of some abstract sense of rationality but because if we choose wrongly we are necessarily, even if unwittingly, risking lives and safety.

Epigraph is from Conrad deFiebre, "Life and Death: Getting Tough on Sex Offenders; Push for Life Sentences Might Cost $1 Billion or More Over 20 Years," *Minneapolis–St. Paul Star Tribune*, April 19 2004, 1A.

And, there are real costs to these laws in addition to the allocation of public funds. These laws have an impact on how we understand sexual violence, what is "real" sexual violence, and what is invisible. They help shape the social environment for sex offenders, the incentives and disincentives for them to seek help and change their behavior, and their ability to achieve reintegration into society. They have an effect on how we think about justice and individual liberty. They affect the legitimacy and solidity of the foundation on which our campaign against sexual violence is based. These costs, too, are very real.

If we are serious about preventing as much sexual violence as we can, then we will demand the best estimates possible about the costs and benefits, not only of the predator approach but also of alternatives. This chapter begins that evaluation process by taking a straightforward look at the direct costs and benefits of sex predator commitments and Megan's laws. Part 2 examines more distal costs, such as the damage these laws may do to our conceptualization of sexual violence and to our system of justice. Part 3 examines the potential costs and benefits of alternate approaches.

This initial examination of the costs and benefits of the predator approach ought to raise serious questions about both predator commitment laws and Megan's laws, but for somewhat distinct reasons. Predator commitment laws cost a huge amount for a return that deals with a very small portion of the sexual violence problem. The money spent on predator commitments might be spent on other approaches with much greater return. The critique of Megan's laws is the obverse. Underfunding impairs their ability to deliver their clearest benefit, the provision of useful information so people can take meaningful measures to protect themselves. When we spend too little on them, we may save money, but we exacerbate their nonmonetary costs without achieving their offsetting benefits.

Predator Commitment Laws

In some important ways, both the costs and the benefits of predator commitment laws are concrete and identifiable. Commitment laws require special buildings and separate treatment programs with explicit budgets. We know with some specificity that predator commitment programs are a large, and growing, expense. The benefits, too, appear concrete: commitment laws produce 100 percent protection from real, identified individuals. We know *these individuals* will not reoffend as long as they remain committed.

Predator commitment costs are high. State by state, the annual cost to house and treat one predator averages $75,000, ranging from $12,680 in South Carolina to over $109,000 in Minnesota.[1] In Minnesota, the annual cost of the predator commitment law was $30.6 million in 2006, up from $20 million in 2002.[2] When Wisconsin enacted its predator commitment law, officials projected an annual operating cost of $3.6 million. Some ten years later, in 2003, operating costs for the Wisconsin program were $26 million a year, with an additional $40 million invested in the physical facility. California is slated to spend $350 million for a facility to house its predator population.[3] Operating costs for the California predator commitment program were $78 million annually as of 2004.[4]

Estimates for the total cost nationally for all sixteen predator laws range from about $225 million to $321 million.[5] Not included in this figure are the one-time litigation costs for new commitments (estimates per case range from $60,000 in Washington to $100,000 in Minnesota) and the capital costs of constructing confinement facilities.[6] In Minnesota, for example, near-term capital costs are estimated at $69 million to add additional beds to the secure treatment centers to house newly committed men.[7] North Dakota's treatment facility is nearly full. Expansion will cost the state an additional $3.1 million.[8]

These figures will increase dramatically. In Minnesota, the rate of admission into the program has for years been one or two per month. But this increased to five or six per month in early 2004 after Dru Sjodin was murdered. The Minnesota commitment population grew from 190 in 2003 to 235 in mid-2004, an increase of almost 24 percent. By the beginning of 2006, the population had grown to nearly 300. Though a government study issued in 2000 projected that the commitment population would be less than 350 by 2010, one newspaper reported that officials in 2006 now expect 800 confined by 2010, at a cost (at current rates) of about $82 million per year.[9] From 2003 to 2004, the Washington program grew 15 percent, from 164 to 190, while California grew 5 percent from 509 to 550.[10] California expects its committed population to triple to 1,500.[11] Florida confined 473 in 2005, but the state estimates this number will reach 1,000 to 1,200 by 2010.[12]

If the estimates for increases hold true for Minnesota, California, and Florida and apply to the other states as well, we would expect to see an annual national expenditure on predator commitments of anywhere from $750 million to almost $1 billion within the next decade.

To decide whether these costs are worth the benefit, we have to get more precise about what the benefits are. How much sexual violence do predator commitment laws prevent? Looking at some concrete information will help us understand that the benefits of predator commitment laws are significantly less than widely perceived.

Let us take Minnesota as an example. How effective is Minnesota's effort to prevent sexual violence by means of its commitment program? One way to get a handle on this question is to compare the amount of recidivist violence prevented by the commitment program to the total recidivist violence attributable to released sex offenders.

In a typical year, Minnesota discharges about four hundred sex offenders from prison. In past studies, the measured sexual recidivism rate for sex offenders released from Minnesota prisons has been about 18 percent with an average follow-up period of 6.5 years.[13] (There is some indication that this rate might now be lower because of better supervision of offenders after their release from prison.) Based on these statistics, we would expect that there are about seventy-two recidivists in a typical cohort of four hundred sex offenders released from prison in any given year.

Over the past several years, Minnesota has committed about 4 or 5 percent of the sex offenders who have completed their sentence in prison. So, the number committed each year has been somewhere between sixteen and twenty. Thus, even if *all* of the *committed* individuals are recidivists, the committed group accounts for at most 27 percent of the recidivists (twenty out of seventy-two). Put another way, even in a state like Minnesota with a predator commitment law, at least 73 percent of the sexually violent recidivists are *released into the community* from prison at the end of their sentences.

Here's another way of thinking about it. California's predator program currently houses 535 men. More than sixty-seven thousand convicted sex offenders have served their sentences and now live in California communities. If the sixty-seven thousand in the community have a recidivism rate of 18 percent (as in Minnesota), we would expect that group to contain 12,060 recidivists. Thus, even if all 535 of those held under civil commitment would have been recidivists had they been released, civil commitment in California confines less than 5 percent of the recidivists. More than 95 percent of the recidivists make their homes in the community.

These numbers probably overestimate the beneficial impact of predator commitments, because they assume that everybody who is committed would be a recidivist if released. But this is not the case. Because there is no perfect method to predict sexual recidivism, some of the people who are committed would not have committed another sex crime even if they had been released to the community.

To understand this, we need to look at some more numbers. Let's consider the sexual recidivism we would expect from a hypothetical cohort of 2,000 sex offenders who are eligible for discharge into the community after conviction. A reasonable assumption is that 60 percent (1,200) of these are *probationers* (convicted but not sent to prison) and 40 percent (800) are being *discharged from prison.*[14] Suppose we want to estimate the annual sex-crime recidivism that we would expect from this group of 2,000. Dividing reported recidivism rates by their follow-up periods gives us estimates of the average annual recidivism rates: 1.2 percent per year for probationers; about 3 percent per year for sex offenders being released from prison. (Since recidivism slows down as time passes, these averages are probably underestimates for the first years out of prison and overestimates for the later years.) Using these figures, we would expect that our hypothetical group of 1,200 probationers would produce 14.4 sexual recidivists per year (1,200 × .012); the released prisoners would produce about 24 sexual recidivists per year (800 × 0.3).

Now let's ask how many of these sex recidivists would have been retained in custody if our hypothetical state enacted a predator commitment law. Assuming an aggressive program, suppose that the state civilly commits 5 percent of those released from prison (.05 × 800 = 40). How many of these forty would have been recidivists had they not been committed? To answer that question, we need to know the accuracy of the state's system for selecting commitment candidates. In the last chapter we saw that actuarial prediction tools—though far from perfect—offer the best method of assessing an individual's risk of sexual recidivism. These methods do not pick out recidivist from nonrecidivists but rather tell us what the proportion of recidivism is among offenders with a given score: the higher the score, the higher the proportion of recidivists. Let us suppose that our hypothetical state is dedicated to ensuring that only the most dangerous are civilly committed, so it commits only offenders whose actuarial scores put them in the very highest risk category. Depending on the actuarial tests used, the "most dangerous" group would recidivate at an annual rate between 3.5 and 11.6 percent per year. If the selection process is less precise, and uses "moderate" risk rather than high risk, the recidivism rate of the commitment group would fall to between 3 and 7 percent per year.

We can use these rates to estimate the number of sexual recidivists that the forty civilly committed individuals would have produced had they been released at the end of their sentences. This number would range from 1.2 recidivists per year at the low end (.03 × 40) to a high-end estimate of 4.6 (.116 × 40) recidivists per year.

The summary table lets us see what percentage of all of the sexual recidivists would be confined by civil commitment. At best, the proportion will be 12 percent (4.6/38.4). At the low end, civil commitment would confine 3 percent (1.2/38.4) of sexual recidivists.

But recall that only one in seven imprisoned sex offenders has a prior sex-crime conviction (we would expect this proportion to be even smaller for sex offenders on probation). Thus, for every sex conviction of a released sex of-

Table 2. Expected recidivism of released sex offenders compared with those confined in predator commitments

Group	Recidivism rate (annual) (%)	Recidivists expected (annual)
Prisoners eligible for release (800)	3	24
Probationers released (1,200)	1.2	14.4
Total eligible for release (2,000)		38.4
Committed (40)— highly selective	3.5–11.6	1.4– 4.6
Committed (40)—moderately selective	3–7	1.2–2.8

fender, we would expect an additional six individuals (who had no prior sex-crime conviction) to be convicted of a sex crime. In other words, if our hypothetical cohort of 2,000 sex convicts could be expected to produce 38.4 convicted sex criminals per year, we might expect another 230.4 sex-crime convictions each year of nonrecidivists (people who had no prior sex-crime conviction). Thus, the total number of sex-crime convictions per year would be 268.8 (38.4 + 230.4). Of that number, civil commitment could be expected to have locked up between 0.4 percent and 1.7 percent of the expected convicted sex criminals each year.

Here is another way of dimensioning the benefits of predator commitment programs. In 2004, California confined 535 men in its predator commitment program, thereby confining between 19 and 62 individuals who would likely have sexually recidivated per year. Compare this with the number of forcible rapes reported to police in California: approximately ten thousand per year. In Minnesota, the commitment program confines 300 or so individuals. Of these, we might expect that somewhere between 9 and 35 would have recidivated each year if they had not been confined.

Compare this number with the 6,469 rapes and sexual assaults that were reported to authorities in 2000 in Minnesota, or to the survey conducted in Minnesota in 2005 that found that 1 percent of women aged 18 to 44 had been sexually assaulted in a sixteen-month period.[15] Based on this finding, the study estimated that about ten thousand women in Minnesota are sexually assaulted every year.

Undeniably, the calculations in this section are estimates. But the conclusion, even from these estimates, is plain. Predator commitments address only a very small portion of the problem of sexual violence. Their cost is high. The question, addressed in chapter 7, is whether the high cost is out of proportion to the sliver of the problem these laws address.

Registration and Notification Laws

Megan's laws present a different cost-benefit calculus. Their costs, in dollars, are much less than predator commitment laws, and harder to pin down. Even more speculative and variable are the nondollar costs—and benefits—to the violence prevention enterprise. When we net the best evidence and thinking to date, the costs seem to outweigh the benefits, though spending more money on the program seems to be able to ameliorate some of the nonmonetary costs.

Community notification programs have three potential benefits. They may give people information so they can more effectively protect themselves and their families from sexual violence. They may reduce sexual recidivism by exposing sex offenders to greater surveillance and community accountability. And they may increase the sense of security and well-being in a community. On the cost side of the ledger, community notification laws require some expenditure of resources, though the level is quite variable. They may pose impediments to the successful (i.e., crime-free) reintegration into the community of newly released sex offenders. Finally, they may give people a distorted sense of the magnitude and source of the risk of sexual violence.

Add to these hoped-for benefits the fact that the laws appeared (when they were passed) to cost the government very little and to put the tools of self-protection in the hands of the citizens themselves. Megan's law thus fit snugly with the ethos of the time, where big government was criticized as expensive and incompetent and reformers sought to put tax money back in the hands of citizens who, it was asserted, were in the best position to decide how to spend it.

Although they vary in many details, state notification and registration laws can be characterized along several major dividing lines. Slightly more than half the states perform an individualized assessment of each sex offender's risk.[16] A common pattern is a three-level classification of offenders into low, moderate, and high risk. This classification then determines the nature of notification to the community. In a typical design, law enforcement agencies are notified of level 1 (low risk) offenders, more vulnerable "need to know" agencies like schools and child-care centers are added to the notification list for level 2 (moderate risk) offenders, and the neighboring public is notified of the release of level 3 (high risk) offenders. The balance of the states use a nonindividualized approach, in which the notification and registration parameters are determined strictly by the nature of individual's criminal record.[17]

Another major divide is that some states use active approaches to community notification (door-to-door notifications, fliers, neighborhood meetings) while others rely on "passive" means such as website lists of offender information.

Little research has been done to determine whether registration and notification laws have fulfilled the hopes of their sponsors, or whether they are wise uses of limited funds. Two studies have failed to find any statistically significant association between implementation of the laws and a reduction in recidivism.[18] One small study has questioned whether the ability of sex offenders to commit crimes in a fairly wide geographic area will render the technique of neighborhood-based notification ineffective. More generally, critics point out that notification laws are premised on a "stranger" rapist model, whereas most perpetrators are known to their victims.[19] Ironically, in some jurisdictions a key part of the notification process is to inform people that the greatest danger to them, statistically, will not come from a registered offender, about whom notification is mandated, but rather from an unregistered relative.[20] A widespread concern is that community notification laws will have an "antitherapeutic" effect, making successful community reentry more difficult for offenders.

The assumption that registration and notification are low-cost programs has proved to be illusory. As law professor Wayne Logan observes, "Jurisdictions have painfully become aware [that] registration and notification, whatever their benefits, are far from cost-free."[21] The failure to allocate sufficient funds has led to fairly widespread concern about the implementation of these programs, in particular the completeness and accuracy of the registration information.[22] Even years after the federal mandate for registration and notification laws began, states report widespread deficiencies and confusion. An AP story in 2003 reported that California "had lost track of at least 33,000 sex offenders."[23] This number accounted for 44 percent of the 76,350 offenders who registered at least once. According to the report, "no one audits California's database for accuracy. State Justice Department officials cannot even say how much the program costs."[24] When confronted with these findings, California's attorney general, who had widely touted the system as an effective tool for the public, said, "our system is inadequate, woefully inadequate. . . . It can only be improved by putting money into the local law enforcement agencies. It's a matter of resources." A month later, a child advocacy group reported on their survey of all fifty states: "States on average were unable to account for 24 percent of sex offenders supposed to be in the databases."[25] Said Laura Ahern, executive director of the nonprofit Parents for Megan's Law: "They're implementing Megan's Law, then turning their backs on it. . . . They need the technology and the staff to track down their sex offenders."

The empirical evidence that community notification prevents or reduces sexual crime is equivocal. A small study of thirty-six offenders incarcerated for sex offenses (who had not been subject to Megan's laws) found that four of their victims would have had a "good" chance of protecting themselves if Megan's law had applied, although the study authors noted that even if those victims had protected themselves, the offenders might have moved on to "more vulnerable targets."[26] Studies in Iowa and Washington found that the recidivism rate of sex offenders is essentially unchanged by registration and community notification—although the Washington study found that rearrest for a new crime came earlier for offenders subject to Megan's laws than for the control group.[27] The results of a study presented in 2003 indicate that notification policies "have not significantly reduced the number of incidents of sexual victimization."[28]

The structure of community notification programs suggests key reasons that may serve to limit the crime prevention goals of Megan's laws. First, the vast majority of victims of sexual assault know the people who assault them. This suggests a limited applicability of the archetypal story in which the disclosure of a stranger's criminal background allows his unsuspecting neighbors to take protective steps they would not otherwise have taken. Second, perhaps as many as six out of seven sexual assaults are committed by people who have no criminal sex offender convictions and are therefore not subject to community notification.[29] Third, community notification laws have limited geographical reach and thus can have no effect if registrants travel outside of the notice area. For Prentky and Burgess, this is a particularly telling criticism. They observe that notification laws "may have their least impact on the most dangerous offenders" because "the *most* dangerous sex offenders rarely are gainfully employed and have stable residences."[30]

Even if it cannot be proved that Megan's laws actually prevent crime, they may have a beneficial effect of increasing a sense of security and control among citizens. Victim advocate Lucy Berliner argues that Megan's laws respond to the perceived needs of the community. A 1997 survey in Washington found 80 percent thought the state's Megan's law was an "important" piece of legislation. Mary Coffee, who heads Florida's sexual predator and offender unit, agrees, calling Megan's law "a safety tool to allow people to make good decisions." In March 2004, Florida's sex offender website had 487,345 hits, and the state's information hot line for the public generates about 2,500 calls a month. "That tells us there's obviously an interest and demand for the information," Coffee said. "We get calls from all kinds: neighbors, parents, people where something's not sitting right with them. They check the Web, call the number and ask questions. . . . That helps them make decisions."[31]

But it is not clear whether community notification helps people make *good* decisions. Many forms of community notification do not provide any practical advice to citizens about how they might protect themselves. Though community notification has been shown to increase protective behavior, such as warning children about strangers and enhancing locks on doors, these behaviors clearly have no relevance to stemming abuse by acquaintances and intimates.[32] Many notification schemes list tens of thousands of names but provide little or no information to the public about each individual. For example, as of 2004, Michigan's public sex offender registry listed 34,000 individuals, including teenagers, who had been convicted of having consensual sex with other teens. In 2006, Calhoun County Circuit Judge Conrad Sindt ordered defendant Jeffrey Haynes, age forty-two, to register as a sex offender. Haynes' only sex crime: sodomizing a sheep.[33] The registry provided no assessment of the risk posed by any of these individuals. The Florida registry list contains a disclaimer that a person's presence on the list "is not intended to indicate that any judgment has been made about the level of risk a particular offender may present to others." Members of the public are advised—not very helpfully—to form "their own risk assessments based on the offender's personal circumstances and conviction history." Connecticut's website states that it "has made no determination that any individual included in the registry is currently dangerous. . . . The main purpose of providing this data on the Internet is to make the information more easily available and accessible, not to warn about any specific individual."[34] Yet if the purpose of the information is not to "warn about any specific individual," how are members of the public supposed to benefit?

These are bare-bones community notification schemes, no doubt adopted because they are relatively cheap to implement. Other states do a much more careful—and expensive—job of providing more meaningful information to communities. They assess the risk posed by individual offenders and use public notification only for a relatively small group of high-risk offenders. Communities are given more complete information both about the offenders and about sexual violence more generally, so that they have some context for interpreting the information.

Advocate Lucy Berliner emphasizes the importance of this kind of careful approach. In Washington, she says, "we do community meetings where police, schools and churches come together to give people a chance to express their fears and deal with them." Many states have successfully implemented community notification procedures that warn about the dangers of ostracizing or harassing offenders and use the meetings as an opportunity to educate the community about the more common sexual offenders who may be family members or friends and how to protect themselves or their children from harm.[35]

Berliner's point is reinforced by the experience in King and Snohomish counties in Washington, where the public notification systems have been designed with principles of "restorative justice" in mind. These systems "allow the offender to present himself as an individual." Sex offender treatment expert Barbara Schwartz reports that "members of the public have been known to help these persons obtain work or housing. . . . If the hope is for the offender to refrain from reoffending, then assisting them with being able to find housing, work, and a social network aids in achieving that goal."[36] Done thoughtfully and sparingly, advocate Berliner says, community notification can help build community by giving people the tools "to look out for each other and each others' children instead of relying on government, which can't possibly protect you from released sex offenders."[37]

But this careful, community-building approach may be more the exception than the rule. In a critique of community notification that is echoed by a number of commentators, law professor Bruce Winick writes:

> The perpetual stigma imposed by registration and community notification laws seems to signal that the possibility of redemption is foreclosed. Sex offenders are given a particularly stigmatizing deviancy label and subjected to social ostracism. . . . This is a message of hopelessness that can only diminish the individual's motivation and ability to change.[38]

These concerns are supported in one of the few empirical studies published to date, which surveyed thirty Wisconsin sex offenders who had been identified as highest risk. Wayne Logan reports that "researchers found that employment problems, harassment, ostracization, residential exclusion, and negative impacts on families and friends were all common consequences of notification."[39] A therapist and sexual abuse consultant, Robert Freeman-Longo (now Robert Longo), has collected a long list of problems with public notification laws. Though largely anecdotal, his information comes from knowledgeable treatment professionals widely dispersed throughout the country. Among the problems he reports: disruption of a long-standing and successful community treatment program for adolescents; family members of offenders being harassed because of the offender's appearance on a registry; reluctance of child protection workers to report juvenile sex abusers out of concern that the adolescent will be branded for life by registration requirements. Prentky and Burgess worry that "we cannot dismiss the possibility that some percentage of offenders will reoffend because of the stress and pressure imposed by a hostile, rejectionist community that has branded the offender as a pariah."[40]

A report by the National Institute of Justice provides an instructive counterpoint. The report cites several studies that conclude that notification provides a strong incentive for offenders to engage in treatment and comply with the conditions of their community placement. The report also states that the "increased community awareness" generated by community notification has led to members of the community being more vigilant and recognizing suspicious activity involving their families.

In the end, whether a Megan's law does good or ill, is useful or not, probably depends in large measure on how much it costs. The National Institute for Justice report emphasizes the cost of Megan's laws and the choices about resource allocation they entail:

> Almost every respondent reported that doing notification is very time consuming and burdensome. The Thurston County detective in Washington State said, "At the beginning, no one realized the staffing impact of this legislation; it's a monster." Furthermore, probation officers in some States are not given reduced caseloads to compensate for labor-intensive supervision of sex offenders.[41]

The report suggests that the burden might decrease over time as communities become more familiar with the process. Nonetheless, at the time of the report,

> only two jurisdictions were identified that have provided additional funding for doing notification. . . . "If notification is unfunded," an expert concluded, "something else will get less attention." A probation officer complained, "We lose time [doing notification] that we should be spending on managing the offender," while a police officer said, "Other work gets shortchanged."

Schwartz summarizes these concerns: Megan's laws will require "significant funds . . . There are more productive ways to spend these public funds."[42]

At bottom, a judgment about the effectiveness of Megan's laws probably will rest largely on the resources and care with which individual states and communities design and carry out these laws. The cheapest implementation—undifferentiated lists on the Internet—provide very little useful information for citizens. Well-designed programs will cost more money, because they require states to make judgments about relative risks and to craft the notification process so that it facilitates both rehabilitation and public safety.

Megan's laws and predator commitment laws share a common provenance: public outrage over government's failure to prevent horrible sexual crimes. Both forms of intervention were adopted without any clear investigation of their costs, monetary and otherwise. Both of these interventions are based on a "stranger-danger" model of sexual violence, clearly at odds with the true nature of sexual violence. We must see these programs in their proper context: as options to be chosen, or rejected, in constructing a comprehensive and systemic approach to sexual violence. It is time to see the problem more broadly, and to choose solutions more carefully, so that our resources can work most effectively.

Part II

CONSEQUENCES

CHAPTER FIVE

Feminism, the Culture Wars, and Sexual Violence

> Collectively, women are more at risk of violence in intimate relations than in public spaces.
>
> —ELIZABETH STANKO

> The institution that most strongly protects mothers and children from domestic abuse and violent crime is marriage.
>
> —Heritage Foundation

We are in danger of being blinded to hard and valuable lessons we have learned about sexual violence. In the "culture war," launched by conservative forces such as the Heritage Foundation in part in a backlash to the women's movement and feminism, our new and enlightened architecture of sexual violence is at risk of becoming collateral damage. The predator laws are vehicles by which this retrograde effort might dismantle the fruits of years of reform and improved understanding of sexual violence. By placing the predator laws in this context, I seek to develop some understanding about the forces that are propelling these laws as well as the harm they can do.

In the traditional view, the paradigmatic example of sexual violence was the rapist who was a deranged stranger. The women's movement challenged this view, making the role of social norms and values a much more visible explana-

---

Epigraphs are from Elizabeth Stanko, "Naturalizing Danger: Women, Fear, and Personal Safety," Dangerous Offenders, ed. John Pratt and Mark Brown (New York: Routledge, 2000), 150; and Robert E. Rector, Patrick F. Fagan, and Kirk A. Johnson, "Marriage: Still the Safest Place for Women and Children," Mar. 9, 2004, http://www.heritage.org/Research/Family/bg1732.cfm.

tion for sexual violence. This was part of an agenda to change foundational aspects of gender relations, to dismantle patriarchy. This aspect of feminism was (and is) threatening to conservative forces in society, because it challenges deeply held beliefs about who we are. It suggests a need for fundamental change. But the seeds planted by feminist reformers have taken root, changing in important ways the received wisdom about sexual violence. So successful has been this change that many aspects of it cannot be challenged directly. But there remains strong resistance to the underlying deep meaning of this new architecture. The predator laws provide an indirect means to reassert the old paradigm and thus undercut the feminist approach. In the process the broadly accepted new insights, what we can call the new architecture of sexual violence, is placed at risk.

Social Attitudes and Mores

The traditional view of gender relations is real and very much in play. The cover story of a 1998 supermarket tabloid headlined the now iconic photo of President Bill Clinton hugging a beaming Monica Lewinsky: "Monica's Sexy Strip Show: How Bill Lost Control When That Little Blue Dress Came Off!"[1] Though a tabloid is just a tabloid, this headline embodied a particular "theory" about how sexual misconduct occurs. Women's provocative behavior triggers a loss of control, even in normal men. Therefore, a man's sexual misbehavior in response is not really his fault. Rather, it can be blamed in part on the woman (she triggered the behavior) and in part on his own biological and psychological makeup, the mechanisms that "made" him lose control when he encountered the woman's inviting behavior. In this story, there is no serious room for Clinton's personal responsibility, no notion that the power relationships between Clinton and Lewinsky played a part, and certainly no suggestion that social attitudes and mores allow sexual misbehavior to flourish.

Although no one accused President Clinton of any sexual crime, this tabloid story is illustrative of the traditional architecture of sexual violence and the steps we take to combat it. It was these values and attitudes that came under attack, beginning in the late 1960s, as part of a new agenda advanced by the women's movement and feminist theorists. Led by this movement, our society has experienced a sea change in how it understands sexual violence.

Yet these changes are at risk. There are powerful conservative forces that do not like the feminist underpinnings of the new architecture of sexual violence. These conservative forces have fought back, declaring a culture war over basic values of American society. The thesis of this chapter is that the new ways of seeing and understanding sexual violence, which can help shape a more effective program for prevention, may become collateral damage in the culture war. Unwittingly, perhaps, the predator laws are a key tool of these conservative forces.

The tabloid model of gender violence is emblematic of a set of values and attitudes that were targeted by the feminist revolution of the last decades of the twentieth century. Feminists achieved fundamental changes in society's understanding of sexual violence. There was a restructuring of gender relations that replaced traditional attitudes and behaviors about women's roles and women's place in society.[2]

The feminist movement was essentially revolutionary in seeking to dismantle what was perceived as a patriarchal system. This agenda provoked fierce resistance from politically conservative circles. In the beginning of the twenty-first century, the culture war was about gay marriage and abortion, evolution and school prayer, among other topics. In the 1980s and 1990s, the culture war was about sexuality and violence, women's roles, and the family. When feminists pushed for fundamental change in the most basic institutions of society such as the family and male-female relations, conservatives fought to preserve traditional ways.

The predator laws support the antifeminist side in the culture wars. The new architecture of sexual violence is at risk because this legislation from the 1990s resurrected the traditional architecture of sexual violence, placing the old ways at the center of the fight against sexual violence. Predator legislation pushes against each of the planks of the new conceptualization.

The new architecture had its origins in the feminist reforms, stemming from a complex social movement with several waves and a myriad of streams.[3] The focus here is on second-wave feminism, whose beginnings are roughly marked by the formation of the National Organization for Women in 1966 and the publication of Kate Millett's *Sexual Politics* in 1970.[4] As described by John D'Emilio and Estelle B. Freedman in their authoritative work *Intimate Matters*, this movement produced "in short order a fairly elaborate body of theory that described and defined a system of gender oppression." The movement examined the most sacred institutions of American life—marriage, family, motherhood—casting them "as institutions that maintained the oppression of women."[5]

Led by theorists such as Catharine MacKinnon and Susan Brownmiller, the women's movement turned substantial attention to sexual violence.[6] Brownmiller saw in rape a key way in which the patriarchal society maintained the oppression of women. Rape, she wrote, is "nothing more or less than a conscious process of intimidation by which all men keep all women in a state of fear."[7] Similarly, according to MacKinnon, feminist theory understood sexual violence as "an act not of [biological] difference but of dominance . . . of gender hierarchy." Sexual violence "flourishes with social support, enforcing and expressing" the socially imposed inferiority of women.[8] In this way of thinking about sexual violence, sociocultural explanations rise to the top because they "locate the causes of rape and sexual assault within the fabric of western culture and society."[9]

This move to a sociocultural explanation for sexual violence de-emphasizes psychological and biological explanations. The implications of this change of viewpoint are central to the perspective on sexual violence that grew out of the feminist movement. If sexual violence is essentially biological—as in the Clinton-Lewinsky tabloid theory—responsibility rests, in part, with the woman for triggering the male's biological impulses. The feminist formulation places responsibility, in contrast, both with society, for providing social support, and with the man, for acting not because of his internal psychological or biological impulses but out of the choices he makes because of the "sexual politics" and "sexual power" inherent in social norms and values. Andrea Dworkin put it this way: "Men are doing it, because of the kind of power that men have over women. That power is real, concrete, exercised from one body to another body, exercised by someone who feels he has a right to exercise it, exercised in public and exercised in private. It is the sum and substance of women's oppression."[10]

It is important to note that the perspective shift is as much normative as it is scientific. It is certainly possible to understand the feminist theorists as making an empirical assertion—that patriarchy *causes* sexual violence. But it is equally plausible that the new way of understanding sexual violence recognizes the complexity of the psychological factors that might predispose some men (and not others) to sexual assault, while simultaneously seeking to elevate the part of the causal equation that has its roots in attitudes and values. Read in this way, the new architecture does not assert that patriarchy *causes* sexual violence. Rather, it requires us to examine and understand the role that social norms and societal attitudes play as they interact with the individual differences inherent in human beings. It laid the groundwork for significant reforms, which were broadly adopted, to stop social structures from tolerating or facilitating sexual violence.

This shift in focus from biology and psychology to culture and norms engendered another key shift. In traditional ways of thinking (and under traditional legal concepts) the family was the "private" domain of the man of the house, whose conduct with respect to his wife and children was, within broad limits, not the province of law. Feminists saw the family as an important site for the expression of the gender hierarchy that preserved male dominance and insisted that violence in the family and among acquaintances, just like violence "in public," needed to be legally prohibited. As history professor Sara Evans put it, "The [women's] movement politicized issues that had long been deemed outside the purview of 'politics,' including sexuality, domestic violence, and the exercise of authority within the family."

This shift had broad consequences, leading eventually to a key structure of the new architecture, the recognition that sexual violence is not a pathologically isolated cancer but a systemic dysfunction, spread broadly throughout the normal relationships of society. It is therefore not surprising, as Evans emphasizes, that the move to politicize the personal struck at the heart of important societal—and politically conservative—values:

> The result was a far more radical challenge (in the sense of *fundamental*, going to the roots) than efforts simply to gain admission for women into the public world of civic and economic rights. . . . It questioned one of the most fundamental and intimate forms of hierarchy, one that has been used in myriad contexts to explain, justify and naturalize other forms of subordination.

"The result of this feminist challenge," said Evans, "has been a political, legal, and cultural maelstrom."[11] The feminist agenda on sexual violence was, for a time, at the center of that maelstrom. And even as the feminist view has gained ascendancy legally and culturally, traditional forces have sought to push back. As we shall see, the predator laws have provided an effective (if not necessarily intended) vehicle for this retrograde campaign.

As they turned their attention to violence against women, feminist reformers sought to expose the underpinnings of the old architecture of sexual violence. They identified a set of rape myths, widely held misperceptions and false beliefs about the nature of sexual violence. The myths hold that rape is essentially a sexual crime of passion perpetrated by strangers; that women can exercise substantial control over whether they are raped, by modulating where they go and how they dress and by resisting hard enough; and that women, at some level, secretly want to be raped. As in the tabloid Clinton-Lewinsky headline, the myths portray men as unable to control their sexual urges when they reach some point during sexual arousal. They characterize "real rape" as that which is committed by a small proportion of men who are mentally deranged.[12] In the myths, women's accusations of rape are often false, designed to shift responsibility onto men for illicit acts invited and welcomed by the woman. Taken as a whole, these societal ideas and attitudes about rape tend to shift responsibility for sexual violence onto women, minimizing not only the harm to the woman but also the responsibility of both the male perpetrator and the larger society.

Empirical work has demonstrated that the myths were both widely held and false.[13] For example, early surveys found that 25 percent of male undergraduates "hold beliefs that rape is provoked by the victim, that any woman can prevent rape and women frequently cried rape falsely."[14] Further, studies showed that men who raped were psychologically similar to "normal" men: "Attitudes and beliefs that lead to rape are extensions of normal sexual behavior and socialization, not products of sexual deviance."[15] For example, in one study, 35 percent of "normal" men "expressed some likelihood of raping."[16] In another study, 62 percent of ninth grade boys and 58 percent of ninth grade girls said that a man has a right to sexual intercourse against his date's consent "if they have dated for a long time."[17] Further, as is described more fully later in this chapter, extensive research showed that sexual assault was more widespread, and much more a product of intimate and family relationships, than portrayed by the rape myths.

Unsurprisingly, the rape myths were not simply part of the popular culture but shaped the legal system's treatment of sexual violence in fundamental ways. A number of aspects of the myth were explicitly espoused in the maxims routinely invoked by the courts.[18] In the 1700s, Sir Matthew Hale, lord chief justice of the Court of King's Bench, penned the maxim that rape is "an accusation easily to be made and hard to be proved, and harder to be defended against by the party accused, though never so innocent."[19] So deeply ingrained in our thinking was this fear of false rape accusations that this maxim was still being used in U.S. courts in the 1980s, as reflected in this 1983 jury instruction in an Oregon case: "[A rape charge] is easily made and once made, difficult to defend against even if the person accused is innocent."[20]

The rape myths shaped the warp and woof of the traditional architecture of sexual violence. No part of the legal system was clean of the taint of these societal attitudes and beliefs. In its formal rules and informal practices, the law reinforced a very specific set of assumptions about sexual violence, its perpetrators, and its victims. Women who made complaints of being raped were often treated hostilely by police and prosecutors, who were skeptical of their claims. The trauma experienced by victims was in this way ignored, and compounded, when they sought help from the legal system. Often, key physical evidence was not collected. The accounts of women whose behavior did not conform to the dictates of conventional morality were especially discounted. The system viewed stranger rapes as the only "real" rape, giving less attention and credit to complaints of acquaintance and date rape. The legal definitions of rape similarly ignored sexual assaults that did not fit a narrow, stereotypical template, in which physical force overpowered physical resistance. Many rape laws required that the accusation be corroborated by a third person, a requirement not present in any other kind of crime of personal violence. When rape cases went to trial, defense lawyers often attacked the woman complainant, putting her life and experiences on trial. Even when men were convicted of sexual assault, sentences often did not reflect the seriousness of the injuries their actions had caused.

Thus, the rape myths both informed and were fostered by the broader architecture of sexual violence. The values of the legal system seemed congruent with those of the larger society in tolerating, or even supporting, a broad range of sexual violence against women. Many feminist thinkers viewed the law's traditional approach to sexual violence (in the words of Carole Goldberg-Ambrose) as "contributing significantly to a system of male dominance."[21] Conversely, the evidence suggested quite strongly that the values, attitudes, and practices of the society—what feminists might call "patriarchy"—could be fairly characterized as tolerant, or even permissive, of the sexual exploitation of women.[22]

Inspired originally by feminist reformers and thinkers, and reflecting many of their ideas, a new architecture of sexual violence began to emerge. In a series of initiatives loosely referred to as "rape reform," during the 1970s and through the early 1990s formal legal definitions and the practices of the legal system were changed in ways that were consistent with the feminist conceptualization of rape.

Beginning with Michigan's comprehensive rewriting of its criminal sexual assault law in 1974,[23] rape reform changed the law of rape in four broad ways. First, the single crime of rape was replaced with a series of criminal sexual offenses covering a broader range of sexual assaults. This broadening sought to capture sexual assaults that took place in the formerly "private" context of family and other close relationships. For example, the new laws captured sexual assault even if it did not involve penetration. The traditional requirement of "force" was broadened to cover misconduct where the perpetrator leveraged nonphysical forms of power (authority, age, incapacity) to abuse the victim.

Second, the legal requirement that the victim "resist to the utmost" was modified or removed, focusing the law's attention on the behavior of the offender rather than that of the victim.

Third, the "corroboration" requirement was eliminated, thus removing the formalized suggestion that women's accusations of rape were somehow inherently untrustworthy.

Fourth, rape shield laws were enacted.[24] These are restrictions on the permissibility of questioning rape victims about their prior sexual behaviors. By

1999, rape shield laws had been adopted by forty-nine states, the federal government, and the military.[25] In addition, penalties for criminal sexual conduct were toughened to recognize the newly acknowledged seriousness of the crimes, particularly those involving family and acquaintances. For example, the average time served by rapists sentenced to prison rose from about forty-one months in 1985 to about sixty-one months in 1996.[26] Finally, rape crisis centers and victims' services were established to reduce the hostility and isolation often experienced by sexual assault victims in the legal system.

The Ideology of Rape Reform and Conservative Backlash

While rape reform had its origins in feminist theory, many aspects of the reform agenda had broad appeal across the political spectrum, including among political conservatives. To be sure, the motivations of feminists and conservatives were different. Feminists sought to "abolish 'boys' rules' to sexual relations,"[27] while political conservatives sought to advance their law-and-order agenda. Conservatives and feminists had common cause to increase sentences for sexual crimes and tighten evidentiary rules at the expense of sex-crime defendants.

But the compatibility of the feminist and conservative agendas was little more than surface deep. For underlying the rape reform movement was the antipatriarchy agenda of feminists that was essentially revolutionary and, hence, deeply offensive to conservatives. Beginning in the 1970s, conservative commentators such as Phyllis Schlafly accused feminists of being "anti-family, anti-children and pro-abortion."[28] Over time, the two sides engaged in battles over day care, abortion, homosexuality, and the role of women in marriage and the workplace. But during the late 1980s and early 1990s the battle focused for a time on the question of sexual misbehavior by men—sexual assault and sexual harassment.[29]

Thus, underneath the broad acceptance of key aspects of the rape reform movement, an intense battle was raging. Evans characterizes the opposition to feminism in the 1980s and 1990s as "intense," suggesting that "one must read [the critics'] venom as a response to something they perceive to be very powerful."[30] Part of the intensity of the conservative opposition sprang from the hyperbole of some feminist rhetoric about sexual violence. Evans, for example, characterizes some "charismatic" feminist theorists as asserting that "most if not all heterosexual sex was comparable to rape."[31] Although such broad-brush accusations were easy targets for caricature, it was the core beliefs of the feminist reforms that presented the most glaring danger to conservative values. For conservatives, the real threat came from the view—originally espoused by feminists, but soon broadly borne out by empirical research—that sexual violence (and violence against women more generally) was not the work of a monstrous few, but was common, mostly took place at the hands of intimates and acquaintances, and was supported by key cultural practices and values.

Beginning in the early 1980s, feminist scholars and social scientists began a sustained project of empirical work that supported this core feminist ideology about sexual violence. Diana Russell's 1982 book *Rape in Marriage* was the first large-scale study of sexual violence from a feminist perspective; it revealed the "commonness of men's violence for a sample of U.S. women. . . . One in six of the women reported some form of incestuous abuse before age eighteen. Nearly one in two of the women reported experiencing some form of sexual abuse at any point in their lives."[32] Research findings published in 1988 by Mary Koss proved further support for the feminist approach.[33] Koss's research reported that one in four college women had been victims of rape or attempted rape at some time in their lives. Other research from the same period found that one in eight women had been the victim of rape at some point in their lives.

Meanwhile, a similar transformation was taking place with respect to child sexual abuse. Operating against a backdrop in which "small girls were seen as 'seductresses,'"[34] Florence Rush published *The Best Kept Secret: Sexual Abuse of Children* in 1980. It recharacterized child sexual abuse as a product of the social institutions, belief systems, and myths of patriarchal societies.[35] Sharon Araji reports that by the mid-1980s "commonly cited estimates suggest that one in four girls and one in nine boys will be sexually abused by the time they reach eighteen."[36]

Debunking many of the prevailing myths about rape, the research findings showed that sexual violence was widespread and perpetrated mainly by nonstrangers. The clear implication was that society bore a heavy responsibility for allowing violence against women to flourish.

As it emerged, this empirical information about sexual violence provoked a vehement backlash from conservative forces. Conservative critics, wrote history professor Ruth Rosen, complained that feminists "have largely hallucinated the many gender crimes they claim to be ubiquitous." Summarizing the position of the conservative Women's Freedom Network, Rosen characterizes the conservative critique as claiming that "radical feminists [are] guilty of cooking their data, exaggerating the victimization of women, targeting men as enemies, and seeking special (governmental) privileges for women."[37]

A leading conservative critic was Christina Hoff Sommers, whose 1994 book *Who Stole Feminism?* leveled a lengthy attack on Koss's findings about the incidence of sexual violence and on her underlying methodology. Sommers argued that Koss defined rape too broadly.[38] As a result, she argued, Koss's "one in four" figure was highly exaggerated. The fight between Sommers and Koss was not about social science methodology. Rather, it was the implications of Koss's numbers—that American society was "divided against itself along the fault line of gender"—that was so worrisome to Sommers.[39] "High rape numbers," Sommers wrote, "promot[e] the belief that American culture is sexist and misogynist."[40] To be sure, Sommers, like other conservatives, saw a "general crisis of violence against persons" in the United States. But "patriarchy is not the primary cause of rape[; rather] rape, along with other crimes against the person, is caused by whatever it is that makes our society among the most violent of the so-called advanced nations."[41]

In two key ways Sommers's critique was on target. First, Koss and other feminists were quite deliberately trying to expand the definition of rape. Much of what feminists called "consciousness raising" was about helping women understand that the sexual violence they suffered at the hands of their families and lovers was not normal or inevitable but rather was properly understood as rape.[42]

Second, Sommers's fear about the implications of the statistics Koss presented was well founded. Empirical findings about the commonness of rape were an important foundation for the feminist antipatriarchy agenda. The new empirical findings provided strong support for the reform of rape laws. But it was the broader implication that most worried traditionalists. As succinctly put by British criminology professor Elizabeth Stanko, the new evidence demonstrated that "collectively women are more at risk of violence in intimate relations than in public spaces."[43] This conclusion challenged core conservative beliefs about the importance of family and that women's proper place was in the home. The new understanding of men's violence against women became not simply a reason to change the technical rules of the criminal law. The nature of the risk and the danger to women became a central feature of the campaign for women's liberation.[44]

By the late 1980s and early 1990s, political conservatives had growing reason to worry. There was clear evidence that the new architecture of sexual violence was gaining the upper hand. "Sexualized expressions of male power" in the form of sexual harassment drew intense media attention.[45] The 1990s began with an onslaught of high-profile cases, including the Tailhook scandal—the 1991 aviators' convention at the Las Vegas Hilton Hotel where more than eighty women were assaulted—and the termination of two senatorial careers on allegations of persistent patterns of sexual harassment. Most memorable were the October 1991 Senate deliberations on the accusations of sexual harassment made by Anita Hill against Supreme Court nominee Clarence Thomas.[46] These incidents were an unmistakable signal that the old gender order was changing.

Meanwhile, further trouble for the traditional architecture of sexual violence was brewing. Beginning in the mid-1980s, the Department of Justice began contemplating changes to its venerable Crime Victimization Survey, one of two key measures of crime that had been used since the early 1970s. Following the approaches pioneered by Koss and others, the department began field testing a redesigned survey in 1989 that "broadened the scope of covered sexual incidents beyond the categories of rape and attempted rape to include sexual assaults and other unwanted sexual contacts."[47] For the first time, the survey measured sexual assault outside of the traditional categories of penetration by force, including unwanted or coerced sexual contact under a threat or attempt to harm.[48]

Results from the redesigned Crime Victimization Survey were first reported in 1994. The redesign results bolstered the feminist position in two important ways. The new statistics showed that sexual violence was both more common and more often perpetrated by acquaintances and intimates than previously reported. The changed methodology of the survey showed a 300–400 percent increase in sexual violence.[49] In 1977, for example, the Crime Victimization Survey reported that the rate for "rape and attempted rape" was 0.9 victimizations per 1,000 persons twelve or older (male and female). The rate for 1985 was 0.7 per 1,000, and it remained steady at or about that level through 1992 (varying between 0.6 and 0.8).

The 1994 survey report (describing victimizations in 1993) included—for the first time—data from the redesign. Reflecting the redesign's broader definitions of sexual violence, 1994 publications changed the reporting category from "rape and attempted rape" to a new category called "rape/sexual assault." The victimization rate reported for this new category was 2.3 per 1,000 persons twelve and older, a figure that was three to four times higher than the rate for "rape and attempted rape" reported in the most recent prior years.

The redesign of the Crime Victimization Survey also resulted in a marked increase in the measured level of nonstranger sexual violence. In a report on 1991 crime rates (published in 1993, immediately before the redesigned survey), the Bureau of Justice Statistics reported that more than half (52%) of rapes were committed by strangers. A post-redesign press release issued by the bureau in 1995 was headlined "Women Usually Victimized by Offenders They Know."[50] The press release stated that "the victim's friends or acquaintances committed more than half of the rapes and sexual assaults, [and] intimates committed 26 percent." According to these official numbers, the measured rate for stranger rape had decreased from 52 percent in 1991 to "about one in five."

This new understanding was further boosted by results of the National Violence against Women Survey, sponsored by the National Institute of Justice and the Centers for Disease Control and Prevention. Data were collected in 1995 and 1996. The survey found that almost one in six (17.6%) U.S. women had experienced a completed or attempted rape as a child or adult,[51] results that clearly confirmed the earlier findings such as those of Koss. The same survey found that 76 percent of the perpetrators of sexual and physical assaults against women after age eighteen were intimate partners (i.e., current and former spouses, cohabiting partners, dates, and boyfriends/girlfriends); 16.8 percent were acquaintances; 8.6 percent were relatives other than spouses; and only 14.1 percent were strangers.[52] Almost 8 percent of women reported that they had been raped by an intimate partner at some time in their lives.[53]

Perhaps the height of the feminist theorists' success came in the mid-1990s. In 1993, UN Resolution 48/104 recognized violence against women as a violation of women's human rights.[54] In 1994, Congress passed the Violence against Women Act (VAWA), providing funding for a variety of rape-prevention services, including programs to combat campus-based sexual assault and rape prevention and education programs. The act "reflected the first comprehensive legislative plan designed to set into motion a national agenda for combating violence perpetrated against women."[55] Significantly, the act created a private legal damages claim for gender-motivated violence.

The passage of the VAWA has meaning on several levels. At one level, it provided important funding for broad-based services, in recognition of the new evidence about the widespread nature of sexual assault, its presence on college campuses and other "normal" settings, and the possibility of combating rape through prevention and education programs, in addition to a more traditional criminal justice approach. But at a more fundamental level, the new federal law had roots deep in feminist theory. By addressing violence in terms of gender, Congress appeared to be siding with the notion that violence against women was a civil rights issue, not just a criminal justice issue, and that violence against women had a political aspect to it. Especially in its adoption of a private legal damages claim, the VAWA seemed to be equating violence against women with racially motivated violence and other forms of civil rights violations motivated by bias.

For conservatives and feminists alike, the Violence against Women Act was seen as a key victory for the feminist notion that sexual violence is about sexual power and politics, just as racial violence was about racial oppression and white supremacy. As conservative commentator Christina Hoff Sommers put it, the Violence against Women Act "buy[s] into the gender feminist ontology of a society divided against itself along the fault line of gender."[56] As a feminist, Elizabeth Stanko's view was similar: "Men's violence is now named as a public, collective harm to women."[57]

The Predator Laws and the Conservative Agenda

The predator laws arrived just in time to provide conservatives with a Trojan horse, a stealth vehicle for pushing back against the "tidal wave" of change wrought by the women's movement. The predator laws resurrect the old architecture of sexual violence, undermining, in almost every respect, the new architecture that had been broadly adopted under the tutelage of the feminist movement. Yet the predator laws were not viewed as part of the culture wars. Their support was not partisan, and it is not at all clear from the historical record that either feminists or conservatives foresaw the potential strength of the retrograde values inherent in these new laws.

Nonetheless, the predator laws provided conservatives a way out of a serious predicament. Despite the rape reform movement's *theoretical* underpinnings in the distinctly unconservative antipatriarchy agenda, conservatives found it difficult to oppose the *practical* reforms that made up the new architecture of sexual violence. In part, opposition would have looked soft on crime. But more important, the agenda originally advanced by feminists had achieved strong empirical and popular support. Conservatives had no way of challenging the feminist theories underlying the rape reform agenda without appearing insensitive to the women and children who are the victims of most sexual violence. As Janice Haaken and Sharon Lamb have written, "Sexual violations have acquired tremendous social symbolic power in American political culture so that any challenge to the gains of [the women's and children's rights] movements is perceived to be a threat to victims."[58]

The predator laws have proved to be a perfect vehicle for conservatives. The predator laws provide a highly visible symbol by which politicians can demonstrate their commitment to fighting sexual violence, while simultaneously resurrecting a set of assumptions about sexual violence—the traditional architecture of sexual violence—that is inconsistent with the fundamental advances inherent in the new architecture of sexual violence.

Three major ways in which the predator laws undercut the new architecture deserve emphasis. First, the predator laws resurrect the archetypal sexual of-fense as stranger violence. Second, predator commitment laws reemphasize a psychological model of the sexual offender as a mentally disordered person who lacks the ability to control his sexual impulses. Third, the predator laws diminish the role that community values and morality play in understanding and eventually controlling sexual violence. In the remainder of this chapter I will briefly explore each of these retrograde constructs.

The predator laws create a very specific archetype for the sex offender—the sex predator. This is the quintessential outsider, the monster or animal who picks out his victims from afar, stalks, and pounces. By focusing intensely on rare but horrific crimes, the predator laws convey a clear message that the fem-inists—and the solid empirical science—are wrong: the "greatest threat" to women is not "within women's intimate relationships."[59] Rather, these laws tell us that the real sex criminals are those who lurk in the bushes and parking lots.[60]

A second way in which the sex predator laws work to undercut the feminist message is by adopting a psychological explanation for sexual violence. In the predator commitment laws, the "most dangerous" are defined to be offenders who are "predisposed" to violence by reason of an abnormal psychologi-cal makeup. Predator commitment laws require a psychological explanation for violence: to qualify for commitment, the offender's violence must be "caused" by a "mental disorder," rather than "chosen" because of bad values and attitudes.

Feminist theories, recall, de-emphasized bio-psychological explanations for sexual violence, instead insisting that society confront the role played by "sys-tems, practices, ideologies that continue to privilege male power." A bio-psy-chological explanation for violence ignores societal responsibility. Further, as the Clinton-Lewinsky tabloid model demonstrates, a bio-psychological expla-nation of violence places at least part of the responsibility for sexual violence on women.

Together, the stranger danger and bio-psychological templates for sexual vi-olence convey a strong message that women can control much of the risk of sexual violence by behaving properly. As Stanko puts it:

> In the literature listing women's "safe" actions in public, there is an assumption that such actions will deter all but the pathological offender. Women then are expected, as part of active citizenship, to be responsible for their own safety. Self-governance, in the form of acting like appropriate "feminine" women, provides the "right" signals to those non-pathological men not to abuse women.[61]

There is a further way in which this identification of sexual violence with psychopathology is at odds with the new architecture of sexual violence. Feminist theorists have argued that sexual violence is an extension of the norms of society and flourishes under those norms. Social science evidence, demonstrating the wide incidence of sexual violence among intimates, is consistent with that feminist view. The predator laws take a small group, label them mentally disordered sexual predators, and lock them up in a symbolic, as well as literal, "ritual exile."[62] The ultrasecure "treatment centers" for predators visibly allow us to demonstrate our rejection of sexual violence by exiling a small, aberrational group of "others." This ritual exile allows the broader society to define itself as not being composed of sexual predators. This cleansing requires no fundamental societal change in order to address sexual violence. Under the predator template, whatever obligation the broader society has to deal with sexual violence is visibly and dramatically fulfilled simply by expelling the symbolic sexual predators.

The bio-psychological model constructed by the predator commitment laws pushes back hard against the new architecture in yet a final way. Recall that the Supreme Court has held that predator commitments are available only to lock up those offenders whom psychologists identify as having "difficulty controlling" their sexual impulses. This is, of course, precisely the Clinton-Lewinsky model, in which Clinton is said to have "lost control" in the face of Lewinsky's flirtatious behavior. Sex predator commitment laws bring the official imprimatur—directly from the United States Supreme Court—to what psychology professor Sharon Lamb calls "the dominant discourse of sexuality widely believed and accepted in our culture"—"men's lack of control over their sex drive."[63]

The language we use to describe sexual violence matters. It reflects the way our society chooses to understand and evaluate the sexual relations of men and women.[64] It is not only descriptive but also normative. The nature of the discourse about hotly contested issues such as sexual violence is shaped by those who have power in the society.[65] The very concepts we use in our language convey important messages about social values.

The notion that a person could not control his or her behavior is common in our everyday conversations. Despite its familiarity, this notion is somewhat opaque. We say that "he had trouble giving up cigarettes" or "she could not stick to her diet." What do we really mean by these expressions? What we often are saying is that the person lacked the will power to overcome contrary desires or urges. At some point, the person gets tired of trying and gives in or acquiesces in the urge to do what he or she, at some level, did not want to do.

We often use the expression in a kind of metaphorical way, roughly invoking the image of a person forced, often through some physical pain or threat, to do something she does not wish to do. And, just as we would excuse the person who acted under such physical duress, the expression "he just couldn't help it" is a way of lightening the blame we might otherwise attribute to a person's undesirable behaviors.

When applied to sexual violence, characterizing a rapist as "lacking control" asserts that the man's urges overwhelmed his will, his choice.[66] This way of talking expresses, in a covert yet powerful way, a normative conclusion that undermines the rapist's moral responsibility for sexual violence.

The "lack of control" discourse is a serious setback to our progress in implementing the new architecture of sexual violence. This discourse provides authoritative social support to rapists themselves. Social scientists report that rapists employ excuses that appeal to "forces outside of their control which, the men argued, compelled them to rape." This way of thinking "allowed the majority of these rapists to view themselves as either non-rapists or 'ex-rapists'."[67]

More problematically, courts themselves buy into the same kind of justificatory reasoning. Typical is this language from a judge's decision acquitting a young man in an acquaintance-rape case:

> Young men must be sensitive to a young woman's right to say no, and *young women, in turn, must realize that when a young man becomes aroused during sexual activity beyond a moderate degree there is a danger that he will be driven by hormones rather than by conscience.*[68] (emphasis in original)

The predator laws' "inability to control" linguistic template does not appear in a vacuum but smack in the middle of the struggle to banish the old rape myths and replace them with a new architecture of sexual violence. The predator laws bring the highest level of support to the discourse of minimization and excuse.

Lastly, the predator laws threaten another key feature of the progress inspired by feminist reformers—an insistence that we must reform social values, attitudes, and beliefs that tolerate, or even facilitate, sexual violence. The predator laws are part of a larger contemporary phenomenon characterized by prominent sociologists as "the death of the social." Among the characteristics of this phenomenon are the transfer of responsibility for solving problems from the society to the individual, paying attention to blocking the symptoms of problems rather than attacking root causes, and "de-moralizing" problems by defining them "not in terms of absolute moral codes but because they risk causing harm to us. . . . Actions are good not because they embody virtue but because they work."[69]

Predator laws de-emphasize the moral aspects of sexual violence, favoring instead a frame that focuses on the morally neutral concept of "risk." Predators are defined in these laws not by their guilt—which would imply a moral judgment—but rather by the risk they are deemed to present. This is an essential, not an accidental, feature of these laws. Because these laws claim to be "civil" rather than "criminal," they cannot be seen as condemning the sexual violence that they target. Risk is a morally neutral concept. It exists in nature. Though the harm from sexual violence is seen as bad, the application of the predator laws is no more a moral condemnation than is a cement cask designed to keep nuclear waste from escaping.

Further, the predator laws do not address the causes of sexual violence. The central task of the laws—assessing and then preventing risk—can be accomplished without knowing the causes of violence. And the success of the laws depends not on changing the conditions that produce violence—a task that would require some notion of causes—but rather on simply preventing risky individuals from reoffending.[70]

Looking specifically at Megan's laws we can see a further manifestation of the death of the social. The message of these laws is that society—acting through government—is in significant ways powerless to protect people from sexual violence. The core responsibility for addressing sexual violence must be turned over to individuals and families. Armed with the proper information about the sex offenders who are their neighbors, each individual is supposed to be able to defend herself and his or her children.

By undercutting the notion that our government—our means of acting collectively as a community—can do anything effective about sexual violence, Megan's laws undercut the idea that sexual violence flourishes in some measure because societal values permit it. Megan's laws transfer responsibility from the community to the individual, who, far from acting communally, will presumably simply take individual precautions.

Led by feminist thinking, our new understanding of sexual violence shows that effective prevention must include some communal effort to change societal values. But Megan's laws encourage a different approach, one that is essentially an individualistic and, one might even say, selfish approach to public safety. The stories are legion of neighborhoods organizing to protest the location of an offender in their midst, often forcing the offender to move to other neighborhoods. Though this may not have been the intent of Megan's laws, it is, to a substantial extent, their effect. Megan's laws promote an ethic that is the equivalent to the not-in-my-backyard phenomenon that is a perversion of environmentalism. Here, however, the ethic is a starker version that might be framed as an assault-my-neighbor ethic.[71]

The predator laws arose out of authentic and deeply felt fear and outrage about horrible crimes. But these laws foster a conceptual architecture that aids and abets the conservative, antifeminist agenda. They threaten some of the real progress we have achieved in shedding the old and destructive myths about sexual violence. The predator laws ignore the root causes of sexual violence. They direct our attention solely to the monster, the other, so that we feel satisfied that we have excised the cancer of sexual violence and can safely ignore the social structures and values that allow sexual violence to flourish more broadly among "normal" members of our society.[72]

CHAPTER SIX

Harbinger of the Preventive State?

Civil Rights Groups Warn against Tipster Training: Workers Who Regularly Go into Homes Would Be Trained to Spot Terrorist, Drug or Sexual Predatory Activities.

—*St. Petersburg Times* headline, July 9, 2004

Today the target is people who are sexually dangerous. Which class of people, who are different from us and who we do not like, will it be tomorrow?

—Minnesota Supreme Court Justice ALAN PAGE

The predator laws are bad public policy. They misdirect public resources away from the bulk of sexual violence, requiring the expenditure of large sums on the smallest, though most visible, fraction of the problem. They undercut the advances inspired by feminist reformers and do little or nothing to attack the root causes of sexual violence. Though the predator laws represent a strong and positive message of condemnation for sexual violence, their unintended consequences cry out for a better way to construct a public policy on sexual violence prevention.

But there is an even more urgent reason for alarm. Two powerful streams of contemporary American public policy are converging on a dangerous course. We are at risk of becoming a "preventive state," in which the paradigm of governmental social control has shifted from solving and punishing crimes that

This chapter is based in part on Eric S. Janus, "The Preventive State, Terrorists, and Sexual Predators: Countering the Threat of a New Outsider Jurisprudence," *Criminal Law Bulletin* 40 (2004): 576–98. Epigraph from Justice Page is from *Matter of Linehan*, 557 N.W.2d 171, 202 (Minn. 1996) (Page, J., dissenting).

have been committed to identifying "dangerous" people and depriving them of their liberty *before* they can do harm.[1]

The impulse for prevention has taken its strongest form in two disparate areas: the antiterrorism efforts since 9/11 and the sexual predator laws. In both areas, the government has erected an "alternate system of justice" in which the normal protections of our civil liberties are substantially degraded in order to make room for an aggressive preventive agenda.[2]

The prevention of harm is, of course, a positive. Our law books are full of beneficial statutes intended to regulate risky behavior in order to prevent harm. But the preventive state heralds a different type of prevention—what might be called radical prevention—that differs fundamentally from routine prevention. Radical prevention operates by substantially curtailing people's liberty *before* harm results, whereas in routine prevention individuals suffer substantial deprivations of liberty *only after* they have caused or attempted actual harm. It is this combination—substantial liberty deprivation in anticipation of harm—that is the hallmark of radical prevention and the preventive state.

Radical prevention is not a new impulse in the United States. Historically, it has featured prominently in U.S. law. A central feature of these historical laws was their focus on outsider groups. This allowed the constraints on liberty to be seen as exceptional and allowed the larger society to sustain its belief that U.S. law protected individual liberty.[3]

In the last half century, the courts have erected important constitutional bulwarks against excessive erosions of our liberty in the name of prevention. Beginning in the 1960s, the civil rights revolution has all but eliminated the legitimate targeting of outsider groups. At the same time, the Supreme Court has identified the fundamental nature of key aspects of liberty, establishing special protections against encroachment. Further, the Court has limited the scope of the criminal law, permitting it to reach only behavior that has a relatively close and direct connection to actual harm.

These constitutional constraints have helped to keep radical prevention in check. But the sexual predator laws provide a model for undoing the constitutional protections of liberty. The laws allow the establishment of an expansive alternate system of justice, in which radical prevention prevails at the expense of liberty. Sexual predator laws do this by reintroducing and relegitimizing the concept of the degraded other. Membership in this outsider group is then used to rationalize a diminished system of justice, in which the normal protections of the Constitution do not apply.

There are growing pressures to expand prevention. The threat of terrorism after the 9/11 attacks is creating a new and tangible sense of vulnerability, bringing with it intense pressure to curtail the hard-won constitutional limits on the expansion of security at the expense of liberty. Here is the cause for alarm: the predator laws, which provide a model for evading those constitutional limits and a roadmap for the expansion of prevention, may jump from the relatively narrow realm of sexual violence to the radically broader universe of providing protection from the risk of crime—and terrorism—in general.

The Push for Radical Prevention to Combat Terrorism

Since the terrorist attacks of September 11, 2001, the federal government has adopted an aggressive policy of prevention in dealing with terrorism. The overall theme of the response is clearly articulated in President George W. Bush's doctrine of preemption. As his National Security Advisor Condoleezza Rice put it in 2002, the United States has the right to attack and wage war before the "smoking gun becomes a mushroom cloud."[4] Or, to quote the president himself, we need to destroy the threat to our nation "before it fully materializes."[5]

The theme of preemption extends from the grand realm of the law of war to the prevention of individual acts of terrorism. Law professor Robert Chesney identifies a "sharp change" following 9/11 in the government's adoption of a "prevention paradigm" in its criminal justice efforts to combat terrorism: "The overriding priority of the Department [of Justice] since 9/11 is to prevent attacks before they occur using all available tools." This has produced "significant internal incentive [for prosecutors] to expand their capacity for prevention."[6]

The major legislative response to the 9/11 attacks was the USA Patriot Act, passed in 2001. The act incorporates the notion of prevention in numerous provisions. It pushes the line for criminal prosecution far from actual harm, allowing the surveillance and criminalization of otherwise legitimate acts of nonviolent political dissent as potentially "dangerous" behavior. The law expands the government's ability to intrude on the private lives of citizens, authorizing expansive interception of electronic communications and government access to library and book sale records.[7]

In its response to the terrorist attacks of 9/11, the government has confined hundreds of noncitizens, and even several citizens, as "enemy combatants," a vaguely defined category that functions to remove almost all of the conventional protections of the criminal law.[8] The stated purpose is not to punish for a crime, but to prevent future harm, and to gather intelligence.[9] Beyond the Patriot Act, massive and intrusive surveillance schemes have been proposed,

in which citizens are to watch each other,[10] and even appliance repair techni-
cians and plumbers will be encouraged to watch for signs of terrorist activity
(and sexual predation) in the homes they visit. Disclosures in late 2005 revealed
that the government claimed the right to intercept international telephone
and e-mail communications without warrants and without compliance with
the Foreign Intelligence Surveillance Act. In early 2006, it issued subpoenas
to Google, the largest Internet search engine, to turn over an entire week's
worth of searches. The former searches were said to be in service to the nation's antiterrorism efforts, while the latter sought information to bolster the
government's defense of a beleaguered anti–child-porn law.[11] The pervasive-
ness of such governmental endeavors, in turn, has prompted criticisms that
First Amendment rights of free speech and access to information are being
curtailed.[12]

Despite the powerful rhetoric emanating from the highest levels of government, and the strong feeling of vulnerability induced by the terrorist attacks,
the push for prevention has met with resistance. Although the Patriot Act was
passed overwhelmingly, and without any significant debate, Congress imposed
a sunset provision on its terms, in recognition that its extreme provisions
would be appropriate (if at all) only in extraordinary times of extreme peril.
Popular opposition to its liberty-curtailing provisions forced the Attorney
General to campaign across the country for its renewal.[13] More than 350 cities
and four states have passed resolutions calling for reform of the act,[14] and federal courts have struck down parts of the act's surveillance provisions as vio-
lating the First and Fourth Amendments.[15] The most extreme proposals for
widespread surveillance have met with broad public rejection,[16] and the
Supreme Court has condemned the view that the detention of "enemy combatants" is totally beyond the reach of the courts.[17] In early 2006, Congress
passed a "compromise" bill reauthorizing the Patriot Act. Though some critics of the original act saw progress toward protecting civil liberties, others,
such as American Civil Liberties Union, lamented that the compromise continues to "not require that there be any individualized suspicion of wrong-
doing by Americans before their financial, medical, library, or other records
can be searched."[18]

Perhaps the public's concern over the aggressive provisions of the Patriot
Act arises from an abstract preference for liberty. More likely, though, it is that
such intrusions are seen as touching *our own liberty*. For the most part, these
post-9/11 enactments have been laws of general applicability. With a few key
exceptions (most notably subjecting certain immigrants to heightened scrutiny
because of their countries of origin), they do not *explicitly* target groups by race

or ethnicity.[19] Thus, as the public reads these laws (especially those relating to information gathering), at least some see their own liberty at stake.

At the same time, the pressure to link terrorism with Muslims and Middle Eastern males is exceedingly strong. This is clearly reflected in the patterns of arrests and interrogations after 9/11.[20] The tension between the ideal of no ethnic profiling and the seemingly intuitive stereotyping of the other produces an unstable equilibrium that is ripe for exploitation. As Minnesota's Republican governor Tim Pawlenty put it recently, "Elevating political correctness over homeland security concerns is not a good plan."[21] It is clear that the balance between liberty and security is close to equipoise—and the president's call for preemption expresses the public's powerful desire for security.

The predator laws—adopted and embraced in what seems like the limited context of the universally despised sex offender—now stand ready to provide a constitutional template for the expansion of intrusive government control on a much more massive scale.

Prevention in U.S. Law: Balancing Liberty and Security

Over the past century, our legal system has struggled to set the proper balance between liberty and security. As we look at the development of preventive legislation in the United States, we observe a progressive narrowing of the means by which legislatures can impose radical restraints on liberty in a preventive posture. The restraints on prevention have been accomplished in three ways. First, most important, the idea that our laws may pick out a disfavored group of others for specially disfavored treatment in the law has been all but eliminated. Second, the Supreme Court has developed a hierarchy of liberty, so that some forms of liberty—those that are "fundamental"—are more carefully protected than others.[22] Third, strict rules for our criminal justice system have been articulated, imposing careful constraints on the government's power to enforce criminal laws that take away privacy and liberty.[23]

These limits, however, have been hard won. Historically, many forms of legislation sought to identify "dangerous" people and restrain their liberty before they could do harm.[24] In U.S. legal history, the most egregious and prominent form of preventive legislation has been racially discriminatory laws. These laws created an alternate system of degraded justice in which the outsider group's rights were reduced in order to prevent some (imagined) future harm to the larger society. In *Dred Scott v. Sandford,* the Supreme Court made explicit the structure of this sort of outsider legislation. Justice Roger B. Taney observed that racial classifications in the United States reflected the degraded status of slaves "as a subordinate and inferior class of beings," who, as a consequence of that degraded status, "had no rights or privileges but such as those who held the power and the Government might choose to grant them."[25]

Although the use of race as a marker of subordinated otherness was explicit in *Dred Scott*, its use in the law became problematic after the ratification of the Fourteenth Amendment's equal protection clause in 1868. Nonetheless, the practice continued explicitly for decades, under the transparently false premise (put forth in *Plessy v. Ferguson*) that race-based discrimination was not hierarchical—that is, that these race-based classifications did not subordinate blacks as the other.[26] Famously, *Plessy* rationalized degradation by asserting that the races, though "separate," were nonetheless "equal."

The preventive nature of race-based laws was vividly evidenced in the Japanese internment cases during World War II. The cases involved a series of wartime orders directing individuals of Japanese descent, both citizens and noncitizens, to vacate their homes in western states and remove themselves to internment camps in California, Oregon, Arizona, and eleven other states. The Supreme Court upheld the laws, in cases that have never been overruled.[27]

In *Korematsu v. United States*, the Court seemed to acknowledge that wholesale restrictions on the liberty of citizens are generally not allowed. According to the Court, "Compulsory exclusion of large groups of citizens from their homes, except under circumstances of direst emergency and peril, is inconsistent with our basic governmental institutions." Justice Frank Murphy's dissent made the same point, referring to the "constitutional rights [of citizens] to live and work where they will, to establish a home where they choose and to move about freely." The fundamental nature of this aspect of liberty is a key point. It is a truism that liberty is not absolute and is potentially subject to government regulation for the common good. But these passages, as well as the overall tenor of the Court's decision, suggest that the liberty to live, work, and move about freely is a fundamental liberty, subject to curtailment only in the "direst emergency and peril."[28]

Sensitive, by 1944, to the use of race as a category in law, the majority in *Korematsu* was at pains to insist that "racism" or "racial antagonism" was not—and could not constitutionally be—a permissible ground for such a curtailment of liberty. But the Court's statements and the logic of the decision belie a reasoning that was group based:

> Exclusion of those of Japanese origin was deemed necessary because of the presence of an unascertained number of disloyal members *of the group*, most of whom we have no doubt were loyal to this country. It was because we could not reject the

finding of the military authorities that it was impossible to bring about an immediate segregation of the disloyal from the loyal that we sustained the validity of the
[internment] order as applying to the *whole group*.[29]

To the Court, it was clear with no need for discussion that the relevant characteristic for defining the group was race. It was reasonable, in the Court's
view, to ascribe some risk to the individual members of the group because of
the (assumed) aggregate risk posed by the entire group. To the Court, individuals of Japanese descent shared, simply by dint of their race, the essential
qualities of the group so that this ascription of risk was appropriate.

Of course, the other key factor about *Korematsu* was that it took place during wartime, a circumstance that in itself might be thought to provide the "dire
emergency" the Court said was needed to justify mass internment. To this, the
Court added that there was no time to determine on an individual basis who
was loyal and who was disloyal. But these emergency circumstances simply
provided the context that the Court thought justified its use of a racial category for the ascription of risk. If the dire circumstances made the restriction
of liberty necessary, it was the targeting of a racial group that made the restriction possible by showing how the restriction would be "safely" confined.

An earlier marker in the law of prevention was the Supreme Court's decision in *Buck v. Bell*.[30] Handed down in 1927, *Buck* upheld mandatory sterilization laws that emerged from the eugenics movement. Combining the new
science of genetics with emerging theories of criminology and notions of Dar-
winism, eugenics asserted that the human race could—and should—improve
its future through control of human breeding:

> When these sterilization laws were written, many subscribed to a simplistic version
> of genetics called eugenics and hoped to improve American society by encouraging
> the "healthy" to reproduce while simultaneously preventing those with "deleteri-
> ous inherited traits" from doing so. Under this rubric, mental retardation, insan-
> ity and even criminal behavior were considered hereditary and the "carriers" of
> these traits a danger to future generations.[31]

Thirty-three states passed eugenic sterilization laws, and some sixty thousand
people were sterilized under these laws.

The preventive rationale was unabashedly manifest in *Buck*. Writing for the
majority, Justice Oliver Wendell Holmes opined that "it is better for all the
world, if instead of waiting to execute degenerate offspring for crime, or to let
them starve for their imbecility, society can prevent those who are manifestly
unfit from continuing their kind."[32] In *Buck*, the Court relied on a case that
expressed the foundation of the state's "preventive" power, the 1905 decision

in *Jacobson v. Massachusetts,* upholding the "public health" power of the state to require smallpox vaccination.[33] But sterilization is hardly analogous to vaccination. And the Court was at pains to make clear that sterilization, unlike universal vaccination, was restricted to a small and vulnerable group of outsiders: "mental defectives" who constitute a "kind" of people who are "degenerate," criminal and imbecilic, and who "sap the strength of the State." As one commentator put it, "Sadly, those targeted for reproductive quarantine were already defined as outcasts by a white majority: the mentally ill or retarded, 'sexual deviants,' the impoverished, African-Americans and immigrants."[34] The state's power to curtail liberty in a radical way, in short, was limited in this case to those who fell outside the civic polity by reason of their degeneracy, dependency, and incompetence.

Buck and its approval of involuntary sterilization based on a theory of eugenics have now been discredited, though *Buck,* like *Korematsu,* has never been formally overruled by the Court. But as with *Korematsu,* the "court of popular opinion" has rejected *Buck* and what it stands for. The Supreme Court has firmly established that reproductive rights are fundamental.[35] No court now would suggest that these rights could be diminished simply by reason of a person's mental incapacity, or some other outsider status.

Korematsu and *Buck* highlight the distance that our society, and the courts, have come in eliminating the last of the outsider classifications traditionally used to justify diminished civic personhood. Developments in the law beginning in the 1970s make clear that gender cannot, in most circumstances, justify diminished rights.[36] The passage of the Americans with Disabilities Act in 1990, suggests that disability status, long a marker of diminished rights, also is removed from the list.[37] In two recent cases, the Supreme Court struck down laws that curtailed the rights of homosexuals. In *Romer v. Evans,* the Court struck down a Colorado constitutional amendment that essentially limited the ability of gays to participate in the political process.[38] And in *Lawrence v. Texas,* the Court struck down a criminal law punishing consensual gay sex.[39] In both cases, the Court essentially ruled that the state may not curtail the liberty rights of a group simply because the majority perceives the group as different and morally undeserving of the protections of the law.

If it has been the demise of an "outsider jurisprudence" that blocks the creation of an alternate system of degraded justice, then it is the "great safeguards which the law adopts in the punishment of crime" that characterize the normal system of justice.[40] These "ordinary criminal processes" are the "normal means of dealing with persistent criminal conduct."[41] And the core requirement in the criminal process is charge and conviction for an actual—not predicted—crime.

During the past half century, constitutional bulwarks against radical prevention have been strengthened by a series of cases prohibiting the creation of "crimes" that are too far distant from actual harm. Prior to the middle of the twentieth century, vagrancy laws were a ubiquitous means of preventive control. These laws "erect[ed] flexible status definitions of possibly dangerous character types, designed to permit the preventive apprehension of supposedly likely criminals."[42] Closely related to the vagrancy laws were the antiloitering laws that replaced them. The courts have since struck down both vagrancy and loitering laws.[43] These laws have generally been invalidated on vagueness grounds, because, as the Supreme Court put it, the laws "vest virtually complete discretion in the hands of the police to determine whether the suspect has satisfied the statute and must be permitted to go on his way."[44]

The disapproval of vagrancy laws is of a kind with the limits placed on the criminal law in the past fifty years in regard to potential, rather than actual, harmful behavior. During World War I, the Supreme Court regularly upheld the criminal punishment of speech that was critical of the war effort without any convincing proof that the speech created any realistic risk of harm to the country's defense.[45] During the cold war, political speech that was similarly distant from concrete harm was punished.[46] But beginning in the 1960s, the Court curtailed the criminalization of speech deemed too distant from harmful behavior.[47] Almost simultaneously, the Court held that a person could not be punished for a "status" such as being an alcoholic or a drug addict.[48] Similarly, while the criminal law permits punishment not only of actually harmful acts but also of inchoate crimes such as attempts and conspiracies, "attempts" can be criminalized only if they satisfy a "dangerous proximity" test,[49] and conspiracy requires some concrete action linked to specific harmful acts.[50]

Thus, the criminal law is constrained not only by strict procedural protections but also because its reach is limited to harmful acts rather than harmful propensities. Despite our long history of radically preventive laws, legal developments, particularly of the past fifty years, have in fundamental ways circumscribed permissible forms of radical prevention in the law.

Sexual Predator Laws as a Ready Template for Outsider Jurisprudence and a Preventive State

The predator laws lay down a road map for the creation of a degraded system of justice that radically curtails the usual protections of the Constitution. They accomplish this by resurrecting the outsider jurisprudence that we have, with such difficulty, discarded over the past half century. Instead of being based on race, gender, sexual orientation, or disability, the new outsider status is based on mental disorder and risk. This mental disorder criterion, however, is exceedingly porous, and in reality the laws use the expansive notion of risk as the real marker of otherness.

The predator template for radical prevention poses a threat to maintaining a sound balance between liberty and security. These laws return us to a path that places no principled limits on the degradation of rights for the outside group. Basing outsider status on risk invites broad expansion of the targeted group and legitimizes not only preventive detention but also broad systemic surveillance of entire populations.

Predator laws demarcate a new outsider group and build their alternate system of justice on that edifice. They harness the authority and legitimacy of science and medicine to make their classification of people into "us" and "them" appear to be natural and inevitable, untainted by the invidious prejudice of the rejected outsider jurisprudence. Focusing mainly on risk and mental disorder as markers of difference, the laws are based on the notion that the risky *person* is different at some essential level—or, to put it another way, that he is a different kind of person.

The sexual predator laws rely on and produce the same kind of "essential difference" between groups of people that we have struggled to eliminate from our law. A central tenet of the predator commitment laws is that their targets constitute an "identifiable" group suffering from a particular "condition."[51] To support this view, sex predator commitment laws employ a flawed effort at diagnosis. Diagnosis claims to identify the essence, discarding or ignoring what is accidental about the individual. Yet the real definitional foundation for this outsider group is the ascription of risk. Risk assessment is possible only to the extent that individuals are said to belong to groups whose statistical probability of exhibiting the target behavior can be measured or estimated. An individual belongs to the group only to the extent that he or she is essentially—rather than accidentally—associated with the group.[52] Predator laws, in short, ascribe the group risk to the individual.[53]

The Supreme Court has held that the key marker of difference in the predator laws is the "mental disorder" of the individual subject to commitment. In *Kansas v. Crane*, the Court held that a "mental disorder" is constitutionally adequate to support civil commitment only if it "*distinguish[es]* a dangerous sexual offender subject to civil commitment from 'other dangerous persons who are perhaps more properly dealt with exclusively through criminal proceedings.'"[54]

The use of mental disorder as the definition of the other allows the creation of a degraded system of justice without triggering widespread concern about the encroachment of radical prevention on civil liberties. The mental disorder classification invokes science and medicine, and we tend to think that those with "mental disorders" really are, in some sense, aberrational and different. This reassures us that the alternate legal system is well limited and does not threaten our own liberty.

But in actuality the Supreme Court's definition of "mental disorder" as "serious difficulty in controlling behavior" is a sham, in no way defining a limited group that is truly different in any sense from the rest of us.[55] Failure of self-control is a characteristic that sex offenders share with most other criminals. Knight and Prentky report that "lifestyle impulsivity" is highly predictive of future sexual reoffending and is a "relatively robust predictor of reoffense risk across domains of criminal behavior."[56] One of the most widely accepted general theories of criminality, that of Gottfredson and Hirschi, argues that criminality stems from an underlying deficit in self-control.[57] Poor self-control is widely thought to be a "stable and robust predictor of reoffending among the general criminal population."[58] As Baumeister, Heatherton, and Tice have pointed out: "The most important generalization about crime and criminality is that they arise from lack of self-control. Most crimes are impulsive actions, and most criminals exhibit broad and multifaceted patterns of lacking self-control."[59] In short, impaired self-control is not a "diagnosis" or a "mental disorder" that makes sex offenders different from other criminals—it is precisely what makes them similar to other criminals.

Behind the "mental disorder" screen, the real work of creating the outsider group is done by the concept of risk as employed in the predator laws. Like diagnosis, risk assessment is seen as an expert endeavor, one that increasingly can claim the mantle of science.[60] Predator laws reify risk, make it concrete, and ascribe it to the individual. Risk assessment "seeks to bring the future into the present," distilling the future into a present "condition" or "propensity."[61] This is necessary because otherwise we could not lock somebody up *now* because of what they might do in the future. While the "causal factors" for violence may be a combination of internal (psychological) and external (environmental) factors,[62] the resultant "risk" is ascribed solely to the individual. He *is* dangerous, he *has* risk, and it is his possession of these characteristics that justifies his incarceration. Under the predator template, we lock people up who "pose a threat to others, not because of what they had done but because of who they are, because their very makeup as a human being made them a threat to 'the community.' "[63]

As constructed by the predator laws, risk tells us something essential— rather than accidental—about the person. This characteristic—sometimes called "dangerousness"—is portrayed as a stable ingredient of the person, a part of him even if it is not now visible.[64] It is this internal characteristic, treated as having long-term stability, that justifies both the prediction of future behavior and the creation of outsider status. The predator is not simply a person who commits a crime but a person whose nature is criminal, "a 'criminal man', a person who by his very nature is driven to commit the most violent of crimes against the most vulnerable of victims."[65]

In the predator template, risk quietly takes the place of race, gender, sexual orientation, and disability as the foundation for an outsider jurisprudence. The concept of risk removes the damning taint of racism, sexism, homophobia, and other forms of rejected prejudice. Risk is seen as something in nature, "an ontological state of the world,"[66] "a material object amenable to objective calculation and measurement."[67] The use of science to measure risk and to demonstrate a condition underlying human violence gives risk a "moral neutrality [and] scientificity."[68]

But this naturalizing of risk is misleading, disguising a strong moral condemnation of "the risky." As noted by a British law professor, Barbara Hudson, "the language of risk plays the same role in contemporary society as stigma and taboo in pre-modern societies. . . . Persistent offenders, especially sex offenders, become the new lepers: diseased, incurable, unable to control outbreaks, themselves to blame for whatever privations society imposes upon them."[69]

Thus, we see that risk functions in much the same way that race did as a marker of degraded status. Of course, risk and race differ in many critical aspects. After all, unlike members of racial groups, the members of the group targeted by the predator laws—sex offenders—have *all* violated the rights of others in egregious ways, and it is at least partly this behavior that has landed them in the risky category. Sex offenders are properly held responsible for the crimes they have committed. But this blame is expiated, so far as the law is concerned, in the criminal punishment that the justice system has meted out. Under the Constitution, the imposition of civil commitment, and the intrusive impositions on privacy and liberty of Megan's laws, cannot be premised on the blameworthy criminal "guilt" of the individuals.[70]

Furthermore, past harmful behavior is only a contingent feature of risk, perhaps an artifact of the limitations on our current ability to measure risk. There is nothing *inherent* in the notion of risk that limits its application to people who have actually engaged in harmful—much less criminal—behavior. Under the logic of risk assessment, a person's "risk" exists even before he or she has exhibited any harmful behavior.

Indeed, there is a long tradition—and a developing science—suggesting that the seeds of future antisocial behavior are present long before they become manifest. For at least a century, researchers have sought to identify something unique and different about criminals. This sort of thinking has inspired a variety of "scientific" attempts to demonstrate a criminal personality, a genetically inferior type, related to the lower species, destined to commit crime.[71] Reflecting this thinking, the Minnesota Supreme Court's 1939 *Pearson* decision referred to "sex psychopaths" as "hopelessly immoral" and as a "type of 'unnaturals'."[72]

In many ways, the early attempts to identify a criminal type have been discredited.[73] But recent developments in science may breathe new life into this notion. In 2003, Grant Harris and Marnie Rice recognized that "the preponderance of scientific evidence supports the idea that the majority of variance in violent criminal conduct (including sexual aggression) can be attributed to genetically and physiologically based enduring traits that, once initiated, exhibit life-long persistence under conditions so far observed."[74] In a similar vein, Vernon Quinsey has noted that a number of distinct psychological tests have been developed in recent years for estimating the risk of future criminal violence. He notes that although each of these approaches uses somewhat different methods and includes somewhat different factors, their results correlate with each other and with future violence. Building on the work of David Rowe, Quinsey wonders whether "a super-factor, called 'd,' underlies all of the disparate correlates of criminal propensity." Quinsey compares d (for deviance) with g, the super-factor that underlies intelligence. Noting that g "is a biological variable reflecting some aspect of neural process speed," Quinsey cautions that "it is much less clear what the nature of d is."[75]

Quinsey's caution, however, may be irrelevant in the development of the law. The predator template provides a ready vehicle to transform this "condition"—the presence of d—into the mark of an outsider status. The logic of the predator laws would provide vast powers of prevention to the state, should it seek to identify, and incapacitate, all those whose level of d crosses some threshold of risk.

Outsider Jurisprudence: An American Addiction

After the Supreme Court's *Lawrence* decision declared that homosexuality may not be used as a degraded status, we might have been tempted to pronounce American outsider jurisprudence all but dead, thus providing a solid bulwark against the radical spread of a risk-based outsider status. But there is evidence that the existence of the degraded other has not been a horrible historical diversion but is rather a central—though tragic—addiction of our liberal democracy. The predator template is not an anomaly but a reversion to a practice that fits all too comfortably into liberal democracies.

The existence of reduced-rights zones for the degraded other flows, in Hudson's terminology, from the "key question for liberal theories of justice: that of membership and exclusion. Who is to be included in the community of justice, and whom is the just community to defend itself against?" She argues that the construction of the "irrational, uncivilized" other is a "necessity" in Western liberal democracies. The role played by the negative other in liberal systems, according to Hudson, is to define what it means to have rights, by showing its opposite: "For rights to have meaning, to be cognitively as well as politically recognized, there must be groups without rights, so that the difference between rights and non-rights can be appreciated." Noting that even John Stuart Mill espouses "despotism" as a "legitimate mode of government in dealing with barbarians," Hudson explains that "we find no guidance from liberalism on questions of the limits that should be placed on measures taken to protect good citizens against the risky and dangerous. . . . They have no real existence for us as moral agents with claims upon us. . . . The tenets of rights-respecting democratic governance do not apply to them."[76]

Hudson's analysis helps explain why the sexual predator template poses a distinctive threat to the balance between rights and security. The predator laws provide outsider jurisprudence with a renewed foothold in our national consciousness. Feeling the fear of terrorism in our homeland, there is a danger that our old addiction to targeting outsiders will reawaken, providing us with an immoral rationale for creating alternative and degraded legal regimes for groups we choose, in the heat of the moment, to define, in Mill's terms, as "barbarians."

Just as threatening is the role that the degraded other plays in defining the meaning and scope of rights that "we the people" retain. By creating an outside group with radically reduced rights, the predator template changes the scale against which we measure and understand the terrorism-related restrictions on our own rights. The existence of an alternate system of justice serves to highlight "our" protected position under the Constitution's umbrella, even as our own liberties are being eroded.

The predator template threatens the traditional liberty-security balance by transitioning from guilt to risk as the key predicate for liberty deprivation. Again, this is not an isolated or aberrational development, but an important move that accelerates and legitimizes major transformations in our society. Law professors Malcolm Feeley and Jonathan Simon have argued that we are becoming "markedly less concerned with responsibility, fault, moral sensibility" and more concerned with "techniques to identify, classify, and manage groupings sorted by dangerousness."[77] Many see this as part of a larger development, the rise of the "risk society." In the "risk society," according to Hudson, governance makes the avoidance of risk "the central object of decision-making processes."[78]

This move from guilt to risk entails increased (and qualitatively different) surveillance of citizens. Traditionally, our criminal justice system has a crime-solving approach. The government intrudes on our liberty only in response to some identified criminal activity. Only those whose behavior suggests a link to the crime are targeted for surveillance. But the state must cast a much broader net if it is to prevent crime before it happens.[79] The more distant the "risk" is from actual crime, the broader must be the gaze of the government. The warrantless eavesdropping by the National Security Agency of international e-mails and telephone calls is a prime example. According to the *New York Times,* computers inspect "hundreds of thousands" of electronic messages, selecting "thousands" for further inspection by humans. Of these, authorities "have dismissed nearly all of them as potential suspects."[80]

We are accustomed to preventive surveillance, but only in limited, public areas of our lives, such as using radar to measure our speed. And in limited "special circumstances" the Supreme Court has approved "suspicionless searches" that intrude more deeply into our privacy.[81]

But the predator template legitimizes broad and intrusive surveillance of entire populations. In this alternative system of justice, surveillance need not be limited only to those who are suspected of having committed a crime. Predator laws transform the government's role from reactive crime solving to proactive risk assessment and control. The latter is much more intrusive and expansive than the former. Crime solving begins when a crime is reported. Risk assessment precedes an actual crime. By definition, its sweep must be much broader than the (future) crime whose "risk" is being assessed. Because it involves finding risk rather than guilt, risk assessment must necessarily touch many more people than does crime solving, by large orders of magnitude. Risk, says Kemshall, "becomes a self-justificatory logic for increased extension of the surveillance network into every aspect of social life."[82]

The science of risk assessment combines with the politics of risk to broaden the scope of surveillance. The development of actuarial risk-assessment tools makes risk assessment much simpler to administer than the traditional clinical psychological examination. Though some of these tools remain rather complex, others are brief screening tools that are relatively simple to score. Risk assessment will increasingly become a practical possibility.

The very possibility of *measuring* risk creates a powerful pressure to *prevent* the risk. As Nikolas Rose, a British sociologist puts it, "Once it seems that today's decisions can be informed by calculations about tomorrow, we can demand that calculations about tomorrow should and must inform all decisions made today. The option of acting in the present in order to manage the future rapidly mutates into something like an obligation."[83] Experience with the predator laws confirms the reality of this "obligation." Risks "are subject to 'hindsight scrutiny,' and with the luxury of hindsight, a key test for risk decisions is their defensibility."[84] There is immense political pressure to translate risk knowledge into risk control. But because risk is a continuous variable (unlike guilt), this pressure has no inherent stopping point. The safest course for politicians is to promote the notion of zero tolerance for risk,[85] to expand preventive control to cover all degrees of risk, broadening the populations being assessed and lowering the risk threshold for intervention.[86] As Hudson puts it, "The demand for safety is insatiable."[87]

Security—as achieved by the control of harmful behavior—is a necessary precondition to the enjoyment of liberty.[88] The question is how security and liberty should be balanced. No one is opposed to punishing people who engage in terrorism or commit rape, or to arresting people who are conspiring to commit terrorist acts or attempting to lure children over the Internet. We can all agree on the value of programs that seek to prevent sexual violence or infectious diseases by changing the conditions that are conducive to violence and disease in the society. The problem is not prevention but radical prevention: invading people's privacy and physical liberty, not in response to harm done but to a perceived "propensity" or "risk" of future harm.

Over the centuries, U.S. jurisprudence has gradually imposed a strong set of safeguards against an overextension of security at the expense of liberty. These safeguards are both constitutional and political. We rely on both the courts and the political process to draw the right balance. But our history—and perhaps the very nature of our liberal democracy—exposes an Achilles heel in these safeguards. When we feel threatened by an outsider group, we have used the law to target it by disabling the normal constitutional and political protections, creating a separate and degraded system of justice.

We are living in a tenuous and vulnerable time. The threat of terrorism damages our sense of security. The pressure to trade liberty for safety is intense. Our unfortunate traditions tempt us to relieve that pressure by sacrificing the rights of outsiders, but hard lessons learned in the past highlight the harmfulness of that move. The predator laws reopen the possibility that targeting outsiders might be legitimate. The mantle of science naturalizes the raw and arbitrary power that is the only foundation for a separate and degraded system of justice. Our sense of justice, our fear for our own rights, are soothed by the mental disorder label, the assurance that these folks are somehow different from us. But the only real difference is risk; and as the science of risk assessment improves and expands, the temptation to intervene earlier and earlier, with a broader and broader segment of the population, may be proving too hard for our political process to resist. We should stop the process now, before we create a legal monster we truly regret.

Part III

COURSE

CORRECTIONS

CHAPTER SEVEN

There Are Alternatives

Sexual assault victims in Comal County [Texas] are being victimized again by the system.

The lack of a sexual assault nurse examiner program at McKenna Memorial Hospital in Comal County means that the evidence needed to prosecute assailants often is not collected in a timely manner or at all.

McKenna officials are hesitant to start a program to handle sexual assault victims because of the expense and the number of rapes in the county.

—*San Antonio Express-News*

The predator laws represent an approach to sexual violence that is out of balance. The great bulk of sexual victimization is perpetrated by men who have not been in the criminal justice system and who are acquaintances and even intimates of the victims. Sexual predator commitment laws confine only a small percentage of the sex offenders who are under correctional control, releasing a large majority of recidivists back into the community. Yet the predator commitment laws are exceedingly expensive and growing, while programs that address a broader swath of violence must struggle for funding. If we simply consider the number of sexual victimizations addressed, the cost of sex predator commitment laws seems grossly out of proportion.

We must reexamine the predator model and the resource allocation it entails, broadening the question we ask when designing sexual violence policy. The predator model focuses on the "worst of the worst" and seeks to identify and lock up the "most dangerous." Instead, we should be asking what combi-

Epigraph is from the editorial "Rape Victims Deserve Prompt Medical Care," Mar. 16, 2004.

nation of approaches to sexual violence has the best prospect of preventing the most sexual violence. This entails a shift from focusing mainly on assessing individual risk to understanding and addressing risk both individually and collectively, from addressing mainly the most obvious and visible dangers to attempting to prevent the hidden and silent crimes that make up the bulk of sexual victimization.

The arguments advanced in this chapter are necessarily somewhat tentative, because we still have much to learn about what kinds of interventions are effective in reducing sexual violence. The main point is that the powerfully attractive premise of the predator laws—that we can prevent the next heinous rape-murder—is blinding us to alternative approaches to prevention, and that there are good reasons why these alternative approaches should get a hefty share of the prevention resources. If we really are serious about preventing the most sexual violence, we must look more comprehensively at the full range of interventions that are available.

Sex predator commitment laws are expensive and growing. But their expense alone is not a reason to condemn them. After all, the prevention of sexual violence ought to be a high priority in our society, and we ought to be willing to spend considerable sums on it. The question presented here is whether these laws consume too big a share of the prevention resources.

In the sixteen states that have predator commitment laws, current expenditures to fund those programs are estimated to be in the range of $275–320 million per year. This sum, which will grow rapidly, pays for the incarceration of about three thousand offenders.[1] Compare this level of expenditure to the level of funding provided by Congress on a national basis for prevention of sexual violence. The rape prevention and education grant program is funded at $45.2 million, but the president's 2006 budget request is a bit less, $44.2 million. The Centers for Disease Control and Prevention community initiatives "supports new community programs aimed at preventing intimate partner violence and strengthening existing community intervention and prevention programs." Its budget is $5.8 million. The campus violence grants program was funded at $10 million in 2003, but its funding would be cut by nearly 10 percent under the president's 2006 budget proposal. These programs are all part of the Violence against Women Act, whose funding addresses not only sexual violence but, more generally, domestic violence. Including the programs mentioned above, the VAWA total funding is $385 million. This is the major funding provided by the federal government for domestic and sexual violence programs. In short, the sixteen states with predator commitment programs spend about as much to lock up the "worst of the worst" as the entire nation spends on violence against women programs, serving and addressing a vastly broader group of victims and potential victims.

In 1996, at the height of the rush to adopt the predator laws, 26 percent of parole and probation officers in a national survey reported that sex offender treatment services were in short supply.[2] In 2004, when Minnesota spent $26 million per year to lock up 235 predators, budget troubles forced Minneapolis to propose cutting 137 of its 778 police officers over a four-year period, bringing its force level to the lowest it has been since 1958.[3] Minnesota eliminated 100 probation officer positions despite rising caseloads. Funding in Minnesota for domestic violence and sexual violence prevention programs was cut by $3.6 million per year. A state sex offender official in Idaho—a state that has not enacted a sex predator commitment law—laments that "limited resources . . . need to be focused on the higher-risk guys" but that "in the everybody else group there are lots of people that are dangerous guys. In that mix there are some real low-risk guys and some real high-risk guys."[4]

A 2000 report to the Minnesota legislature from the Department of Corrections noted that the highly effective "intensive supervised release" program for sex offenders was not available in about half of the state's counties and was significantly underfunded in the large metropolitan counties. The report also stated that "routinely, [parole] agents report that caseload sizes are too large to allow them to utilize all of the tools available to best supervise sex offenders in the community" and that "in many jurisdictions, caseload sizes continue to remain at levels that allow only minimum supervision techniques."[5]

Nationally, correctional treatment programs for sex offenders are underfunded and overwhelmed.[6] The National Center for Missing & Exploited Children warns that "while community supervision and oversight is widely recognized as essential, the system for providing such supervision is overwhelmed" and that "state-sponsored [sex offender] treatment programs are under attack and are disappearing around the country."[7]

California, for example, spent more than $78 million in 2004 to lock up 535 predators, while providing no substantial sex offender treatment for the seventeen thousand sex offenders in its prisons, most of whom will return to the community eventually. And, the director of governmental affairs for a Massachusetts antiviolence coalition warns that there are "shrinking resources" in the state for services for sexual assault victims and prevention programs, warning that prevention efforts are "lowest on the totem pole" in funding priorities for the state. Meanwhile, Massachusetts is pouring millions into its predator commitment program.

There are alternatives to the predator approach. What follows is a sampling, not a comprehensive review, of the creative ideas that ought to be considered if we really want to reduce sexual violence. These, and others, are widely supported proposals that could form a more hopeful and effective program to fight sexual violence.

All of these alternative strategies share a common difference from the predator approach. They turn from "zero tolerance" to "harm reduction" as the guiding value.[8] Instead of asking how we can guarantee no more sexual violence from the worst of the worst, we ask how we can most effectively reduce sexual violence overall. The zero-tolerance approach seems to be tougher, thus serving the emotive needs of our society. But, in reality, it is only tougher if we ignore and render invisible the ubiquitous sexual violence that is excluded by the predator paradigm. If the harm-reduction approaches appear to tolerate more risk, it is only because they more honestly acknowledge the true incidence of sexual violence.

The Public Health Approach

Many of the most thoughtful commentators on the prevention of sexual violence urge a public health approach to the problem of sexual violence. Sexual violence, like the classic infectious diseases (smallpox, measles, polio), has widespread negative effects on our society. The public health approach, a systematic application of scientific learning aimed at understanding and addressing root causes, could help effectively reduce sexual violence in the same way that it has controlled many infectious diseases.

The public health approach entails a systematic method of analysis, a way of seeing the problem in a larger, more contextualized framework. It divides interventions into three categories: primary, secondary, and tertiary. Primary prevention efforts focus on stopping sexually abusive behaviors before they start. They aim at changing the conditions that produce the problem—attacking the root causes of sexual violence. Secondary programs focus on "those at high risk for offending as well as stopping recent sexual offenders from re-offending." Tertiary prevention "involves trying to stop future violence by those who have a history of offending behaviors."[9]

The public health approach uses systematic and empirically based information for deciding how best to attack a public health problem like sexual violence. It consciously looks beyond individual characteristics of offenders to identify causes that exist at a societal or community level. These classic steps that enabled public health to conquer infectious disease aim to address sexual violence comprehensively. The first step is "ongoing systematic collection, analysis, and interpretation of data on the incidence, prevalence, and risk factors." The second step is "identifying causes" through research. The third step is the "development and evaluation of programs." Finally, the public health model engages in "dissemination and implementation . . . communicating which preventive programs work based on evaluation of data and putting these programs into practice."[10]

The public health approach helps us understand the difference between thinking about a problem like sexual violence at the scale of individuals and thinking about it from the perspective of the population as a whole. The public health approach allows us to see that there is collective risk as well as individual risk, and that the worst of the worst account for only a fraction of the collective risk posed by sexual violence. The public health approach, by insisting on empirically based policies for reducing sexual violence, puts "prevention efforts foremost."[11] Unlike the conventional narrow and politicized approach that values only punishment, public health advocates understand the need for a "comprehensive approach addressing all levels of prevention (i.e., primary, secondary, and tertiary)."[12]

The predator laws exemplify an approach that is 180 degrees from these public health principles. The predator laws were not based on research. They make no pretense of attacking the root causes of sexual violence or changing the conditions that produce it. Rather, they take a simple containment approach to those who are already identified as dangerous offenders. Far from being comprehensive, they focus only on a small part of the problem, a part that is far removed from the root causes or the experiences of most victims of sexual violence. There has been little research about the effectiveness of the predator law approaches and little reason to believe that they have reduced the scope of sexual violence in any meaningful way. Robert Prentky and Ann Burgess are leading scholars of sexual violence and the design of systems for attempting to reduce it. They point out that despite the "hypervigilant" and "draconian" responses to sexual violence, "by and large, those who sexually intimidate and sexually coerce others do so with impunity." Along with many other experts, they urge a model that "treats sexual assault as a public health problem."[13]

The public health approach helps us see what a focus on identified individual offenders hides: the value and necessity of primary prevention. Because most sexual violence does not show up in the criminal justice system, most will remain unaddressed by secondary and tertiary interventions. Primary prevention is proactive, while the secondary and tertiary methods are reactive. Primary prevention aims at addressing sexual violence before it happens. Secondary and tertiary approaches become applicable only after an offender has begun abusing victims.

Although primary prevention programs are in their infancy, and their effectiveness is as yet unproven, they have a number of attractions. They are relatively cheap and can reach large numbers of people. They aim to change root causes of sexual violence by addressing attitudes, beliefs, and behaviors and thus stop sexual violence before it begins. Secondary and tertiary approaches, in contrast, do not address new entrants into sexual offending, but confine their attention to those who have already offended.

Stop It Now! is a grassroots organization founded by Fran Henry, a survivor of childhood sexual abuse. The group advocates a paradigm shift, the creation of "a new pathway for preventing child sexual abuse—a path that uses the powerful tools of public health and prevents abuse before it happens." A recent publication explains:

> While individual cases are extremely important, we now recognize that child sexual abuse is not just the result of individual pathologies and aberrant families; it is a widespread social illness, requiring social action and change, and primary, 'front end' prevention strategies. . . . We need a proactive, prevention-based model that will address the root causes of abuse on a social systems scale: that is what public health can offer.[14]

Another key advocate of public health approaches is Kathleen Basile, an official with the Centers for Disease Control and Prevention. Citing a long list of other authors, Basile states that "more attention should be given to primary prevention of sexual violence if real gains are to be made in decreasing this problem." Basile argues that "national campaigns against sexual violence in the media could affect rates of sexual offending by gradually influencing societal norms that condone sexual aggression." She cites campaigns regarding the use of automobile seat belts, noting that today about two-thirds of the population uses seat belts, "largely because the norms about wearing seat belts have changed through public awareness combined with changes in laws." Smoking cessation campaigns provide another example of the larger society getting involved in preventing a widespread problem. She states that "the same societal urgency needs to be established around decreasing sexual violence perpetration by involving the public in large-scale sexual violence preventive efforts."[15]

Primary prevention programs are largely in the developmental stage. Some experimental programs seek to change attitudes and behaviors among school-age populations. Safe Dates, a program offered to middle school students in rural South Carolina, seeks to change norms around dating violence, to decrease gender stereotyping, and to enhance conflict management. The program also offers services for adolescents in abusive relationships. Early research indicates that the program is successful in reducing sexual violence on dates.[16] Another program, in a midsize city in the Pacific Northwest, was designed to challenge high school students' "attitudes about coercive sexual behavior" and teach them "ways to deal with unwanted sexual advances through clear communication." The program was subjected to a controlled evaluation, which indicated that "students with more negative attitudes about sexual assault benefited the most from the program."[17] Other programs, aimed at high-risk adolescent males, report some success at decreasing rape-myth acceptance.

Another approach advocated by Stop It Now! and other groups is to facilitate early intervention where there is a risk of sexual abuse. This involves public education about the signs that sexual deviancy is developing in a child or that an adult is engaging in sexually exploitive or abusive behavior. It also involves helping people know what to do and where to turn to obtain help to stop sexual abuse. Stop It Now! produced a social marketing campaign aimed at abusers and potential abusers. Employing "provocative ads that highlighted the effectiveness of treatment," they "encouraged abusers to stop hurting children, urged offenders to get help, and prompted family members to call for assistance." Evaluation suggested that the program produced "several dramatic changes" in the public's knowledge about child sexual abuse. In addition, the Stop It Now! campaign recognizes and attempts to remove the barriers for abusers seeking help without exposing themselves to unduly harsh consequences of shaming and exclusion. In a pilot program in Vermont, fifteen adults and ten adolescents self-reported their abusive behavior to authorities, and clinicians reported that twenty adults and ninety-eight juveniles voluntarily entered treatment without a direct victim report.[18]

A report commissioned by the Centers for Disease Control discussed very preliminary results from a program to identify and evaluate primary prevention approaches to sexual violence.[19] Preliminary results from the study found some significant increases in participants' knowledge regarding consent and in their intentions to prevent disrespectful behavior, though there were some results in the opposite direction. The report states:

> Participant feedback measures have demonstrated strong positive response to the intervention by youth. Qualitative data from focus groups in three sites indicates that programs are changing participants' concepts of healthy and unhealthy relationships and enhancing their ability to recognize and respond to sexual harassment.[20]

Primary prevention efforts "are essentially at the drawing boards."[21] Pursuing these promising leads will require additional resources for experimentation and careful evaluations, and dissemination and implementation of the approaches that are shown to be most effective.

A Continuum of Interventions

The strength of the public health approach is that it demands an examination of all levels of intervention. Though primary prevention approaches deserve substantial attention, secondary and tertiary approaches in the criminal justice system remain important options for intervention. The public health approach demands that we understand how best to use all intervention options to achieve the goal of maximum violence reduction. The strength of the criminal justice system is that it is the principal means of exerting coercive control over a substantial number of known offenders, and it is the main way we have of expressing strong moral disapproval of sexual violence. Among its limitations: most sexual abusers never find their way into the system, and most sexual violence is committed by individuals who have not been in the system.

Our society has taken two types of approaches to reforming the criminal justice system's approach to sexual violence. First, the feminist-inspired rape reforms have attempted to cast a wider net for the criminal justice system and to reform the procedures and rules so the system is less hostile to the victims of sexual violence. There is still more work to do in this regard, especially in lessening the trauma experienced by victims in the criminal justice system. Second, over the past two or three decades, states have increased penalties for sexual crimes, so that more people are now spending more time incarcerated for sexual violence.

Though there is clearly some momentum remaining in this punitive trend, many commentators urge that greater use of incarceration may have reached a point of diminishing returns. Writing from a feminist perspective, for example, Patricia Rozee and Mary Koss argue that "we may have to reconsider our need to punish perpetrators using traditional criminal justice methods (e.g., imprisonment) if we are to be open to new ways of dealing with the problem of rape." They point out that the traditional criminal justice system fails women victims of rape in three ways. First, men are not held accountable due to lack of reporting and failure of prosecutors to file charges, and because of acquittals. "Second, men who are arrested for rape have most likely gotten away with this behavior for some time and have an established pattern of behavior that is difficult to change through rehabilitation or prison. Third, women are revictimized by the criminal justice process."[22]

A paradigm shift is required. Though punishment through incarceration has an appropriate role, a rational approach to prevention would use a wide range of other criminal justice approaches to provide broader, more effective reduction in sexual violence. Providing a full "continuum of interventions" recognizes the fact that even in the criminal justice system most sex offenders will remain in, or return to, the community. It is for this reason that a central recommendation of the Minnesota Governor's Commission on Sex Offender Policy is the establishment of a "true continuum" of interventions.[23]

Offenders present a range of risk (varying both from offender to offender and from time to time in the same person), and a range of interventions corresponding to the range of risks ought to be available. These interventions need to be well managed and changeable as an offender's change in risk warrants.

In light of this reality, many experts recommend a shift from risk prediction to risk management.[24] The risk prediction model, relying primarily on historical and static variables, seeks to assess the long-term risk posed by an individual so that an appropriate level of intervention (confinement, supervision) may be imposed. Risk is seen as a static, unchanging characteristic of the person, and risk prediction leads to a one-time assignment of the individual to a disposition corresponding to the static assessment of risk. In contrast, the risk management model acknowledges that the risk posed by an individual may change over time, as characteristics of the individual or his environment change, responding, for example, to treatment, physical condition, aging, changes in family circumstances, increased supervision, and so on. In the risk management model, "the focus is on the reduction of risk through compliance and progress with risk interventions"; interventions are "sensitive to changes in risk status." The nature and intensity of the intervention should be tailored to the individual and should recognize that this can change over time.[25]

Many experts believe that supervision in the community, if properly designed and administered, "can be made sufficiently 'tight' to reduce risk to a minimum for many offenders."[26] As Prentky and Burgess put it, for high-risk offenders long-term and intensive community supervision and aftercare "should be the centerpiece of any secondary intervention strategy."[27] But this entails increasing the resources for community treatment and supervision so that the required level of intensity and length of supervision can be achieved.

The state-of-the-art model for delivering this type of aftercare supervision to sex offenders in the community is the containment model, developed in Colorado. The approach is called "containment" because its main focus is the reduction of recidivist sexual violence through the effective and coordinated deployment of both external and internal controls. A multidisciplinary team is assigned to each offender. Key players are a parole or probation officer, a treatment provider, and a polygraph examiner.[28] The parole or probation officer represents the coercive power of the state, the "external" control. The treatment provider seeks to work with the offender to develop insight and skills at self-regulation, while monitoring the offender's behavior in order to interfere with the offender's opportunity to assault again.[29] Consistency of approach and sharing of accurate information are critical features of this approach, enabling the team to "decrease or eliminate an individual's privacy, opportunity, and access to potential or past victims."[30] The combination of accurate information, correctional supervision, and treatment is seen as a powerful tool in reducing recidivism.

A key feature of the approach is the use of polygraph examinations to get accurate information about offenders and their behavior, focusing on holding offenders accountable. Deception is a key feature of sexual offending, so use of the polygraph is thought to be an important tool in verifying what offenders tell treatment and probation personnel, akin to using urine testing with drug offenders. Sharing information, the supervisors "identify precursor behaviors and at-risk situations," allowing intervention before the offender commits a new crime.[31]

But the required "intensity of supervision" is "significant," and the developers of the containment approach recommend caseloads limited to twenty or twenty-five sex offenders, with flexibility to monitor the offender's activities at night and on weekends. Halfway houses should be available "so a safe, residential option is available to criminal justice officials managing these cases." As the developers put it: "Criminal justice policymakers must explore the reallocation of resources if they intend to take the leadership role necessary to implement a containment approach."[32]

John LaFond and Bruce Winick are two law professors who have specialized in sex offender policy. They propose to take the containment approach developed in Colorado and add an additional component to it—a reentry court. At the heart of LaFond and Winick's approach is the notion that a plan for facilitating the successful reentry of offenders into the community is "an essential goal of any sensible correctional process." This entails "community reintegration," both as a means to safety and as a goal in itself. To accomplish this, they recommend a "graduated release strategy" in which supervised release is accompanied by services designed to help reintegration.[33]

Beginning with drug treatment courts founded in the late 1980s, the judicial system has spawned a variety of problem-solving courts, including domestic violence and mental health courts. According to LaFond and Winick, the interaction between the judge and the offender is an "essential ingredient . . . of these new judicial models." The judge takes on a role that goes well beyond the rather distant and impersonal role in the normal courtroom. In these problem-solving courts, the judge and the offender develop an ongoing relationship as the offender works his or her way through the period of correctional supervision. LaFond and Winick report that "the judge serves as a behavioral motivator, shaping successful performance in treatment through praise and other types of positive reinforcement, and punishing lack of required participation in treatment or instances of relapse through the application of agreed-upon sanctions." They observe that "there is a kind of 'magic' in the judicial robe" in that the judge's "direct participation and interaction . . . makes an important difference in offender compliance and rehabilitation." As the offender succeeds, the judge gradually lessens restrictions.[34]

The involvement of the judge and the court system—through periodic appearances by the offender as the process of reentry progresses—helps produce in the offender a sense that he is being treated with "dignity and respect . . . demonstrating concern for his well-being." There is good evidence that affording people this kind of participation in hearings that they regard as fair has positive psychological value. This approach creates and manages "powerful incentives for sex offenders to invest in rehabilitation, thereby reducing sexual recidivism and increasing community protection."[35]

The containment approach and the reentry court idea both acknowledge that most offenders will return to the community, and if we wish to prevent further victimization by these individuals we need to devote attention and resources to their reintegration. Restorative justice approaches take this insight one step further.

Restorative Justice

Restorative justice approaches seek to facilitate offender reintegration while emphasizing the importance of accountability and community safety. The restorative justice movement argues that restorative approaches produce greater prospects of safety, because they place offenders within a web of relationships that helps ensure accountability and safe behavior. The primary focus of restorative justice is on redressing harm to the victim.[36] These programs operate at both the internal and external levels, providing "opportunities for hope and recovery"[37] and a feeling of acceptance, along with the kinds of family and community connections that enable the community to exert its normal forms of control. The key is the ability of these programs to accommodate and promote both "accountability and understanding."[38] According to sociology professor Lois Presser and criminal justice professor Elaine Gunnison, "Restorative justice stresses the need to repair the harms caused by crime and to reintegrate victims, offenders, and communities."[39]

Mary Koss, Karen Bachar, and C. Quince Hopkins run a program called RESTORE (Responsibility and Equity for Sexual Transgressions Offering a Restorative Experience) in Pima County, Arizona. The program deals with date and acquaintance rape and nonpenetration sexual offenses. The RESTORE program "emphasizes offender accountability through reparations and rehabilitation rather than punishment and aims to transform the community's role in addressing crime."[40] RESTORE is a victim-centered diversion program, offering victims the option of addressing the sexual violence through a process that consciously is designed to eliminate the kinds of trauma associated with the formal systems of criminal adjudication.

This program uses a restorative justice technique called community conferencing that brings together "victims, offenders, and their supporters for a face-to-face meeting in the presence of a facilitator." At this conference, the participants "discuss the effects of the incident on them" and "make a plan to repair the damage done and minimize the likelihood of further harm."[41] The aim is to have the offender accept responsibility, make things right, and earn redemption. Similar restorative programs, most of which address programs for juvenile offenders, have high success rates: 90 percent of restitution agreements made in restorative programs are completed within a year, compared with 20–30 percent compliance in more typical court-ordered restitution programs.

Another example of restorative justice is the Canadian Circles of Support and Accountability, operated by the Mennonite Church and supported by a small grant from the Correctional Service of Canada, discussed at some length in Jon Silverman and David Wilson's book about responses to pedophilia, *Innocence Betrayed*. Working with offenders as they are released from prison, six people form a virtual circle around the offender in the community. The members of the circle visit the "core member" each day, "both to support [the offender] and hold him accountable for his attitudes and actions within the community." The circles are not treatment. Rather, they provide support and accountability. The process seeks to acknowledge the harm but also works with the offender and the community to prevent further harm. The "intended result is to reduce reoffending through deterrence and prevention, rather than relying on punishment." The approach has gotten support not only from the Canadian Correctional Service but also from Toronto's Sexual Abuse Squad. In their description of the project, Silverman and Wilson quote an officer on the squad, Detective Constable Brian Thomson, whom they call "as traditional a 'cop' as you could ever hope to find." Thomson finds the circles indispensable in supervising sex offenders in the community. Eileen Henderson, a "typical Canadian 'soccer mum'" who coordinates the Circles, posits that it is the idea of community that is at the heart of the Circles' success: "I think it's about people forming a community, and not excluding anyone. Looking at everyone as people." Said one of the volunteers: "The bottom line is that these people are not monsters sent from another planet. They came out of our communities and we have to find ways of working with them in the community while at the same time keeping that community safe." Silverman and Wilson characterize the Circles as "controlling through inclusion."[42]

Assessing the Alternatives

If we want to design an effective public policy to address sexual violence, we ought to begin by trying to "dimension" the concrete benefits of the predator laws in comparison to the alternatives. This is not an easy task. Predator commitment laws may prevent only a miniscule amount of sexual violence, but what they prevent is concrete and visible. Real—dangerous—offenders are incapacitated so that we know they will not hurt anyone. The benefits of the alternative approaches are harder to see. They are doubly invisible. The crimes these approaches prevent are not the crimes that make the headlines; they are the hidden assaults and rapes whose ubiquity makes them almost invisible. And, of course, potential crimes that are prevented are even less visible.

This invisibility is one of the most pernicious effects of the predator laws. Their focus on the predator—the worst of the worst—blinds us to the great bulk of sexual violence and to the interventions that might well provide effective prevention. If we are serious about preventing sexual violence, we must make the invisible visible.

We must examine the pot of money now spent by states on sexual violence prevention and ask whether that money is being allocated most effectively to protect all potential victims. This is a complex task. Many of the approaches are in their infancy. There is a dearth of research, and little consensus, on the effectiveness of various interventions.

What follows is a series of "thought experiments" that sketch some of the questions that a comprehensive plan for intervention must address. The numbers used in these thought experiments are snapshots at different moments; many are estimates; some are optimistic results of studies that are not necessarily consensus results. These are "thought" experiments, and they may not reflect the complexity of real life. But they are the beginnings of further inquiry and are intended to invite others with expertise in sex offender management and cost-benefit analysis to join the undertaking. These experiments do not prove that reallocating resources would be better. They merely suggest that it is worth asking these questions if we want to be most effective.

Experiment one. By orders of magnitude, predator commitments are more expensive than other effective societal interventions that save lives. The cost per life saved by flu vaccinations is $500, by breast cancer screening is $17,000, and by highway improvements is $60,000.[43] In contrast, I estimate the cost of preventing a single sexual crime by means of civil commitment to be at least $200,000 and perhaps as much as $3.25 million.[44]

Experiment two. Instead of civilly committing the twenty most dangerous offenders next year, what if we provided residential sex offender treatment in the community? Residential treatment costs about one-third as much as civil commitment, so for the cost of committing the twenty, we could provide these services for the sixty most dangerous offenders. Residential treatment generally lasts about a year, whereas civil commitment appears to go on indefinitely. So, each year we could provide residential treatment to the sixty most dangerous offenders set to be released from prison. Over a ten-year period, we would serve six hundred of the most dangerous. Though there is no consensus as to whether sex offender treatment works, at least one comprehensive study on sex offender treatment suggests that effective treatment can reduce recidivism by 30 to 40 percent.[45] Civil commitment would provide 100 percent protection from twenty high-risk offenders. For the same amount of money, the alternate plan might provide (under the results of this optimistic study) 30–40 percent protection from six hundred offenders of similar risk.

Experiment three. The year after next, if we again forego committing the twenty most dangerous, we could use the savings to beef up community supervision of released sex offenders. Under intensive supervision, a probation officer's case load is fifteen offenders. A normal case load for one officer is one hundred offenders.[46] The incremental cost per offender to provide intensive rather than normal supervision is about $15 per day,[47] so we could fund this intensive supervision for about four hundred offenders every day. Many experts believe that intensive community supervision of sex offenders is the best way to reduce recidivism.[48] Mark Carey, former commissioner of the Minnesota Department of Corrections, thinks that proper probation supervision can reduce recidivism by 30 to 40 percent.[49] Even if Carey is off by a factor of five, this alternative might produce greater protection than the civil commitment option.

Experiment four. In 2004, California confined 17,000 sex offenders in its prisons, and 535 in its predator commitment program. The daily cost for each committed individual was about $400, which is about five times the daily cost of keeping a prisoner. According to the *San Francisco Chronicle,* California offers "no significant" sex offender treatment programs in its prisons.[50] Based on data from Minnesota, I estimate that an expenditure of about $3.50 per day per sex offender in the prison population would provide sufficient treatment capacity to successfully involve 40–50 percent of sex offenders who are released from prison.

If California confined 144 fewer men in its predator commitment program, this would free up sufficient money to fund sex offender treatment in the prison system. Let us make an optimistic assumption that this treatment reduces recidivism by 40 percent (as some research shows). Assuming that the recidivism rate for sex offenders released in California is similar to that in Minnesota (18% over 6.5 years), we would expect the 17,000 inmates, when released, to include 3,060 recidivists during their first 6.5 years of release. If 40 percent of the inmates participated in treatment, a reduction of *their* recidivism by 40 percent would reduce the recidivists by 490. (Even if we used a more pessimistic figure for treatment efficacy, say 10%, the reduction in recidivists would be about 122.) If we assume that the 144 men not committed would recidivate at a rate of 50 percent over the same period (the selection process for civil commitment would need to be very, very good to achieve this kind of result), civil commitment would have confined 67 individuals who would have been arrested or convicted for recidivist crimes during the period. Thus, the transfer of predator commitment funds to prison-based sex offender treatment might multiply the prevention effect of the funds by sevenfold (a reduction of 490 recidivists as compared to 67). Even using a more conservative estimate of treatment effectiveness, the prevention effect of the funds would be increased by a factor of 1.8.

Experiment five. In Minnesota, the statewide budget for sexual assault victims services, to serve 8,699 victims of sexual assault, was $4.5 million in 2003. The budget for civil commitment in that year was about $20 million, which perhaps prevented between 7 and 23 recidivists from reoffending in the community.

Experiment six. In 2004, the total state expenditure in Minnesota on treatment and supervision of convicted sex offenders (in prison and after release in the community) was approximately $4.2 million. Added to the 2004 budget of $26 million for predator commitments, the total equals the state's "sexual violence prevention" fund. Commitments eat up about 87 percent of this prevention fund but account for at most 12 percent of recidivist sexual crime. The state devotes only 13 percent of its sexual violence prevention fund to addressing the remaining 88 percent of the recidivist crime.

Experiment seven. Jeanne Martin runs a violence reduction program in southern Minnesota. Her program provides some direct services for victims of sexual violence. Funding for these services was cut by 25 percent recently. Her program also funds theater productions that educate elementary and junior high school students about sexual violence prevention. At a cost of $125 per school, these programs reached 4,000 elementary school students and 2,500 junior high school students in a year. Pre- and postevaluations showed substantial changes in students' attitudes toward sexual violence. Martin's budget for this unit was cut in 2002–03 and restored in 2003–04. Due to budget restraints, the governor of Minnesota recommended the elimination of existing funding for programs such as violence prevention programs in public schools.[51]

Experiment eight. Over the past decade, the rate of rape and sexual assault has decreased nationwide. But the welcome decrease has not been confined to states with predator commitment laws. Minnesota's predator commitment law has been at work since the early 1990s, yet a Minnesota violence task force reported in 2004: "The total number of sexual assaults has dropped nearly 50 percent in the U.S. from 1993 to 2002 . . . but only 2 percent in Minnesota." Furthermore, during the period *prior* to the implementation of the predator law in Minnesota (1960 to 1993), "Minnesota's rape rate was lower than the nation's. Since 1993, Minnesota's rape rate has been higher than the national average."[52] The rape rate in the fifty states and the District of Columbia fell, on average, from 37.9 per thousand in 1995 to 33.9 per thousand in 2000. Of the fifteen states with predator commitment laws in operation during this period, eight did better than the national average, but seven did worse.

Choosing the right mix of programs to address sexual violence is a serious matter with serious consequences. It is not simply that poor choices might be a waste of money. Rejecting more effective interventions in favor of less effective approaches also costs lives and permits preventable harm.

There are many variables and many unknowns. But we do know that sex predator commitment laws address only a small part of the problem while consuming a large part of the resources. We know there are many alternative approaches and that these approaches are, relatively speaking, starved for funds.

In this chapter I have not proved that a different allocation of resources would be more effective in preventing sexual violence. The argument made here is that there is a good possibility that we could prevent more violence with a resource allocation mix that put more money into primary prevention, treatment, and community supervision and reentry of sex offenders than in trying to find and incapacitate the worst of the worst. But, as the thought experiments suggest, this is a complex problem, the data on many forms of intervention are preliminary or inconclusive, and there are many factors to consider.

Where should we go from here? First, we ought to resolve that sex offender policy will be made rationally, based on the best available evidence. Second, we should understand that this policy involves allocation of resources among a variety of approaches. Though we might wish to expand the pot of money available for prevention, the reality is that funds are limited. Deciding to fund a sex predator commitment program is a *choice* that necessarily limits funds for other approaches.

There is no question that research into the efficacy of various approaches should be strengthened and speeded up. With better research, we can achieve more effective resource allocation.

But we must act even in the absence of full knowledge. Though we do not know conclusively, there is evidence that treatment and community supervision are effective in reducing recidivism. We can act on the hypothesis that reentry and reintegration of offenders are both critical. There is good reason to believe that primary prevention programs can reduce sexual violence by changing social norms. It would be rational to conclude (at least tentatively) that carefully controlling the growth of predator commitment programs and shifting the resources to these other approaches will achieve increased prevention.

Do we know what mix of interventions is the best? Clearly we do not. But not deciding is deciding. By funding the predator approaches at the expense of the other approaches, we have made a choice. And there is good reason to think that it is not the best choice.

If we change the question we are asking about sexual violence, we have a better chance of figuring out what is the best approach. We should be asking what is the best way to prevent the most violence, rather than simply who are the worst of the worst or how can we lock up the most dangerous. Once we shift perspective, we can see that there are choices, and those choices ought to be exercised in the most thoughtful, knowledgeable way possible.

CHAPTER EIGHT

The Politics of Sexual Violence

I don't want to understand pedophiles, I want to put them in prison.
—Representative MATT SALMON, R-Arizona

Seventy-four-year-old Robert Carney sat in the Milwaukee courtroom, a small, balding man. His frame reflected the toll taken by three years of
chemotherapy for lymphoma. Manacled and in an orange prison jumpsuit, he
was a "patient" in Wisconsin's sex offender commitment program. More than a
year before this court appearance, a judge had ordered him conditionally released
from custody. A state psychologist described Carney as "at relatively low risk for
future sexually violent behavior." But the outrage of his potential neighbors in
the community had thwarted the enforcement of the judge's order. Now Carney
was back in court to seek enforcement of the court's conditional release order.
The judge gave the state a few months more to comply. He worried that the state's
failure to release Carney into the community endangered not only Carney's constitutional rights but also the viability of the state's commitment program.[1]

How did it come about that a predator commitment law—an extraordinary
intrusion on constitutional liberties, justified because its reach would be limited to the most dangerous—was being used to continue the confinement of a
frail aging cancer victim, despite professional and judicial determinations that
he ought to be supervised in the community? The answer, in a phrase, is the
politics of sexual violence. Quoting a Wisconsin official, a Milwaukee news re-

This chapter is based in part on Eric S. Janus, "Closing Pandora's Box: Sexual Predators
and the Politics of Sexual Violence," *Seton Hall Law Review* 34 (2004): 1233. Epigraph is from
Kelly Patricia O'Meara, "Innocence Lost?" *Insight on the News*, June 14, 1999, http://www.
insightmag.com/media/paper441/news/1999/06/14/CoverStory/Innocence.Lost-
209148.shtml.

port summed it up in this way: "In urban areas, people may be divided on many issues but manage to unite in opposition to sex offenders moving nearby, he said. 'When it comes to this group of characters, it's something people can coalesce around—we all hate them. . . . They become each community's Osama bin Laden.'"[2]

Sex offender commitment laws offer a dangerous but attractive promise. In exchange for perfect protection against a few of the most reviled and dangerous criminals, those who prey sexually on women and children, we need only trade in our most fundamental constitutional limitations on government power—but only with respect to those most dangerous individuals. We reassure ourselves that our molestation of these constitutional protections is safely limited. We have also been reassured that these extraordinary intrusions on fundamental liberties are time-limited, unfortunate necessities born of a temporary prevention gap. We can be done with the cost, and the embarrassment, of these laws just as soon as we can fix the criminal justice system to eliminate the prevention gap.

But fifteen years after the birth of predator commitment laws, they are growing. It is not simply their budget that grows without limit. Of equal concern is that the predator template they espouse becomes more and more central to how we think and talk about sexual violence. The seductive power of these laws, their ability to shape and motivate private and public fear and action, are too strong. These laws entail a logic, a way of framing the issue of sexual violence, that pushes our thinking and approach to sexual violence ever further off balance. Like Pandora's box, these new laws, which seemed attractive at first, now seem deceptively alluring. But given the political context in which they exist, we are unable to limit or abandon them.

Consider this snapshot from Minnesota. When the state first adopted a sex predator commitment program in the early 1990s, its supporters described it as a temporary fix that would become unnecessary in a decade or so when tougher prison sentences would finally close the "prevention gap." But for fifteen years, the commitment scheme continued undiminished. And, in response to the tragic murder of Dru Sjodin in 2003, the rate of commitments has increased dramatically, growing from about eighteen per year to about sixty per year. Now state officials warn that the number of commitments might continue to grow. The total population under confinement has increased from 77 in 1995 to 306 in 2005. State officials predict a population of 500 by 2011.[3]

Events in several states trace this politics and its consequences. There is increasingly myopic focus on the "predator" as personifying the danger to the community. Civil commitment is seen as the solution to the predator. When the system fails to provide perfect protection—as is inevitable—pressure develops to solve the problem by expanding the net cast by civil commitment. At the same time, the fear of predators generates intense community impediments to their release. The predator commitment programs—and their budgets—grow on both counts.

Throughout the nation, there is a growing intolerance for solutions that do not conform to the narrow scenario that underlies the predator laws. Worse, when scientifically derived findings and professionally designed programs stray from straight and narrow answers, they are shouted down in a moralistic and politically motivated firestorm.

The virulent politics makes even the study or discussion of alternative approaches to sexual violence seem to be a third-rail issue—instant political death for anyone proposing serious consideration of alternative approaches. In 1998, three academic researchers published an article in the *Psychological Bulletin,* a peer-reviewed academic journal of the American Psychological Association. The article examined the widely held belief that "child sexual abuse [CSA] causes intense harm, regardless of gender." Examining fifty-nine studies of CSA, the authors concluded that "basic beliefs about CSA in the general population were not supported." They concluded that the "negative effects were neither pervasive nor typically intense."[4] The study did not conclude that CSA was *never* harmful, nor did it dispute the fact that many children exposed to CSA do, in fact, suffer harm. Rather, the authors argued for a more careful and scientific definition of CSA, one that would help sort out the true nature of the harm arising from sex between adults and children or adolescents. Finally, the authors emphasized that their study concerned psychology, not morality or legality: "Moral codes of a society with respect to sexual behavior need not be, and often have not been, based on considerations of psychological harmfulness or health." Their findings, therefore, did not imply any change in current legal or moral approaches to CSA.

When the article was discovered by the news media and politicians it provoked an intensely negative firestorm of criticism. The matter reached as far as the United States House of Representatives, which voted unanimously (355–0) to denounce the study. Representative Matt Salmon (R–Ariz.), sponsor of the resolution, called the article the "emancipation proclamation of pedophiles." Referring to the authors of the article, he observed: "Those who excuse this evil conduct, particularly those in positions of influence, are also pretty low on the food chain and deserve the harshest possible condemnation."[5]

Though the American Psychological Association, the publisher, initially defended the article as valid science, the organization eventually bowed to the intense pressure and vowed to adopt new procedures for reviewing articles to be published: "We acknowledge our social responsibility as a scientific organization to take into account not only the scientific merit of articles but also their implication for public policy. Some of the language in the article, when examined from a public policy perspective, is inflammatory."[6] The conservative Family Research Council asked for more: "APA needs to root out the pro-pedophilic academicians who are trying to normalize child abuse."[7]

Many researchers might have taken issue with this article's conclusions. A recent review article in another respected journal, the *Journal of Psychiatry and Law,* reflected the more prevalent view that "psychological damage associated with childhood sexual abuse is substantial and quite well documented."[8] But this just serves to underline the point that the nature of the harm caused by child sexual abuse is an empirical issue. If we want to develop effective programs and policies to assist the victims of sexual abuse, we ought to invite full scientific knowledge of its nature and consequences. The political response to the earlier article placed the moral condemnation of child sexual abuse in direct conflict with increasing empirical knowledge of it.

The same political dynamics have overwhelmed the development of sound public policy in states across the nation. Here are the stories of how the politics of sexual violence has deflected the fight against sexual violence in Minnesota, Wisconsin, and California.

Minnesota

Despite its origins as a political response to public outrage, the actual development of the Minnesota Sex Offender Program (MSOP) was delegated by the state to Dr. Michael Farnsworth, at that time the state's director of forensic psychiatry. The program's design was based on Farnsworth's research into the state of the art of sex offender treatment nationwide. As late as 1995, the Minnesota Supreme Court stated that "an average patient is expected to complete the program in a minimum of twenty-four months."[9] This would have been a crucial aspect to Farnsworth, whose background and professional orientation was in the treatment of severely mentally ill persons. He would have been extremely sensitive to charges, such as those made later by a task force of the American Psychiatric Association, that sex offender commitment laws entail a "bending [of] civil commitment to serve essentially nonmedical purposes" and are "an unacceptable misuse of psychiatry."[10] He designed the sex offender program in the good-faith belief that it was intended, like other forms of psychiatric treatment, for treatment and release.

There were indications that Minnesota took its constitutional and programmatic mandates seriously. The per diem expense for the Minnesota program has been among the highest in the nation, and the Minnesota treatment program is cited as a national model.[11] While other states housed their sex offender programs in correctional settings,[12] or delegated supervision of the facility to correctional officials, or used old jail buildings (e.g., New Jersey), Minnesota built a new facility, administered by the Department of Human Services and disconnected from any prison, to house the sex offender program.[13] When the rural community of Moose Lake, where the new sex offender program was located, was surprised that the economic boon of high-paying state jobs meant that a building full of pedophiles could watch cablecasts of their elementary school plays, the state (at least initially) took the position that these men were patients, not prisoners, and there was no apparent basis for restricting their First Amendment rights.[14] In response to the need for assessments of future risk in order to implement the sex offender law, the state funded the development of an actuarial tool to assess the risk of recidivism, so that the selection process for commitment would rest on science rather than clinical guesswork.[15]

Of course, there were many ways in which the assurances about the law were belied in Minnesota. The most significant of these was that the promise of progress through the treatment program simply did not materialize. The population of the MSOP kept growing as new commitments continued apace; no patients were released; and only a small handful of detainees managed to achieve, and maintain, the highest levels of treatment success at which some form of release might be contemplated.[16]

By 1998, the failed promise of the treatment program began to be noticed. Concerns among government officials about the growing cost of the program led the legislature to mandate a study by the Department of Corrections. In its report to the legislature in 1998, the Department of Corrections projected a rapid growth in the population under commitment and a concomitant growth in the cost of the sex offender program. The report projected that costs in the twelve years between 1998 and 2010 would increase by 450 percent (from $17 million to $76.9 million).[17] The report characterized the cost of the current system as "considerable."

These concerns led to several changes in the MSOP. For example, the state developed a satellite replica of the program in a prison. This program was aimed at imprisoned sex offenders in an effort to reduce the number of released offenders who required civil commitment. Officials also began to examine why the treatment program had an almost nonexistent completion rate. Officials focused on the fact that committed individuals were not all equally competent in navigating the rather complex cognitive-behavioral treatment program and that committed individuals varied widely in the level and nature of the risk they posed.[18] For example, clinical director Anita Schlank reported at a symposium held in November 2002 that about 25 percent of the committed men could be managed, with proper supervision, in the community. The Minnesota Department of Human Services proposed to address these issues by developing an alternative treatment pathway for "patients whose treatment needs are not currently being adequately met (as indicated via lack of progress toward less restrictive settings)."[19] The idea was that some of the moderately risky patients could be moved into the community, even though they had not been able to master the lengthy treatment program that was otherwise required for release.

All of this planning ran into an apparently immovable obstacle in June, 2003, when the *Minneapolis–St. Paul Star Tribune* published an article entitled "State Looks to Release Sexual Psychopaths: Is Concern for Offenders, or the Lock-up Program's High Cost, Driving Change?"[20] Referring to the planning just described, the article characterized officials as "looking for ways to release into the community some of the 190 sexual psychopaths. . . . These [are] repeat rapists and pedophiles, who . . . have been declared sexually dangerous by judges." According to the article, treatment officials felt they had fulfilled only part of their legal obligation—to protect the public—and had neglected the other part—"giving sexual psychopaths in their care individualized treatment in the least prison-like settings possible." The article stated that "sex psychopaths" would be released under strict supervision, and that officials can "manage—but not eliminate—risk to the community." The article suggested that intense supervision in the community could achieve a recidivism rate of 10 percent. It painted the officials as discounting this risk to the community in order to satisfy the rights of the sex offenders: "More important [than the risk to the community], they say, the state has a legal obligation to provide effective treatment."[21]

The issue immediately was politicized. Even though the plan was developed by the clinical staff and not by politicians, Attorney General Mike Hatch, a Democrat, characterized the plan as a consequence of the Republican governor's "no new taxes pledge":

> "This whole no-new-tax pledge is having an unyielding consequence to the public," said Attorney General Mike Hatch, whose office petitions to have sexually dangerous offenders committed for many counties. "To keep a few bucks in people's pockets, we are going to let sexual predators out to harm people."[22]

A prominent prosecutor was quoted as mocking the claim that offenders released into the community would be adequately supervised. Referring to the projected 10 percent recidivism rate for released offenders, the article stated:

"Some prosecutors don't see a one-in-10 recidivism rate as a success story," adding, somewhat ironically in light of the underlying premise that only the most dangerous are committed, "especially since no one can predict which sex offender will rape again."[23]

The story remained in the headlines for several weeks, while the attorney general and the governor attacked and blamed each other. Finally, the governor issued an executive order that directed Department of Human Services officials not to release anyone unless "required by law or ordered by a court." The governor's chief of staff was quoted as explaining, "The governor doesn't want these guys to get out, and he's made that clear ever since he was running for office."[24]

The Minnesota sex offender crisis entered a second stage in November 2003 with the tragic disappearance of college student Dru Sjodin and the arrest, ten days later, of Alfonso Rodriguez Jr.

In many ways, the case was an archetypal case and immediately was in the national spotlight. Sjodin was a young, blond college student, abducted and (many assumed) raped and murdered by a stranger, an older male, a repeat sex offender. (That Rodriguez is a Mexican-American probably made the archetypal salience of the alleged crime even stronger, tapping into conscious and unconscious racial stereotyping and prejudice.) One newspaper article, assessing why the Sjodin case caught the nation's attention, surmised that "part of the answer may be in Dru Sjodin's smile: Beauty to the Beast some people see in Rodriguez, released from captivity in May after serving 23 years for vicious attacks on women."[25] The case reignited the political finger-pointing between the governor and the attorney general. The debate was now transformed, moving as if scripted to the next dramatic level. In place of the hypothetical future release from commitment of moderate-risk offenders, the new story focused on a real victim and a real offender and a real crime.

The story immediately focused on why and how this "level 3 sex offender" had not been civilly committed on his release from prison. The attorney general accused Governor Pawlenty of allowing Rodriguez to be released; the governor and his commissioner of corrections, Joan Fabian, blamed their subordinates for "bad judgment" and promised to seek disciplinary action and "removal" of the state workers responsible for recommending against commitment. The governor proposed reinstating the death penalty in Minnesota, which had abolished the ultimate penalty some one hundred years earlier.[26]

The crisis focused attention on the process by which offenders are selected for commitment. As if it were reporting a scoop, a *Star Tribune* headline disclosed: "Hurdles High for Offender Commitment: Many Most Likely to Commit Sex Crimes Again Are Released after Prison Rather Than Institutionalized." The body of the article gave the details: "Since 1999, three-fourths of the rapists and pedophiles most likely to reoffend were released in Minnesota instead of being committed for indefinite treatment at a secure psychiatric facility." The article continued:

> The data show that commitment of offenders like Rodriguez is not driven only by how dangerous they are. It is also governed by the very high standards set by state law and the courts. And all along the way, the individual judgments of psychologists, prosecutors and judges can influence the outcome, making it appear almost arbitrary.

The article reported that "controversy is becoming focused on the validity of how corrections and justice officials choose who should be committed and why." The newspaper noted that some offenders who had been assessed in the actuarial risk assessment as being in the highest risk group had not been committed, while others assessed as more moderate risk were committed.[27]

An editorial in the *Star Tribune* shaped, and reflected, the nature of the debate. The question was whether the system was "too lax." How could an offender "officially classified by the state as a sexual predator" not be referred for civil commitment? Releasing a person like Rodriguez seemed "wildly risky." The editorial then posed a question to which Minnesotans deserved "a better explanation": "Did they make a serious error, or did they take a gamble—hoping to save the cash a commitment would consume?"[28]

Eventually, the governor and the commissioner of corrections settled on a strategy of referring all level 3 sex offenders to county prosecutors for consideration of civil commitment. The corrections commissioner explained that she had "ordered the change to ensure that prosecutors familiar with the laws review all Level 3 offenders for possible civil commitments. Now only corrections officials do the initial reviews and referrals."[29] This amounted to shifting the responsibility (and, hence, the blame) for making judgments about sex offender commitments from a centralized process at the Department of Corrections to eighty-seven county attorneys. The commissioner of corrections "defended that response as necessary to ensure 'that we don't miss somebody who should be committed.'"[30] The effect of the change was immediate. During the first two months of 2004, sixteen men were civilly committed, more than the number committed annually in most years, and approaching the highest *annual* rate of twenty-two in the year 2000.[31]

Meanwhile, at the legislature over fifty bills were introduced to address the problem.[32] In the midst of this legislative frenzy, the Democratic Party began running "a caustic television commercial" accusing the Republican governor of "bungling the release of sexual predators."[33] The *Star Tribune* described the ad in a front-page story: "Over foreboding music, the camera narrows in on [Governor] Pawlenty's eyes and a narrator says: 'These eyes just watched as administrative bungling and the wrong budget priorities let rapists and sexual predators back on our streets.'"

As the legislative session drew to a close, state policymakers began to settle on their legislative proposals. "Prodded by fear and anger over the Dru Sjodin case, Minnesota is now poised to dramatically expand its efforts to punish and prevent violent crime by sending hundreds, and eventually thousands, of sex offenders to prison for life."[34] The cost of the proposed legislation would exceed $1 billion over a twenty-year period and could increase the number of prisoners in Minnesota with life sentences from four hundred to over nine thousand by midcentury. "I'll concede that there are costs on the horizon," one Republican legislator said. "We will meet those costs. We thought it was worth it. We don't want sexual predators loose in society." As another legislator put it: "What is the price of yet another victim . . . the innocence stolen from another child, the sense of safety at night for another woman?"[35] Other legislators expressed doubt about the policy but despair at the debate: "When you think of the costs, it boggles the mind. I'd rather fund early childhood education. But it's easy to demagogue the crime issue."[36]

Wisconsin

The developments in Wisconsin offer an instructive comparative case study. A Midwestern state similar in many ways to Minnesota, Wisconsin's sex offender program was, like Minnesota's, one of the original three modern sex offender commitment laws. Both programs grew consistently but moderately over the initial years of their operation, with Wisconsin reaching a population of 260 in the fall of 2003, compared with Minnesota's 200.[37]

Wisconsin's program differed from Minnesota's in two notable respects. First, the Wisconsin and Minnesota courts diverged in their interpretations of their respective discharge standards. In Wisconsin, the courts held that an individual must be released if his risk of reoffense fell below the threshold for commitment, which was substantial probability of reoffense.[38] The Minnesota courts, in contrast, held that discharge would be permitted only if the individual could make an acceptable adjustment to society, a standard that suggests a lower level of risk than the "highly likely" standard required for commitment in Minnesota.[39] To put the difference is simple terms, Wisconsin would release people if they no longer fit into the "most dangerous" category, whereas Minnesota would release only those who fit into the "least dangerous" category.

There was a second critical difference between Wisconsin and Minnesota, highlighted by the story of Robert Carney, the seventy-four-year-old cancer victim whose supervised release was discussed at the beginning of the chapter. Despite the political and legal wrangling about his release, Carney was lucky to live in Wisconsin and not Minnesota. Minnesota officials would not have taken into account that his advancing age and frailty might moderate his risk for reoffense for the simple reason that he had not completed the prescribed sex offender treatment program. Before 2000, Wisconsin had a similar policy limiting supervised releases to individuals who had completed the prescribed treatment program. In 2000, Wisconsin treatment officials expanded the release criteria employed by state evaluators to include individuals whose risk could be "managed safely" in the community, even if the individuals had not successfully completed the treatment program. Carney fit that profile. According to news accounts, this change caused the rate of recommendations for supervised release to double. By the fall of 2003, the number of persons who had been released, either conditionally or absolutely, from Wisconsin's program reached about thirty-nine. Of that number, a fair proportion had been returned to the institution because of "rule violations," but the news media reported no instances of sexual reoffenses by released individuals.[40] In contrast, Minnesota had released only one person. After living uneventfully in the community for a number of years, this individual was returned to the institution in 2003 because of a violation of the conditions imposed on his release.

As described above, Minnesota officials were working on a similar change in policy in the summer of 2003 when the press disclosed the plans, triggering the political firestorm and effectively putting a stop to those plans. In September of the same year, some three months later, the press in Wisconsin discovered and exposed Wisconsin's liberal standards for release. A front page headline in Milwaukee's *Journal Sentinel* blared "State Tops in Release of Sexual Predators."[41]

In a subsequent article, the *Journal Sentinel* described the state's liberal policy as "a practice quietly implemented within the state DHFS [Department of Health and Family Services]" and characterized it as having "turned the law upside down."[42] This sentiment was echoed in an editorial in the *Appleton Post-Crescent* supporting tightening of standards. The paper opined that the "idea" of the sex offender law was to "minimize[e]" the risk to the community and criticized the legal standard for release:

> An offender has to be deemed "substantially probable" to re-offend to be denied release. That means an offender who is only "probable" or, say, "slightly probable" would have to be released. Someone who is "probable" to commit another sexual offense can rejoin the community, with supervision? No way. No wonder communities are rejecting these guys.[43]

The news reports triggered immediate legislative proposals to tighten release standards. Within two days, the original sponsors of Wisconsin's sex offender law proposed lowering the standard for commitment from "substantially probable" to "probable" to reoffend, thereby tightening the standard for discharge as well. The proposal also required "progress in treatment" as a condition for supervised release. The article quoted the director of the secure facility as pointing out that the existing discharge standards would allow community placements of individuals whose risk of reoffense was below 75 percent, pointing out that "it's not a determination that the person is safe." One of the sponsors of the legislation stated: "The standard needs to fall to the side of protecting of public safety."[44] Within months, the legislature passed a bill tightening the standards for release from sex offender commitment programs, effectively reversing the policy that had led, without serious incident, to the supervised release of more than thirty-nine men from the sex offender program.

Meanwhile, the state's effort to find community placements for committed offenders was meeting another obstacle as citizens voiced "virulent opposition" to proposals to house offenders, like Robert Carney, in their neighborhoods.[45] In September, the Wisconsin press reported that the third proposed location for convicted child molester Billy Lee Morford—a home on a dead-end street in a mostly industrial area—was scuttled when "a homeowner bowed to public pressure and withdrew an offer to rent." The president of the local apartment association was quoted as saying that he "would advise against anyone renting to Morford. . . . 'Nobody wants to touch this,' [he] said. 'You don't want to have your neighbors protesting and marching in front of your house. You can't blame people for not renting to him.'"[46] The case of pedophile Shawn Schulpius was even more extreme. A judge had ordered him released to a community placement in 1997, but the state claimed to be unable to locate a placement that would accept him. In 2004, Schulpius sought a remedy from the state court of appeals, but the court rejected his claim, holding, in a split decision, that "the state acted in good faith in attempting to find placement for Schulpius and that its failure to do so did not rise to the level of a violation of his due process rights."[47]

California

The story of sex offender Patrick Ghilotti and a California community's response to him echoes the experiences in Minnesota and Wisconsin. In 2004, forty-seven-year-old Ghilotti was one of the first "sexually violent predators" slated to be released from the California sex offender commitment program. He had been convicted multiple times of violent rape and had spent six years in the California sex offender commitment program at Atascadero State Hospital, where he was "chemically castrated." State officials determined that he had made sufficient progress to be conditionally released and planned for him to move in with his wife, a nurse he had met during his treatment at Atascadero but had never lived with, at her home in Vacaville.

On learning of Ghilotti's impending release, his future neighbors organized in opposition. A story in the *Marin Independent Journal* reported on a rally held by fifty neighbors. The paper quoted one neighbor as saying, "We'd become prisoners in our own home. . . . People might look at this and say, 'Maybe he looked at dirty pictures,' . . . This is not that. There's an animal coming here. . . . I know it takes all types to make the world go round, but this is something else." Though there were 139 registered sex offenders (and an unknown number who were not registered because they had not yet been apprehended) living in the town, the deputy police chief opined that Ghilotti was a "very special case" and would pose an "unacceptable risk to the community." Most upsetting, perhaps, was the not-in-my-backyard approach taken by the neighbors. "I think he has a place already," said one of the neighbors. "He should stay where he is at." Proclaimed a lawn sign, "Experiment with Rehabilitation Somewhere Else."

By constructing a prototype of the "real" sexual criminal as an animal, outside the home, the predator laws minimize and marginalize the majority of sexual violence and its victims that do not fit this narrow prototype. The role of the community in this narrative is seen as cramped and selfish. Involvement means keeping the highly visible danger out. Addressing sexual and other violence against women at a root level is not the subject of the community's energy. These neighbors will have accomplished their goal if some other neighborhood, perhaps not as well organized, is saddled with Ghilotti. But we, as a society, will be no closer to dealing with the causes, or facilitators, of sexual violence.

The same story is being repeated throughout California, as a trickle of offenders is released from the state's predator commitment program. As the *Salinas Californian* reported: "Brian DeVries, the first graduate of a special state treatment program for violent sexual predators, ended up in a trailer at the Correctional Training Facility on a judge's order after more than 100 Santa Clara County landlords refused to rent to him."[48] Cary Verse, a multiple offender, had been "run out" of his homes in Mill Valley and then Oakland by "angry residents."[49] After he finally found a place to live in San Jose, a new law required him to move back to Contra Costa County, where he had committed his last offense. Ninety landlords turned him down. Finally, a couple—both lawyers—offered to rent him a small cottage on land they owned. State officials approved the plan. When the public was notified, the local paper published a special "Community Alert" issue. At a public meeting, neighbors "took turns questioning the couple's intent. Were they in it for the publicity? For the $1,200-a-month rent they'd pull down from the state?" A protest was organized outside of the couple's law office. Several hundred neighbors chanted, "Why here, why here? We don't want Cary here." Protesters held up signs that read, "Put Him in Orinda." While awaiting a judge's decision about whether he could move into the cottage, Verse lived for a year in a "motel room along a grimy stretch of Monterey Highway in San Jose." When he first moved in, protesters blocked the motel driveway for a week before they tired of the vigil. Under the terms of his release, Verse logged the details of his days. He was required to call his probation agent before going out, reporting all of his moves. He wore a GPS device when he went out. Finally, after a year or more of searching for a place to live, the judge approved his move to the cottage.

Lessons about the Politics of Sexual Violence

In some ways, Verse got off easy. In Bellingham, Washington, thirty-six-year-old Michael Anthony Mullen, a local resident with a history of petty crimes, allegedly shot and killed Hank Eisses and Victor Vasquez, two level 3 sex offenders. He allegedly killed them in the apartment they shared with a third sex offender. Mullen told police that he was "outraged" by the Idaho case in which released sex offender Joseph Edward Duncan III had been arrested in connection with the murders of four members of a family and the kidnapping of two children. Mullen was able to locate his victims by visiting a county website that listed the names and addresses of all level 3 sex offenders.[50]

Fortunately, vigilantism of this severity has been relatively rare. But the Bellingham killings share the visceral intensity that characterizes the politics of sexual violence. And just as the vigilante murders are a perversion of the healthy revulsion we all feel toward sexual violence, the politics have dragged us into a vicious feedback loop that is increasingly disrupting our bearings as we seek to prevent sexual violence.

In a nutshell, this is how the politics of sexual violence is getting us off track. The public is naturally horrified at sexually motivated violence, especially murders. The media follows suit. But by selecting only certain crimes of sexual violence for intense coverage, the media narrows the public's focus to a narrow slice of sexual violence—the pattern we have come to call the "sexual predator." The predator laws give an official imprimatur to this archetype, strengthening the focus on the predator as symbolic of the entire problem of sexual violence.

As "predators" become the archetype of the sex offender, the predator laws become the template for the solution to sexual violence. Inevitably, a further tragedy occurs: another rape-murder is committed by a released sex offender. The new crime is characterized as a failure of the system, whose sole goal is said to be to locate and neutralize sexual predators. Responding to the new outcry, policymakers cast the predator net wider. Efforts to keep reasonable limits on the use of the predator laws, or to develop alternative strategies, are subjected to intense political condemnation and are halted. More and more resources are required for the predator strategy. Then, predictably, another horrendous crime happens, and the process begins again.

The core of these destructive politics is plain. The laser focus on the predator has led us to the promise that we can identify the predator before he strikes, and this has led us to loudly proclaim we will have zero tolerance for risk, and that we will spare no expense. When, inevitably, the first promise fails, politicians and the media seek cover in ever louder avowals of their allegiance to the latter.

Tragically, all are conceits. Finding the next rapist-murderer, like finding a needle in a haystack, is largely a matter of chance. Both Alfonso Rodriguez Jr. and Joseph Edward Duncan III were individually evaluated for civil commitment and passed over. Noting that the state of Washington "boasts one of the most stringent laws controlling sex offenders in the country," the *Seattle Times* offered this explanation for the state's failure to commit Duncan: "It's easy to now second-guess that decision, but the psychologists who make those recommendations are very skilled, said Sarah Sappington, head of the state Attorney General's sexually violent–predator unit."[51]

So too do the claims of zero tolerance and spare no expense ring hollow. In the aftermath of Rodriguez's arrest, as Minnesota politicians exchanged blame and legislators fell over one another in drafting tougher laws for sex offenders, a small group of women and men protested state cuts of $5 million in domestic violence funding.[52] The story, buried in the B section of the newspaper, was a whisper compared to the cacophony generated by the crises of the previous summer and fall. In an open letter to community leaders, the chief judge of the Hennepin County (Minnesota) District Court issued a plea for adequate funding for domestic abuse programs. Citing an annual rate of "over 30,000 calls to 911 regarding domestic violence," the judge noted the toll of domestic violence: "In the last five years 132 women and 68 children under the age of 13 died because of domestic violence."[53] Where was the outrage when these 200 victims fell?

The consequences of the politics of sexual violence are deadly. Limited resources are a reality. Despite the mantra of "zero tolerance" for risk, most risks will necessarily go unaddressed. A media commentator in California highlighted the irony in the enormous public outcry over the supervised release of three graduates of California's sex offender commitment program:

> It's worth asking whether such strident resistance is proportional to the potential threat these ex-convicts pose. . . .
> Care to guess how many convicted sex offenders are believed living freely in California, either paroled or simply released without significant treatment? It's about 67,000.[54]

The politics of sexual violence forces the majority of the risks of sexual violence underground, making them invisible in the political discourse. Risks that fall outside the predator template simply cannot figure into the public discourse. Because the risks must remain invisible, we are deflected from a sensible and effective fight against sexual violence.

CHAPTER NINE

Righting Public Policy against Sexual Violence

Society would "spare no expense" to eradicate a childhood disease that affected 20% of girls and 14% of boys; caused intrapersonal, interpersonal, and health-related difficulties; and replicated itself across generations. This description characterizes [childhood sexual abuse (CSA)], but a comprehensive national campaign to address CSA has not been forthcoming.

—J. A. MERCY, sexual violence expert

The predator laws are a paradox. They loudly proclaim our societal condemnation of sexual violence, yet they seem to reject the consensus advice of many experts about how best to prevent sexual violence. They adopt the feminist-inspired call to fight sexual violence but ignore the clear evidence that it is acquaintance danger, not stranger danger, that poses collectively the biggest threat to women and children. They take on the mantle of the campaign to end sexual violence, but they do nothing to understand and address its root causes.

In short, the predator laws give loud expression to our collective disapproval of sexual violence. They empower victims and other innocent members of society by giving voice to their hurt and their fears. They demonstrate that the powers that be are responsive to the concerns of ordinary citizens who are fed up with years of public policy that minimized much sexual violence. But at the

Epigraph is from James A. Mercy, "Having New Eyes: Viewing Child Sexual Abuse as a Public Health Problem," *Sexual Abuse* 11, no. 4 (1999): 317–22, quoted in Keith Kaufman et al., "Reconceptualizing Child Sexual Abuse," in *Preventing Violence in Relationships,* ed. Paul A. Shewe (Washington, D.C.: American Psychological Association, 2003), 33.

same time they deny the insight that sexual violence is a systemic problem, intertwined in a complex way with who we are as a society. Instead, current predator policy—to identify, stigmatize, and exclude—distorts the true nature and extent of sexual violence, focuses on a small fraction of the problem, ignores the great majority of victims and their trauma, and does little or nothing to deal with the root causes of sexual violence.

To right our public policy on sexual violence will require some paradigm shifts, a willingness and ability of policymakers to see nuance, and a new understanding of the conflicting interests that public policy must seek to accommodate.

It is tempting to construct an overly simple explanation for how our sexual violence policy has become so distorted. In this scenario, science and empiricism have lost the battle against mindless emotionalism and pandering politics. An irresponsible press, we might surmise, has whipped the public into a hysterical moral panic, and opportunistic legislators, afraid to think independently, have served up the predator laws and other draconian and punitive measures. Lost in the hysteria is any reliance on science or concern for policies that might best contribute to a decrease in sexual violence.

There is much about this scenario that is true. Robert Prentky and Ann Burgess, who between them have over fifty years of expertise in the management of sex offenders, express a sentiment that is shared by many professionals and experts: "Unfortunately, we must conclude that the social debate over management of sexual offenders is fueled by impassioned feelings about sex offenders, and typically is insensitive to rational input and uninformed by empirical data."[1] They offer a crisp dictum for the development of sex offender policy: it ought to be based on "sound, reliable information."

To understand why this simple prescription seems so difficult to attain, we need to appreciate that the public policy about sexual violence operates on at least two levels, and ideally serves at least two different goals. On one level, our laws and policies should have as their purpose the reduction of sexual violence. From this perspective, our public policy ought to be grounded in scientifically based empirical knowledge about sexual violence. We might call this the "rational" level.

On the second level, laws and public policy serve an emotive and expressive function. They respond to and address the emotional reactions of fear and disgust that we feel about sexual violence. They express our disapproval and condemnation. We can label this the "emotive" level. Both levels—rational and emotive—are legitimate and important.

But there are constraints that we must recognize as we seek to meet these two needs. Resources are limited. Despite the pronouncements of politicians that cost is no object, it is. Politics also matters. As described in chapter 8, there is a politics of sexual violence that punishes those that appear soft or tolerant of sexual violence. In addition, politics on a grander level makes a difference. As explained in chapter 5, the culture war provides one possible explanation for the ready acceptance of the predator approach.

Our goal in designing a public policy ought to be to achieve some convergence of the rational and the emotive. We should, in other words, seek to design a policy that is best designed, according to our current empirical knowledge, to reducing sexual violence *and,* at the same time, expresses adequately our condemnation of sexual violence.

But the two levels can pull at cross-purposes. The social science research, as well as the feminist perspective, tells us that the ubiquity of sexual violence is connected to our values, attitudes, myths, and practices. The predator laws send a clear message rejecting sexual violence. But in condemning sexual violence through the ritual exile of the worst of the worst, constructing the most atypical crime as the archetype, the expressive message from these laws is that we are distancing ourselves from the most common forms of sexual violence and thereby renouncing responsibility for our societal role in fostering sexual violence. To put it much more concretely, the predator laws telegraph the notion that the only real rape is stranger rape and that intimate and acquaintance rapes are not real crimes.[2] The emotive message of the predator laws undercuts the empirical truth about sexual violence and the real pain suffered by thousands.

There is no inherent reason why our sexual violence policy cannot properly express our condemnation of sexual violence while simultaneously embracing the knowledge gained from social science and the insights gained from feminist perspectives. But political and fiscal undercurrents may block such convergence. The antifeminist tilt of the predator laws may, in fact, be why they have engendered such widespread support. And the financial support may arise from the same reason that the predator laws are so effectively expressive of social disapproval—that they target the most obvious, the worst, and the most distant aspects of sexual violence. Most sexual violence is relatively hidden, perpetrated by family and acquaintances, not newsworthy. Our condemnation of these behaviors is consequently quieter, more nuanced, and less noticed. Politics, and funding, are tied to media exposure, which tilts in the same direction.

The question addressed in this chapter is whether—and how—the public's enthusiasm and legislators' support for the predator laws can be transformed into support for approaches that, while less flashy, are based on sound science and, as such, more likely to get at root causes and much broader swatches of sexual violence.

The complexity of sexual violence requires complex solutions. The right public policy on sexual violence requires negotiating a set of nuanced dualities. We must, at once, both own the problem of sexual violence and condemn it. We must express our outrage at the high visibility but rare rape-murders, while not discounting the common and invisible sexual violence that occurs day in and day out in relationships and among acquaintances. We must hold offenders accountable for the harm they have done, giving support to the victims of their crimes, while at the same time fostering the reintegration of those offenders into the ties of family and community that will provide the most effective control of antisocial behavior.

And we must accept the inevitable uncertainties in policy development, given our growing but still incomplete knowledge about the causes and cures of sexual violence. In our desire to express clear condemnation of sexual violence, we seek a zero-tolerance approach. But realistically, we cannot guarantee zero risk, and we must face the question how we are going to deal with imperfect and uncertain approaches to the risk of sexual violence.

In a sense, we need to redefine the moral high ground. We need to understand that true commitment to reducing sexual violence means focusing on the entire problem, not just the tip of the iceberg; it means addressing root causes; it means understanding and addressing the trauma of victims in the system. And it means understanding, and paying attention to, the best of what the experts have to offer on how we should design our approaches to sexual violence.

We should seek policies that express our condemnation of sexual violence by addressing the *most* sexual violence (not just the most visible). Our policies should hold offenders accountable *and* enable many of them to earn reintegration into the society. We should learn to condemn sexual violence *while* we, collectively, take responsibility for addressing its root causes in our own society. We need to focus our attention both on the individual perpetrator *and* on the conditions that foster or prevent sexual violence.

In this book I have argued that the predator laws stand in the way of these nuanced approaches. But these laws have grown out of authentic, grassroots movements of ordinary people. The movements have centered on true tragedies; the laws express real feelings of solidarity and support for the victims of those tragedies. Political responsiveness to the perceived and articulated needs of the public, especially when it comes to preventing sexual violence and enhancing the safety of a vulnerable part of the population, must be counted as a good. We need to find a way that both validates the strong public condemnation of sexual violence and that is based on sound science.

Restructuring Public Policy

As we have seen in chapter 7, there are probably many effective ways to address sexual violence as it really exists. These ways seek to address its root causes, to produce accountability and safety in a system that is not hostile to victims, and to provide effective containment while offenders are reintegrating into the fabric of society. Yet legislators keep pouring resources into highly punitive approaches that do nothing to address the root causes of sexual violence, or to ameliorate the hostility experienced by victims in the criminal justice system, or to assure safety from the great proportion of sex offenders who remain in or return to the community. Further, the policies that are funded and enacted seem to get the emotive message only half right. They express our condemnation of sexual violence but fail to take responsibility for its existence, and, even more important, they render less visible the vast amount of sexual violence that does not conform to the predator template. Our system for making sexual violence policy is broken. To achieve a more sensible policy, we need to take some concrete steps to reform the process by which our laws and programs on sexual violence are constructed.

The core fears and needs of victims and citizens must be acknowledged. The first, critical step in righting our public policy is to repair the rift—if there truly is one—between the public and the experts. We must be able to envision and create a public policy that incorporates the truths of both. The growing knowledge that empirical research brings to the field should not be ignored. But it is equally a mistake to characterize policy design as solely a matter of incorporating the teachings of good science. The laws we pass to address sexual violence are also necessarily a means for the expression of the values and fears of the public.

It is demeaning and counterproductive to marginalize the public's role in the creation of the predator laws. The moving forces behind the spread of Megan's law—families who have lost children to horrible crimes—cannot be said to be hysterical or in a moral panic.[3] These were regular people who suffered horrible loses and sought to make things better. And the public at large has felt and expressed appropriate solidarity with their loss and outrage. Paul Slovic, a scholar of risk management and regulation, notes, "The public is not irrational. The public is influenced by emotion and affect in a way that is both simple and sophisticated." He continues, "Perhaps the most important message from the research done to date is that there is wisdom as well as error in public attitudes and perceptions."[4]

Rather than dismissing the public's views as emotional and unhelpful, we must understand the truth in them, even though public opinion might be based on inaccurate information about the risks of sexual violence. Examining the movements that have led to the predator laws, four clear truths emerge. First, there is genuine fear and a desire to protect women and children from sexual violence.[5] Second, there is a desire for justice, to hold offenders accountable for the harm they have done. The third message is a clear expression of societal condemnation of sexual violence. And fourth, people seek some sense of control over their own safety and involvement in the construction of public policy that affects them and their families.

We can, and should, recognize these as a set of legitimate, indeed desirable, outcomes for policy. But that recognition ought not to excuse the predator laws—and the implications they bring—from critical evaluation. The predator template is not the only approach to achieving these appropriate goals. Properly understood, an approach that rejects the predator template and its implications is much more likely to accomplish much of what the public wants.

Victims and professionals should form alliances to work for policies that serve both rational and emotive goals. It is not at all clear that there is really a rift between the recommendations of the experts and the agendas of many victims' advocates. Tom McBride, executive director of the Washington State Association of Prosecuting Attorneys, who favors a more flexible and victim-centered approach to sentencing sex offenders, put it like this:

> Particularly in intrafamily situations, it is possible to find support from victims and their families for preventative programs and less incarceration—but you have to really talk at length with just them, without the advocates or groups around them. They see the gray in all this and that the policy choices are not just black and white like talk radio makes it out to be.[6]

Listening carefully to victims and their advocates may reveal much more congruence with the experts than some assume. Take, for example, the Massachusetts Coalition against Sexual Assault and Domestic Violence, operating under the name Jane Doe Inc. In early 2002, the group declared a "state of emergency on matters of sexual violence" and began a campaign to influence the policy of the state. Their agenda: "[To] improve services to victims of sexual assault, while also working to identify and address root causes of sexual violence."[7] Embracing the empirical research that "clearly pointed to the home and family as primary sources of violence against women and children," the group advocated comprehensive and coordinated services and sought to identify gaps in the state's current provision of services. Nowhere in its recommendations did the group endorse an expansion of the predator approach or a more central place for highly punitive responses. Rather, the group meticulously detailed the shortcomings of the state's efforts to prevent sexual assault, to treat victims and offenders, and to make the criminal justice system "more accessible to sexual assault victims seeking justice."

Nancy Sabin, executive director of the Jacob Wetterling Foundation, a national group seeking stronger prevention efforts, was described in a newspaper story as concerned that "stiffer prison terms and more restrictions can actually backfire and make victims more reluctant to report such crimes because the assailant is their father, uncle or brother." The story quoted her as saying, "My concern is that there's no funding for prevention or early intervention, no investment at the front end, to find out why our boys are growing up to be sex offenders."[8]

Another advocacy group, the California-based Generation Five, seeks to "bring together diverse community leaders working to end child sexual abuse within five generations."[9] Adopting a "restorative justice approach," they advocate "developing new means of accountability for child sexual abuse offenders while offering a continuum of services aimed at recovery and appropriate restitution." Janet Carter, vice president of the Family Violence Prevention Fund, which focuses on legislation to stop the cycle of violence through prevention, early intervention, and support, expresses a similar sentiment:

> To date, we have put nearly all our energy and resources into punishing batterers and helping victims. . . . To make real progress in ending abuse, much more of our collective energy and resources should focus on a different phase of the problem. We should be doing more to stop violence before it starts—by teaching the next generation of boys that violence against women is always wrong; by implementing dating violence education in schools; and by encouraging parents, teachers, coaches and other adults to speak with children and teens about abuse.[10]

These sentiments are echoed by victims' advocates around the country.

But the voices of victims and their advocates are too often silenced or unheard. An activist associated with a Florida group opposed to sexual violence told my research assistant in a 2005 interview that people who favor a prevention approach "are lacking a national voice and national advocate. . . . The criminal justice approach is so attractive because it focuses on punishment and taking people off the streets; the crime lobby is very strong. . . . They are all politically savvy and connected. We don't have that kind of clout."[11]

The experts and the public, including the victims' advocacy movement, can make substantial common cause. Professionals and victims and their advocates need to form alliances and view each other as partners in the development of sexual violence policy. Slovic, the expert on risk protection legislation, argues that a "new approach" to legislating about risk is needed, one that "focuses on introducing more public participation" into the process.[12] Laurie Robinson, a Justice Department official in the Clinton administration, agrees about the importance of ensuring that victim groups are part of the policy development process. She refers to the "strategic—and moral—importance of making the victim advocate community a key ally and focusing on the goal of reducing victimization."[13]

Victim advocates, citizens, and professionals should be seen as partners in policy development. The Center for Sex Offender Management is a nonprofit agency funded collaboratively by Department of Justice, the National Institute of Corrections, and the State Justice Institute. Emphasizing that the public has "the power to shape legislation," CSOM recommends that professionals "recognize the public as a legitimate partner in deciding how to effectively manage sex offenders." The group reports that "after learning about a criminal justice issue and having a chance to deliberate over it, the public is much more open to change than conventional wisdom would suggest." They urge an approach that welcomes the public as partner, rather than adversary or customer:

> Such a view may require a public engagement strategy in which leadership understands and respects public opinion and takes the public's concerns seriously. According to this approach, the public is a resource that has the capacity and the willingness to help develop and execute sound criminal justice policy, rather than a reactionary adversary to be ignored, or a group of misinformed consumers that needs to be sold on an idea.[14]

The agency recommends a series of steps, including giving the public sound information about the nature of the problem (e.g., "that it is not feasible to incarcerate all sex offenders indefinitely") and the potential solutions (e.g., "how supervision and treatment programs are effective in protecting the community from convicted sex offenders"), and then creating opportunities for meaningful participation in both the development and implementation of the policy, in a process that takes the concerns of the public seriously.

Legislation should be developed in a structure that ensures systemic design and comprehensive attention to sexual violence. Lawmakers must begin to see sexual violence as a whole, to look at it systemically. William Edwards and Christopher Hensley are among the few scholars who have studied the process by which sexual violence prevention policy is made. They observe that sexual violence is a complex phenomenon and that attempts to address it that are quite narrowly focused—as, for example, community notification and registration laws—may "unintentionally affect other aspects of sexual victimization and intervention, and that ignoring these complex relationships ultimately limits their capacity to effectively address both specific and broader aspects of the problem."[15] They criticize the current approaches as excluding "virtually all of the other aspects of offender functioning that are not immediately recognizable as being related to their management and tracking." They suggest a systems or functional approach in which "one part of a given problem is viewed as being highly integrated with its other parts."[16]

The approach prescribed by these academics is echoed by experts and advocates. A resource paper prepared for the California Coalition on Sexual Offending on the subject of Internet community notification of sexual offenders stated: "Any system of Internet notification will be most effective when it is part of a carefully designed, internally consistent strategy for managing sexual offenders who reside in the community. California lacks such an overall strategy."[17] This approach is echoed by Carla Ferrucci, executive director of the Minnesota Coalition against Sexual Assault, who recommends a comprehensive approach developed with input from key groups and stakeholders:

> The problem is that the decisions are all made so quickly without much thinking. . . . As you know most people who commit sexual assaults know their victims, they aren't strangers. All of these discussions are focusing on a small percentage of the offenders out there. We need a much broader approach to the whole problem.[18]

The spare-no-expense mentality should be transferred from the failed predator model to the public health approach. This follows from the insight that policy must address the problem of sexual violence in all of its complexity. Legislators seem willing to spend millions on programs like predator commitment laws, while underfunding services and interventions that address the problem more comprehensively. By envisioning sexual violence as a whole, the question of resource allocation among the various parts of the problem becomes much more visible, and the funds allocated to the predator laws become a potential source for other approaches to prevention.

The role of the media in shaping the discourse should be understood, and steps should be taken to reshape its message to be more in keeping with the reality of sexual violence. The last piece of the policy puzzle is the media, which is commonly assumed to play a major role in shaping the public's (mis)perception of sexual violence through its portrayal of the atypical and rare forms of sexual violence as typical and representative. It would be helpful to know the source of this form of media bias in order to construct a strategy for countering it. There is certainly some evidence that the media's construction of the predator paradigm might be attributable to some larger agenda, such as male bias and anti-feminism. Jenny Kitzinger, for example, writes in connection with a study of the media treatment of "false memory syndrome" that the media coverage was "shaped by anti-feminism, and by male power and class influence." "Gender-politics fundamentally shape the production of news and need to be a central consideration for those studying the media," she writes.[19] And Paula Skidmore, another academic who studies the media, concludes that "gender is at the heart of such [sex] crimes—in the perpetration and their subsequent reporting by the media."[20]

It is also possible that the media's distortion reflects the (politically neutral) news values that seem to shape all media reporting. As Kitzinger notes, "A death from an airplane accident is 6,000 times more likely to make front-page news than a death from cancer. Assaults on children by strangers are more likely to receive coverage than abuse within the home." Media tend to focus on "serious but rare risks. . . . Reporting tends to be 'event' orientated rather than issue orientated."[21]

But media construction of sexual violence is not an intractable problem. First, the role of the media in shaping the public's perception of the risk of sexual violence must be recognized. The media, notes Slovic, "are a dominant source of risk information," and this role is "worthy of explicit, sustained attention." The media must understand the real contours of the risk. And they must be made aware that their portrayal of sexual violence can distort public policy, with harmful consequences to real people. Policymakers, advocates, and experts can help by making these consequences, and their alternatives, visible in a form that both underlines media responsibly and provides the kinds of newsworthy "events" that accommodate the reality of news production.

Much more attention—and money—should be devoted to study and evaluation. It is necessary—but not sufficient—for policymakers and the media to seek to incorporate empirical knowledge about sexual violence. Though increasing, our level of knowledge remains incomplete. A recent study undertaken for the California Coalition on Sexual Offending underlined the need for more information about "the nature and degree to which various forms of sex offender notification enhance community safety and at what price these enhancements are achieved." The same can be said for other critical approaches to fighting sexual violence: more research is needed into the efficacy of treatment and various forms of community supervision, the best forms of primary prevention, the cost and effectiveness of electronic monitoring systems and residential segregation rules for sex offenders. As the California Coalition noted, the need for such research is "urgent."[22]

But the lack of perfect information does not mean that attempting rational-ity in policymaking is hopeless. Rather, policy should be made based on the best available information, and research and evaluation should be automatic components of all aspects of our strategies.

Promoting Better Policy

At this time, the prospects for righting our public policy on sexual violence are mixed—guarded but not without some hope. First, the bad news. Policymak-ers and media outlets around the country continue in their unnuanced embrace of flashy but unproven approaches. The toughness of these initiatives serves well to demonstrate the resolve to fight sexual violence, but the initiatives have been adopted without careful study, lack empirical support, fail to address root causes or broad-based risks, and they bring with them a high likelihood of un-intended consequences.

News media continue to take the rape-murders of young women and girls—riveting human tragedies—and transform them from horrible aberrations into manifestations of the norm. Typical is a news posting on the Fox News web-site. Though the subject of the story was the recent sexual murders of two young girls—events that all responsible commentators agree are extremely rare—the article through slick innuendo suggested again and again that "such crimes" are, in fact, common. The headline—"Molesters Often Strike Again"—is doubly misleading, suggesting that these awful crimes occur "often" and that recidivism is high. Two more times in the lead paragraphs, the article leaves the same impression—but with careful deniability. Sentences like "Criminol-ogists say it's *all too frequent* that the perpetrator in *such* cases is a pathological sexual predator" may be technically true, in the sense that rape-murders are probably perpetrated by "pathological sexual predators." Similarly, "The dan-gerous ones have a high recidivism rate" is also technically true—after all, the definition of "dangerous" is that the individual is highly likely to reoffend. But both invite a counterfactual impression that rape-murders are common and that sex offenders have high recidivism rates. The misunderstanding is rein-forced throughout the article: "Many, if not all, will molest children until the day they die. They're dangerous and they're going to reoffend." Finally, the article powerfully suggests that the problem of sexual violence is simply a mat-ter of fixing the mistakes we are currently making—"doing the job right"—and that these mistakes are simply interstitial, not systemic: "We need to find the loopholes, find the cracks."[23]

Articles like this help to channel public distress over brutal sexualized murders into what the *Palm Beach Post* described as "molester mania": "Fueled by outrage over the inexplicable tragedies, neighborhood associations have turned into vigilante groups. Handmade signs have been planted in sex offenders' yards, and fliers with their pictures on them have been plastered on trees, stop signs and telephone poles."[24]

Unfortunately, instead of exercising leadership and using public energy to develop laws and policies that reflect a sensible allocation of public resources, Florida policymakers rushed through legislation without time for study. The Jessica Lunsford Act was passed by the Florida legislature and was signed by Governor Jeb Bush in thirty-two days, "warp speed by Tallahassee standards."[25]

The breadth of the law is staggering, a good example of the risks of unintended consequences that such rushed and unthoughtful policymaking brings. The law imposes life in prison or a twenty-five-year mandatory sentence followed by lifelong electronic monitoring of persons convicted of "lewd molestation" of a child under twelve. The crime includes touching "in a lewd or lascivious manner" the clothing covering the genital area or buttocks of a child. The act provides $11 million for monitoring devices and prison beds but nothing for sex offender treatment. In a move being replicated in many other cities, Miami Beach passed an ordinance prohibiting sex offenders from living within 2,500 feet of a school, playground, bus stop, park, or any other place where children gather.[26]

Many of the people raising questions about the wisdom of these approaches are treatment experts and victims' advocates. For example, the Miami Beach exclusion law might well exclude sex offenders from almost the entire city, given that the narrow city contains more than a dozen schools and thirty-seven parks. This has raised concerns among many, including national sexual violence prevention professionals and advocates. Nancy Sabin of the Jacob Wetterling Foundation worried that residential-exclusion laws will render other laws, such as registration and community notification laws, ineffective: "If you give them a place to live and work and watch them carefully, they just might not re-offend."[27] A report by the California Coalition on Sexual Offending similarly worries that the new laws "tend to drive [offenders] into poorer neighborhoods." According to a national study, "children from the lowest income families were eighteen times more likely to be sexually abused . . . than children from the higher income families."[28] And an editorial in the *Times-Republican* of Iowa points out that the Iowa two-thousand-foot exclusion zone for sex offenders may be forcing offenders into rural areas. "Farms, acreages— those sort of places are fast becoming the only ones left for sex offenders to live. With many now heading for the rural areas, we question how much safer our children really are. Rural areas are more secluded, more quiet and, sadly, a perfect place for someone to commit another offense."[29]

Other advocates worry that the Lunsford law goes radically overboard. Said Jennifer Dritt, executive director of the Florida Council against Sexual Violence, "You can't paint people with such a broad brush."[30] And, according to the *Palm Beach Post,* local sex offender experts worry that "the state is squandering limited resources that could be better spent tracking people who are serious threats or providing treatment to the thousands who could benefit from it."[31] Florida provides no sex offender treatment in its prisons.[32] John Couey, accused of murdering Jessica Lunsford, reportedly "requested mental health assistance for nearly three decades. He told police in 1991 that he had a problem but had not received help to 'control his sexual attraction for young children.'"[33] Neither he nor David Onstott, accused of murdering thirteen-year-old Sarah Lunde, has ever received sex offender treatment.[34] It is not simply that treatment might have reduced the risk posed by these two men. As important, it might have raised red flags about the magnitude of the risks they posed.

Across the country, patterns are similar. At least twelve states have enacted some form of residency restrictions for sex offenders. These restrictions follow various patterns. Some apply to all sex offenders, some to more limited groups. Some apply to only those on parole or other forms of supervised release, and some purport to apply to even those offenders who are no longer under any form of correctional control.[35] Many states are adopting requirements that offenders be tracked with global positioning system (GPS) monitors, in what one newspaper called a "a national GPS tracking frenzy."[36] Minnesota's governor Tim Pawlenty touted the benefits of such a requirement, reportedly saying that "the technology would allow the average citizen—armed only with an Internet-connected cell phone—to enter a shopping mall parking lot, punch in a code and scan for registered sex offenders."[37]

Jumping on the GPS bandwagon, California governor Arnold Schwarzenegger proposed subjecting all eighty-five thousand California sex offenders to lifetime GPS monitoring and would bar them from living in many neighborhoods. The governor gave the legislature less than a month to consider the legislation, threatened to put it on the ballot if they did not act, and injected partisan politics into the equation, "stating that Republicans are more interested than Democrats in public safety," according to a newspaper editorial. The timing gave the legislature no time to examine the proposal, and Schwarzenegger said he did not know how much his proposed legislation would cost.[38] In an editorial criticizing the governor's proposal, one California newspaper pointed out the complexity of the decisions that might be made if such a proposal were to be carefully evaluated. The editorial's bottom line: "Haste and threats result in bad laws."[39] As of March 2006, the legislature was deadlocked, but supporters of the measure claimed that they had more than the 373,816 signatures needed to put it on the fall ballot. As a dozen other states considered similarly broad legislation, conservative talk show hosts, such as Fox News' Bill O'Reilly, devoted several shows to the law and sold window decals and bumper stickers supporting its passage.[40]

Neither the residential-exclusion strategy nor the GPS technology can provide a silver bullet for dealing with sex offenders. And both can have undesirable consequences if used excessively or unwisely. GPS is not cheap—and its effectiveness depends on careful monitoring. "GPS is a tool, but not a silver bullet," said Nancy Sabin. "My concern is that there's no funding for prevention or early intervention, no investment at the front end, to find out why our boys are growing up to be sex offenders."[41]

But there are some hopeful developments. Recently, the Senate passed Dru's law, named in memory of Dru Sjodin. This is a sensible development, supported by advocates and passed only after some deliberation, which would set up a national registry for sex offenders. Underlying the need for such a law is the patchwork of laws that has made it difficult for local officials to track offenders who move there from other states. But though the law would provide for federal funding for the registry, the law's requirement that local officials monitor high-risk offenders released into their jurisdictions is not funded.[42]

Another hopeful sign is the package of sex offender legislation that finally passed in Minnesota during the summer of 2005. Like the response in Florida, the Minnesota legislation was triggered initially by a heinous crime—the murder of Dru Sjodin in 2003. But Minnesota policymakers resisted the knee-jerk, fast-track legislation that has marked so many of the legislative innovations responding to high-profile sex crimes. Though the crime spawned scores of legislative proposals, the legislature wisely stayed its hand, mandating a nonpartisan, multidisciplinary study. Headed by a thoughtful retired Supreme Court justice, the study commission held seventeen meetings and in a four-month period produced a report with recommendations that attempted to look systemically and empirically at the prevention of sexual violence. The report recognized that most sex offenders are in the community—not in prison—and that therefore "effective supervision" policies are an "essential element of public safety." Again based on its view of the empirical research, the commission recommended that community supervision be "intensive," carried out by officers with specialized sex offender caseloads.

The commission also addressed a problem that had led to adoption of the predator laws in the beginning—the lack of flexibility at the end of determinate sentences. Taking a nuanced view, the commission recommended a blended determinate-indeterminate sentencing system for offenders. In the commission's view, this system would provide long periods of supervision—and the flexibility to adapt the conditions of the supervision to dynamic assessments of the offender's risk. The commission also made a number of recommendations for a more comprehensive, empirically based sex offender policy, such as developing a statewide approach to sex offender management and studying the proper allocation of resources between criminal justice and public health approaches to sexual violence.

Legislative action followed in due course. Two competing bills worked their ways through the house and senate. One of the bills would have enacted a set of extreme measures including castrating child molesters and putting "predatory offender" markings on license plates of released sex offenders. It contained provisions that would have added eleven thousand inmates to state prisons by mandating sentences of life without parole for a broad range of sexual offenses (even for first-time offenders), doubling the prison population and requiring seven new prisons.

In the end, a more moderate approach prevailed, which followed in material respects the commission's recommendations. The final legislation imposes life sentences on a small group, limited to those convicted of the most disturbed and heinous crimes, and adopts a flexible indeterminate sentencing approach for other serious sex offenses. It increases funding for GPS monitoring of sex offenders, housing options for released sex offenders, intensive supervision in the community, extended periods of supervision post release, and sex offender assessment and treatment (providing a range of sex offender programs and treatment, especially for juveniles).

Perhaps most encouraging about the Minnesota legislation is its mandate for ongoing evaluation. It requires reports on GPS monitoring (including its costs and impact on public safety), data collection on program effectiveness (and providing funding priority to effective programs), and the appointment of a working group on sex offender management to study a range of issues, including best practices in the supervision of sex offenders in the community.

During the legislative debate, media treatment of the sex offender issue struck a more temperate tone, providing space for politicians to address issues in a more nuanced manner. An editorial in the *Star Tribune* in May 2005, just as the legislature was negotiating the final form of the legislation, specifically called out the political posturing that so often characterizes the politics of sexual violence—using mild satire to put this posturing in its proper place. The editorial proceeded to make the case against the otherwise obligatory get-tough rhetoric, arguing that overly tough posturing might have unintended and undesired consequences. The editorial adopted a systemic and contextual attitude, observing that since most sex offenses are not reported to authorities, draconian measures might provide a disincentive for broader reporting. It warned that overreaching in setting prison sentences would entail huge expenditures on prisons, while "[a] lot of sensible crime control could be bought for far less cost."[43] Other state newspapers echoed the same themes. The *Duluth News Tribune,* at around the same time, ran a feature story headlined "State Puts Squeeze on Probation Programs," which began with the observation that "lawmakers are quick to send money to prisons, but they are more shy about paying for community probation officers."[44]

A July 2005 story in the *St. Paul Pioneer Press* took a nuanced look at approaches to prevention, pointing out that GPS monitoring is "not a panacea" and suggesting that the state, by expanding its use of this technology, had hopped on a national bandwagon.[45] The *St. Cloud Times* ran a story in August 2005 titled "Uproar Aside, No Level 3 Offenders Live in Area."[46] Almost simultaneously, *Finance and Commerce,* a trade publication for lawyers, featured a newly funded program that provides transitional housing for offenders (including many sex offenders) in Minnesota. Headlined, "MN Program Offers Stable Housing for Parolees," the story's last line emphasized the key elements of resource allocation and effective use of limited funds: "By providing housing options for offenders coming out of prison, we not only increase public safety, we also increase the effective use of the public dollar."[47]

The horror we all feel in response to horrible crimes of sexual murder is real and natural, and represents the best human instincts. But it is neither natural nor inevitable that these atypical crimes should come to fill our entire field of vision, forcing into near invisibility the much more typical, and much more frequent, types of sexual abuse.

Sexual violence is a complex problem. Making headway against it will require clear vision, undistorted by the myopia of the sexual predator paradigm. It will require perseverance and patience and investment, as we increase our knowledge and seek the most effective—rather than the flashiest—approaches to increased safety. Sensible lawmakers and policymakers will partner with victims' advocates and with the social scientists who study sexual abuse. The media must understand and convey the real extent and nature of sexual offending, creating space for the public and its representatives to engage in debate as they seek to achieve both a loud condemnation of sexual violence and effective programs to combat it.

In the end, it will require attention to issues of justice, because solutions built on principles that cannot be generalized, that do not represent the best in our jurisprudence, are doomed to fail.

NOTES

Introduction The Worst of the Worst?

1. Mary P. Koss, "Hidden Rape: Sexual Aggression and Victimization in a National Sample of Students in Higher Education," in *Rape and Sexual Assault*, vol. 2, ed. Ann W. Burgess (New York: Garland, 1988).

2. Carol Steiker, "Foreword: The Limits of the Preventive State," *Journal of Criminal Law & Criminology* 88 (1998): 774.

3. Catharine A. MacKinnon, "A Sex Equality Approach to Sexual Assault," in *Sexually Coercive Behavior: Understanding and Management*, ed. Robert A. Prentky, Eric S. Janus, and Michael C. Seto (New York: New York Academy of Sciences, 2003), 266.

4. Scott Harshbarger, "The Role of Citizen Education and Political Engagement in Framing the Issues," in *Sexually Coercive Behavior*, ed. Prentky et al., 8.

Chapter 1 New Legislative Approaches

1. John Q. LaFond, "Washington's Violent Predator Statute: Law or Lottery? A Response to Professor Brooks," *University of Puget Sound Law Review* 15 (1992): 755.

2. J. Christopher Rideout, "So What's in a Name? A Rhetorical Reading of Washington's Sexually Violent Predators Act," *University of Puget Sound Law Review* 15 (1992): 781.

3. Ibid.

4. Ibid.

5. Conrad deFiebre, "Life and Death: Getting Tough on Sex Offenders," *Minneapolis–Saint Paul Star Tribune*, Apr. 19, 2004, A6.

6. Daniel M. Filler, "Making the Case for Megan's Law: A Study in Legislative Rhetoric," *Indiana Law Review* 76 (2001): 331.

7. Ibid.

8. Ibid., 316.

9. Laurie O. Robinson, "Sex Offender Management: The Public Policy Challenges," in *Sexually Coercive Behavior: Understanding and Management*, ed. Robert A. Prentky, Eric S. Janus, and Michael C. Seto (New York: New York Academy of Sciences, 2003), 6.

10. Robert E. Freeman-Longo, "Revisiting Megan's Law and Sex Offender Registration: Prevention or Problem," on file with author, 2001.

11. Michael Petrunik, 2002, "Models of Dangerousness: A Cross-Jurisdictional Review of Dangerousness Legislation and Practice," http://www.psepc-sppcc.gc.ca/publications/corrections/199402_e.asp.

12. Ibid.

13. Ibid., citing David Boerner, "Confronting Violence: In the Act and in the Word," *University of Puget Sound Law Review* 15 (2001): 548.

14. Lucy Berliner, "Victim and Citizen Perspectives on Sexual Offender Policy," in *Sexually Coercive Behavior,* ed. Prentky et al., 470.

15. John Pratt, *Governing the Dangerous: Dangerousness, Law and Social Change* (Sydney: Federation Press, 1997).

16. Michael Tonry and Kathleen Hatlestad, "Sentencing Reform in the United States," in *Sentencing Reform in Overcrowded Times: A Comparative Perspective,* ed. Tonry and Hatlestad (New York: Oxford University Press, 1997), 6.

17. John D'Emilio and Estelle B. Freedman, *Intimate Matters: A History of Sexuality in America,* 2nd ed. (Chicago: University of Chicago Press, 1997), 314.

18. Tonry and Hatlestad, "Sentencing Reform," 6; R. Lieb, "Washington State: A Decade of Sentencing Reform," in *Sentencing Reform in Overcrowded Times,* ed. Tonry and Hatlestad, 20; Debra Dailey, "Minnesota's Sentencing Guidelines—Past and Future," in *Sentencing Reform in Overcrowded Times,* 35.

19. Boerner, "Confronting Violence," 548; Office of the Attorney General, State of Minnesota, *Attorney General's Task Force on the Prevention of Sexual Violence against Women* (Saint Paul, 1989), 19.

20. Governor's Task Force on Community Protection, State of Washington, *Final Report to Booth Gardner, Governor, State of Washington* (Olympia, 1989), II–5.

21. Office of the Attorney General, *Attorney General's Task Force,* 10, 19.

22. Franklin E. Zimring and Gordon Hawkins, *Incapacitation: Penal Confinement and the Restraint of Crime* (New York: Oxford University Press, 1995), 10–16.

23. Ibid., 12.

24. Lieb, "Washington State," 27; Dailey, "Minnesota's Sentencing Guidelines," 38.

25. Boerner, "Confronting Violence," 572; John L. Kirwin, "Civil Commitment of Sexual Predators: Statutory and Case Law Developments," *Hennepin Lawyer* 66, no. 7 (1995): 25.

26. Boerner, "Confronting Violence," 548.

27. Psychopathic Personalities Subcommittee, "Report," in *Minnesota Dept. of Human Services, Report to the Commissioner: Commitment Act Task Force* (1988), 45, 48–50.

28. *Smith v. Doe,* 538 U.S. 84 (1949).

29. *Millard v. Harris,* 132 U.S. App D.C. 146, 151 (1968).

30. Edwin Sutherland, "The Diffusion of Sexual Psychopath Laws," *American Journal of Sociology* 56 (Sept. 1950): 142–48, reprinted in *The Collective Definition of Deviance,* ed. Floyd Davis and Richard Stivers (New York: Free Press, 1975): 281–89, quoted in Petrunik, "Models of Dangerousness."

31. William D. Erickson, "Critical Analysis of the Psychopathic Personality Statute," on file with author.

32. Samuel J. Brakel, John Parry, and Barbara A. Weiner, *The Mentally Disabled and the Law,* 3rd ed. (Chicago: American Bar Association, 1985).

33. Group for the Advancement of Psychiatry, *Psychiatry and Sex Psychopath Legislation: The '30s to the '80s* (New York: Mental Health Materials Center, 1977), 942, 935.

34. Brian G. Bodine, "Washington's New Violent Sexual Predator Commitment System: An Unconstitutional Law and an Unwise Policy Choice," *University of Puget Sound Law Review* 14, no. 1 (1990): 109–10.

35. Estelle B. Freedman, "Uncontrolled Desires: The Response to the Sexual Psychopath," *Journal of American History* 74 (1987): 83–106.

36. Minnesota Psychiatric Society, "Problems with the Current Psychopathic Personality Statute," on file with author, 1992, p. 3.

37. American Psychiatric Association, *Task Force Report on Sexually Dangerous Offenders* (Washington, D.C.: APA, 1996).

38. American Psychiatric Association, *Dangerous Sex Offenders: A Task Force Report on Sexually Dangerous Offenders* (Washington, D.C.: APA, 1999), 173–74.

39. National Association of State Mental Health Program Directors, "Policy Statement on Laws Providing for the Civil Commitment of Sexually Violent Criminal Offenders" (1997), http://www.nasmhpd.org/general_files/position_statement/sexpred.htm.

40. W. Lawrence Fitch, "NASHMPD Update: Civil Commitment of Sex Offenders in the U.S. (A Quick and Dirty Survey)," a paper presented at the 19th annual conference of the National Association of State Mental Health Program Directors, Forensic Division; St. Petersburg Beach, Florida, 1998.

41. Joel Stashenko, "Father of Slain Florida Girl Pleads for Civil Commitment for Sexual Predators," Apr. 28, 2004, APALERTPOLITICS 20:27:40.

42. Garcia, *Sex Offender Management*, New Mexico Senate Bill 2005, NM S.B. 442(SN); *Sex Offenders—Secretary of Public Safety—Sex Offender Management Board Member*, New Mexico House Bill, NM LEGIS 19 (2005).

43. Coughlin, *Civil Commitment*, Ohio Senate Bill 2003, OH S.B. 262(SN).

44. AP Newswires, "Governor Pushes 'Civil Commitment' Proposal," Aug. 26, 2004, APALERTPOLITICS 18:11:06.

45. Karen Kane, "Young Sex Offender Won't Get Out at 21," *Pittsburgh Post-Gazette*, Dec. 17, 2004, A1.

46. Parents for Megan's Law, "Message from the Director," http://www.parentsformegans law.com/html/message.lasso?action=detail&uid=11.

Chapter 2 Judicial Promises and Betrayals

1. *Cooper v. Oklahoma, 517 U.S. 348, 366* (1996), quoting *United States v. Chisolm,* 149 F. 284, 288 (S.D. Ala. 1906).

2. *In re Linehan,* 557 N.W.2d 171 (Minn. 1996), *certiorari granted,* judgment vacated, 118 S.Ct. 596 (1997).

3. Gail F. Stevens, "Applying the Diagnosis Antisocial Personality to Imprisoned Offenders: Looking for Hay in a Haystack," *Journal of Offender Rehabilitation* 19 (1993): 1–26.

4. American Psychiatric Association, *Diagnostic and Statistical Manual of Mental Disorders Fourth Edition, Text Revision* (Arlington, Va.: American Psychiatric Association, 2000), xxx.

5. Eric S. Janus and Nancy H. Walbek, "Sex Offender Commitments in Minnesota: A Descriptive Study of Second Generation Commitments," *Behavioral Sciences and Law* 18 (2000); Andrew Harris, "A Prospective Analysis of Sexually Violent Predator Commitment Policies," PhD diss., New York University, 2003.

6. Jill S. Levenson, "Reliability of Sexually Violent Predator Civil Commitment Criteria in Florida," *International Journal of Offender Therapy and Comparative Criminology* 48 (2004): 638–48.

7. The Wisconsin program has released 15% of the committed men into supervised settings in the community, with no reported incidents of sexual recidivism. The director of the Minnesota program reported in 2002 that about 25% of the men in the program could be managed adequately under careful supervision in the community. (She subsequently backed away from this statement.)

8. Rebecca L. Jackson, Richard Rogers, and Daniel W. Shuman, "The Adequacy and Accuracy of Sexually Violent Predator Evaluations: Contextualized Risk Assessment in Clinical Practice," *International Journal of Forensic Mental Health* 3, no. 2 (2004): 115–29.

9. Josephine Marcotty, "State Looks to Release Sexual Psychopaths: Is Concern for Offenders or the Lock-up Program's High Cost Driving Change?" *Minneapolis–St. Paul Star Tribune,* June 22, 2003, 1A.

Chapter 3   A Factual Primer on Sexual Violence

1. U.S. Department of Justice, Office of Justice Programs, Bureau of Justice Statistics, *Sex Offenses and Offenders: An Analysis of Data on Rape and Sexual Assault,* by Lawrence A. Greenfield (Washington, D.C.: Government Printing Office, 1997), 22.

2. The National Crime Victimization Survey (NCVS) was begun in 1972 as an effort to complement the FBI's annual enumeration of crimes reported to law enforcement agencies. The NCVS collects data every year from a sample of about 50,000 households, and measures crime from the victim's perspective. U.S. Department of Justice, Office of Justice Programs, Bureau of Justice Statistics, *National Crime Victimization Survey Redesign* (Washington, D.C.: Government Printing Office, 1995).

3. Bureau of Justice Statistics, *Sex Offenses and Offenders,* 1.

4. U.S. Department of Justice, Office of Justice Programs, National Institute of Justice, *Full Report of the Prevalence, Incidence, and Consequences of Violence against Women: Findings from the National Violence against Women Survey,* by Patricia Tjaden and Nancy Thoeness (Washington, D.C.: Government Printing Office, 2000), 22, exhibit 6.

5. U.S. Department of Justice, Office of Justice Programs, Bureau of Justice Statistics, *Criminal Victimization 1994,* by Craig Perkins and Patty Klaus (Washington, D.C.: Government Printing Office, 1996), 7.

6. U.S. Department of Justice, Office of Justice Programs, National Institute of Justice, *Managing Adult Sex Offenders in the Community—A Containment Approach,* by Kim English, Suzanne Pullen, and Linda Jones (Washington, D.C.: Government Printing Office, 1997), 1, http://www.ncjrs.org/pdffiles/sexoff.pdf.

7. Bureau of Justice Statistics, *Sex Offenses and Offenders,* 24, table 3.

8. U.S. Department of Justice, Office of Justice Programs, Bureau of Justice Statistics, *National Crime Victimization Survey: Criminal Victimization 2002,* by Callie M. Rennison and Michael R. Rand (Washington, D.C.: Government Printing Office, 2003), 10, table 9.

9. U.S. Department of Justice, Office of Justice Programs, National Institute of Justice, *Full Report of the Prevalence, Incidence, and Consequences of Violence against Women,* by Patricia Tjaden and Nancy Thoeness, 26, exhibit 9.

10. Gene G. Abel, M.D., and Nora Harlow, "The Abel and Harlow Child Molestation Prevention Study," 2002, 1 (on file with author).

11. Bureau of Justice Statistics, *Sex Offenses and Offenders,* 11.

12. U.S. Department of Justice, Office of Justice Programs, Bureau of Justice Statistics, *Violence against Women: A National Crime Victimization Survey Report* (Washington, D.C.: Government Printing Office, 1994), 12, table 23.

13. U.S. Department of Justice, Office of Justice Programs, Bureau of Justice Statistics, *Reporting Crime to the Police, 1992–2000,* by Timothy Hart and Callie M. Rennison (Washington, D.C.: Government Printing Office, 2000), 5; Kim English and others, "Sexual Offender Containment: Use of the Postconviction Polygraph," in *Sexually Coercive Behavior: Understanding and Management,* ed. Robert A. Prentky, Eric S. Janus, and Michael C. Seto (New York: New York Academy of Sciences, 2003), 411–423 (reporting on a study by Watson and Newcomb).

14. U.S. Department of Justice, Federal Bureau of Investigation, *Crime in the United States 2003: Uniform Crime Report* (Washington, D.C.: Government Printing Office, 2004), 28.

15. Bureau of Justice Statistics, *Sex Offenses and Offenders*, 12.

16. Ibid., 15.

17. Wendy Koch, "Despite High-Profile Cases, Sex Crimes against Kids Fall," *USA Today*, Aug. 25, 2005, final ed., 1A.

18. Franklin E. Zimring, *An American Travesty: Legal Responses to Adolescent Sexual Offending* (Chicago: University of Chicago Press, 2004), 25–26.

19. Roxanne Lieb, Vernon Quinsey, and Lucy Berliner, "Sexual Predators and Social Policy," in *Crime and Justice: A Review of Research*, ed. Michael Tonry (Chicago: University of Chicago Press, 1992), 43–114.

20. RCWA § 71.09.010.

21. F.S.A. § 775.21.

22. Randy Furst, "Study: New Take on Sex Offenders; While Legislators Propose Dramatic Increases in Sentences, Researchers Suggest That, in Fact, Sex Offenders Are Less Likely to Commit New Crimes," *Minneapolis–St. Paul Star Tribune*, May 3, 2004, 1B.

23. R. Karl Hanson, Kelly E. Morton, and Andrew J. R. Harris, "Sexual Offender Recidivism Risk: What We Know and What We Need to Know," in *Sexually Coercive Behavior*, ed. Prentky et al., 157.

24. U.S. Department of Justice, Office of Justice Programs, Bureau of Justice Statistics, *Recidivism of Prisoners Released in 1983*, by Allen Beck and Bernard Shipley (Washington, D.C.: Government Printing Office, 1989), 6, table 9.

25. *Smith v. Doe*, 538 U.S. 84, 103 (2003).

26. Hanson, Morton, and Harris, "Sexual Offender Recidivism Risk," 155.

27. Minnesota Department of Corrections, Sex Offender/Chemical Dependency Services Unit, Community-Based Sex Offender Program Evaluation Project, *Report to the Legislature* (Saint Paul, 1997), 4; this is consistent with later findings that reported the six-year recidivism rate for probationers who completed treatment at 5%, compared to 11% for those who did not. Minnesota Department of Corrections, *Sex Offender Supervision: 2000 Report to the Legislature* (Saint Paul, 2000), 15–16.

28. Grant T. Harris, Marnie E. Rice, and Vernon L. Quinsey, "Appraisal and Management of Risk in Sexual Aggressors: Implications for Criminal Justice Policy," *Psychology, Public Policy, and Law* 4, nos. 1–2 (1998): 81; Judith V. Becker and William D. Murphy, "What We Know and Do Not Know about Assessing and Treating Sex Offenders," *Psychology, Public Policy, and Law* 4, nos. 1–2 (1998): 119–21.

29. Becker and Murphy, "What We Know," 120; John Kip Cornwell, John V. Jacobi, and Phillip H. Witt, "The New Jersey Sexually Violent Predator Act: Analysis and Recommendations for the Treatment of Sexual Offenders in New Jersey," *Seton Hall Legislative Journal* 24 (1999): 12.

30. Ibid., 13.

31. Harris, Rice, and Quinsey, "Appraisal and Management," 78.

32. Leonore M. J. Simon, "Matching Legal Policies with Known Offenders," in *Protecting Society from Dangerous Offenders: Law, Justice, and Therapy*, ed. Bruce J. Winick and John Q. LaFond (Washington, D.C.: American Psychological Association, 2003), 149–63; Cornwell, Jacobi, and Witt, "New Jersey Sexually Violent Predator Act," 12, citing Raymond A. Knight and Robert Alan Prentky, "Classifying Sexual Offenders: The Development and Corroboration of Taxonomic Models," in *The Handbook of Sexual Assault: Issues, Theories, and Treatment of the Offender*, ed. William L. Marshall, D. R. Laws, and Howard E. Barberee (New York: Plenum, 1990), 23.

33. Cornwell, Jacobi, and Witt, "New Jersey Sexually Violent Predator Act," 12.

34. Abel and Harlow, "Child Molestation Prevention Study," 1.

35. Bureau of Justice Statistics, *Sex Offenses and Offenders*, 23.

36. Robert A. Prentky and Ann Wolbert Burgess, *Forensic Management of Sexual Offenders* (New York: Plenum, 2000), 245.

37. Ibid.

38. Ibid., 30.

39. Margaret Talbot, "The Bad Mother," *New Yorker,* Aug. 16, 2004, 62.

40. W. L. Marshall and W. D. Pithers, "A Reconsideration of Treatment Outcome with Sex Offenders," *Criminal Justice and Behavior* 21, no. 1 (1994): 10–27.

41. Estelle B. Freedman, "Uncontrolled Desires: The Response to the Sexual Psychopath, 1920–1960," *Journal of American History* 74 (1987): 87–88.

42. Group for the Advancement of Psychiatry, *Psychiatry and Sex Psychopath Legislation: The '30s to the '80s* (New York: Group for the Advancement of Psychiatry, 1977).

43. Lita Furby, Mark R. Weinrott, and Lyn Blackshaw, "Sex Offender Recidivism: A Review," *Psychological Bulletin* 105, no. 1 (Jan. 1989): 27.

44. Marshall and Pithers, "Reconsideration of Treatment Outcome," 11.

45. Robert A. Prentky, "A Rationale for the Treatment of Sex Offenders: Pro Bono Publico," in *What Works: Reducing Reoffending–Guidelines from Research and Practice,* ed. James McGuire (New York: John Wiley, 1995), 167.

46. Lieb, Quinsey, and Berliner, "Sexual Predators and Social Policy," 93.

47. Gordon C. Nagayama Hall, "Sexual Offender Recidivism Revisited: A Meta-Analysis of Recent Treatment Studies," *Journal of Consulting and Clinical Psychology* 63 (Oct. 1995): 802.

48. R. Karl Hanson et al., "First Report of the Collaborative Outcome Data Project on the Effectiveness of Psychological Treatment for Sexual Offenders," *Sexual Abuse: A Journal of Research and Treatment* 14 (2002): 169.

49. Solicitor General of Canada, Public Safety and Emergency Preparedness Canada, *The Effectiveness of Treatment for Sexual Offenders,* July 2002, http://www.psepc-sppcc.gc.ca/publications/corrections/200207_e.asp (accessed Mar. 24, 2005).

50. Janice K. Marques et al., "Effects of a Relapse Prevention Program on Sexual Recidivism: Final Results from California's Sex Offender Treatment and Evaluation Project (SOTEP)," *Sexual Abuse: A Journal of Research and Treatment* 17, no. 1 (Jan. 2005): 102, citing D. A. Andrews and James Bonta, *The Psychology of Criminal Conduct,* 3rd ed. (Cincinnati: Anderson, 2003).

51. Marnie E. Rice and Grant T. Harris, "The Treatment of Mentally Disordered Offenders," *Psychology, Public Policy, and Law* 3 (1997): 153–54.

52. Ibid., 154.

53. Ibid., 155.

54. American Psychiatric Association, *Dangerous Sex Offenders: A Task Force Report on Sexually Dangerous Offenders* (Washington, D.C.: APA, 1999), 118–19.

55. Rice and Harris, "Treatment of Mentally Disordered," 154.

56. L. S. Grossman, B. Martin, and C. G. Fichtner, "Are Sex Offenders Treatable? A Research Overview," *Psychiatric Services* 50, no. 3 (1999): 354.

57. Rice and Harris, "Treatment of Mentally Disordered," 155.

58. Grossman, Martin, and Fichtner, "Are Sex Offenders Treatable?" 354.

59. American Psychiatric Association, *Dangerous Sex Offenders,* 146.

60. Marques et al., "Effects of Relapse Prevention Program," 101.

61. Robyn M. Dawes, David Faust, and Paul Meehl, "Clinical versus Actuarial Judgment," *Science* 243 (1989): 1668.

62. Douglas L. Epperson et al., *Minnesota Sex Offender Screening Tool—Revised: Development, Effectiveness, and Recommended Risk Level Cut Level Scores,* Dec. 2003, http://www.psychology.iastate.edu/faculty/epperson/TechUpdatePaper12–03.pdf.

63. Solicitor General of Canada, *Research Summary: Guidelines for Offender Risk Assessment,* Feb. 2002, http://www.psepcsppcc.gc.ca/publications/corrections/200211_e.asp (accessed Sept. 22, 2005).

64. R. Karl Hanson and David Thornton, *STATIC 99: Improving Actuarial Risk Assessments for Sex Offenders,* Feb. 1999, 2, http://nicic.org/library/D15355 (accessed Mar. 12, 2006).

65. Ibid., appendix 1.
66. Ibid., 15, table 5.
67. Ibid.
68. Epperson et al., *Minnesota Sex Offender Screening Tool*, 43.
69. R. Karl Hanson, *The Development of a Brief Actuarial Risk Scale for Sexual Offense Recidivism*, http://ww2.psepc-sppcc.gc.ca/publications/corrections/199704_e.pdf, 16.
70. Hanson and Thornton, *Static 99*, 15, table 5.
71. The following discussion of actuarial risk assessment is based in part on Eric S. Janus and Robert A. Prentky, "The Forensic Use of Actuarial Risk Assessment with Sex Offenders: Accuracy, Admissibility and Accountability," *American Criminal Law Review* 40 (2003): 1443.

Chapter 4 Benefits and Costs

1. Washington State Institute for Public Policy, *Involuntary Commitment of Sexually Violent Predators: Comparing State Laws* (Olympia, 2005), 6.
2. Rachel E. Stassen-Berger, "Costs of New Sex Crime Laws Add Up," *St. Paul Pioneer Press*, Feb. 13, 2006, 1A; Minnesota Department of Human Services, Bulletin 02–77–01 (June 24, 2002), indicates two hundred held at cost of $20 million.
3. Jessica McBride and Reid J. Epstein, "State Tops in Release of Sexual Predators," *Milwaukee Journal-Sentinel*, Sept. 22, 2003, 1A.
4. Jim Doyle, "Costly Care for Rapists, Molesters under Fire: Critics Question Effectiveness of Law Hospitalizing Ex-cons," *San Francisco Chronicle*, July 11, 2004.
5. Washington State Institute for Public Policy, *Involuntary Commitment of Sexually Violent Predators*, 2; Terrence W. Campbell, *Assessing Sex Offenders: Problems and Pitfalls* (Springfield, Ill.: Charles C. Thomas, 2004), 6.
6. Andrew J. Harris, "A Prospective Analysis of Sexually Violent Predator Civil Commitment Policies," PhD diss., New York University, Sept. 2003, 12, quoting John Q. LaFond, "The Costs of Enacting a Sexual Predator Law and Recommendations for Keeping Them from Skyrocketing," in *Protecting Society from Sexually Dangerous Offenders*, ed. B. J. Winick and John Q. LaFond (Washington, D.C.: APA Books, 2003).
7. Bill Salisbury, "Tab Coming Due on State Sentencing Policies: Prisons, Hospitals Seek $140 Million for Construction," *St. Paul Pioneer Press*, Sept. 6, 2005, 1A.
8. "Administrator Seeks to Expand State's Sex Offender Unit," *Grand Forks Herald*, Sept. 14, 2005, 1.
9. Minnesota Department of Corrections, *Sex Offender Policy and Management Board Study* (Saint Paul, 2000). Rachel E. Stassen-Berger, "Costs of New Sex Crime Laws Add Up," *St. Paul Pioneer Press*, Feb. 13, 2006, 1A.
10. Amy Lindblom, "Sex Offender Denied Release," *Union Democrat Online*, Mar. 2, 2005, http://www.uniondemocrat.com/news/story.cfm?story_no=16686.
11. LaFond, "Costs of Enacting."
12. Greg Martin, "What's the Mission," *Sun and Weekly Herald*, Mar. 7, 2005, http://www.sun-herald.com/NewsArchive2/030705/tp1ch12.htm?date=030705&story=tp1ch12.htm; Campbell, *Assessing Sex Offenders*, 7, citing LaFond, "Costs of Enacting."
13. Minnesota Department of Corrections, Board Study, 19. Sex offenders released during a later period have shown a somewhat lower recidivism rate. Stephen Huot, *Sex Offender Treatment and Recidivism: 2002 Update and Preliminary Analysis* (on file with author).
14. Lawrence A. Greenfield, "Sixty Percent of Convicted Sex Offenders Are on Parole or Probation," *Bureau of Justice Statistics News Release*, Feb. 2, 1997, WL 53093 (DOJ).
15. Maura Lerner, "3% of Minnesota Women Report Attack by Their Partner," *Minneapolis–St. Paul Star Tribune*, Mar. 10, 2005, 6B.
16. Wayne Logan, "Sex Offender Registration and Community Notification: Emerging Le-

gal and Research Issues," in *Sexually Coercive Behavior: Understanding and Management,* ed. Robert A. Prentky, Eric S. Janus, and Michael C. Seto (New York: New York Academy of Sciences, 2003), 340.

17. Ibid., 338.

18. Ibid., 342.

19. Ibid., 343.

20. National Institute of Justice (NIJ), *Sex Offender Community Notification.* Series: NIJ Research in Action, Feb. 1997.

21. Logan, "Sex Offender Registration," 345.

22. Ibid., 343.

23. "Thousands of Sex Offenders 'Lost,'" *CBS News,* Feb. 6, 2003, http://www.cbsnews.com/stories/2003/02/06/national/main539717.shtml.

24. Kim A. Curtis, "California 'Loses' 33,000 Sex Offenders," CBS News, Jan. 8, 2003, http://www.cbsnews.com/stories/2003/01/08/national/main535654.shtml.

25. "Thousands of Sex Offenders 'Lost.'"

26. Logan, "Sex Offender Registration," 342, citing Anthony J. Petrosino and Carolyn Petrosino, "The Public Safety Potential of Megan's Law in Massachusetts: An Assessment from a Sample of Criminal Sexual Psychopaths," *Crime & Delinquency* 45 (1999): 140.

27. Logan, "Sex Offender Registration," 342.

28. Victoria Simpson Beck, James Clingermayer, Robert J. Ramsey, "Community Response to Sex Offenders," *Journal of Psychiatry & Law* 23 (2004): 141, citing Jeffrey T. Walker, S. Madden, and Amy VanHouten, "The General Deterrent Effects of Sex Offender Registration and Notification Laws in the United States," paper presented at 55th Annual Meeting of the American Society of Criminology, Denver, November 2003.

29. U.S. Department of Justice, Office of Justice Programs, Bureau of Justice Statistics, *Recidivism of Sex Offenders Released in 1994,* by Patrick Langan, Erica Schmitt, and Matthew Durose (Washington, D.C.: Government Printing Office, 2003), table 5, http://www.ojp.usdoj.gov/bjs/pub/pdf/rsorp94.pdf.

30. Robert A. Prentky and Ann W. Burgess, *Forensic Management of Sexual Offenders* (New York: Kluwer Academic/Plenum Publishers, 2000), 173.

31. Wendy Fullerton, "Tracking Sexual Offenders; Lee Sheriff's Program Provides 24/7 Monitoring," *Lee County* (Fla.) *News-Press,* Apr. 18, 2004.

32. Beck et al., "Community Response," 165.

33. George Hunter, "Teens May Avoid Sex Registry; Exemption Granted for Offenders Close in Age to Minors," *Detroit News,* July 7, 2004, 1B. Jim Schaefer, "Sheep Abuser Is Center of Debate: Man Fights Inclusion on Sex Registry," *Detroit Free Press,* Mar. 3, 2006, http://www.freep.com/apps/pbcs.dll/article?AID=/20060303/NEWS06/603030417/1008/NEWS.

34. *Connecticut Department of Public Safety v. John Doe,* 581 U.S. 1, 5.

35. Lucy Berliner, "Victim and Citizen Perspectives on Sexual Offender Policy," in *Sexually Coercive Behavior,* ed. Prentky et al., 470.

36. Barbara K. Schwartz, "Overview of Rehabilitative Efforts in Understanding and Managing Sexually Coercive Behaviors," in *Sexually Coercive Behavior,* ed. Prentky et al., 377.

37. Patricia Lopez Baden, "Proposal Would Require That Sex Offenders Be Identified to Neighbors," *Minneapolis–St. Paul Star Tribune,* Feb. 13, 1995, 1A.

38. Bruce J. Winick, "A Therapeutic Jurisprudence Analysis of Sex Offender Registration and Community Notification Laws," in *Protecting Society from Sexually Dangerous Offenders,* ed. Winick and LaFond.

39. Logan, "Sex Offender Registration," 343–44.

40. Prentky and Burgess, *Forensic Management,* 173.

41. NIJ, *Sex Offender Community Notification.*

42. Schwartz, "Overview," 360.

Chapter 5 Feminism, the Culture Wars, and Sexual Violence

1. *Star,* "Monica's Sexy Strip Show: How Bill Lost Control When That Little Blue Dress Came Off!" Aug. 18, 1998.

2. Frances Heidensohn, *Sexual Politics and Social Control* (Buckingham: Open University Press, 2000), 14.

3. Sara M. Evans, *Tidal Wave: How Women Changed America at Century's End* (New York: Free Press, 2003).

4. John D'Emilio and Estelle B. Freedman, *Intimate Matters: A History of Sexuality in America,* 2nd ed. (Chicago: University of Chicago Press, 1997), 310.

5. Ibid., 311.

6. Heidensohn, *Sexual Politics and Social Control,* 27.

7. Susan Brownmiller, *Against Our Will: Men, Women, and Rape* (New York: Simon and Schuster, 1975), quoted in John Murray, "The Role of Situational Factors in Sexual Offending," in *Sex and Violence: The Psychology of Crime and Risk Assessment,* ed. David P. Farrington, Clive R. Hollin, and Mary McMurran (New York: Routledge, 2001), 176 and 177.

8. Catharine A. MacKinnon, "A Sex Equality Approach to Sexual Assault," in *Sexually Coercive Behavior: Understanding and Management,* ed. Robert A. Prentky, Eric S. Janus, and Michael C. Seto (New York: New York Academy of Sciences, 2003), 266.

9. Murray, "Role of Situational Factors in Sexual Offending."

10. Andrea Dworkin, "I Want a Twenty-four-hour Truce," in *Transforming a Rape Culture,* ed. Emilie Buchwald et al. (Minneapolis: Milkweed Editions, 1994), 14.

11. Evans, *Tidal Wave,* 3.

12. Nancy E. Snow, "Evaluating Rape Shield Laws: Why the Law Continues to Fail Rape Victims," in *A Most Detestable Crime: New Philosophical Essays on Rape,* ed. Keith Burgess-Jackson (New York: Oxford University Press, 1999), 255.

13. Murray, "Role of Situational Factors in Sexual Offending," 177.

14. Ibid.

15. Snow, "Evaluating Rape Shield Laws," 254.

16. Neil M. Malamuth, "Rape Proclivity among Males," *Journal of Social Issues* 37, no. 4 (1981): 138, cited in Murray, "Role of Situational Factors in Sexual Offending," 177.

17. "Adolescent Dating Attitudes, 1998 Survey Results" (Providence: Sexual Assault and Trauma Resource Center of Rhode Island, 1999), cited in *Taking Action against Sexual Assault,* Jane Doe Inc. (Massachusetts Coalition against Sexual Assault and Domestic Violence, http://www.janedoe.org/Images/sa.pdf), 2001.

18. Snow, "Evaluating Rape Shield Laws," 246.

19. Ibid.

20. *State v. Bashaw,* 672 P.2d 48 (Oregon, 1983), quoted in Joshua Dressler, "Where We Have Been, and Where We Might Be Going: Some Cautionary Reflections on Rape Law Reform," *Cleveland State Law Review* 46 (1998): 409, 416.

21. Carole Goldberg-Ambrose, "Unfinished Business in Rape Law Reform," *Journal of Social Issues* 48, no. 1 (1992): 173.

22. Robert A. Prentky and Ann W. Burgess, *Forensic Management of Sexual Offenders* (Dordrecht, Netherlands: Kluwer Academic/Plenum, 2000), 246.

23. Ronet Bachman and Raymond Paternoster, "A Contemporary Look at the Effects of Rape Law Reform: How Far Have We Really Come?" *Journal of Criminal Law* 84 (1993): 554, 559.

24. Ibid., 559–60.

25. Snow, "Evaluating Rape Shield Laws," 245.

26. Bureau of Justice Statistics, "National Corrections Reporting Program." The figures represent actual time served by prisoners released in that year.

27. Joshua Dressler, "Where We Have Been," 409, 412.

28. Evans, *Tidal Wave,* 6.

29. Elizabeth Stanko, "Naturalizing Danger," 149.

30. Evans, *Tidal Wave,* 8.

31. Ibid., 222.

32. Elizabeth Stanko, "Naturalizing Danger," 160.

33. Mary P. Koss, "Hidden Rape: Sexual Aggression and Victimization in a National Sample of Students in Higher Education," in *Rape and Sexual Assault,* vol. 2, ed. Ann W. Burgess (New York: Garland, 1988).

34. Sharon Lamb, "Constructing the Victim: Popular Images and Lasting Labels," in *New Versions of Victims: Feminists Struggle with the Concept,* ed. Lamb (New York: New York University Press, 1999).

35. Florence Rush, "The Best Kept Secret: Sexual Abuse of Children," cited in Sharon K. Araji, "Sexual Violence and Abuse," *Encyclopedia of Sociology,* vol. 4 (New York: Macmillan, 1992), 1775.

36. Sharon Araji, "Sexual Violence and Abuse," *Encyclopedia of Sociology,* vol. 4 (New York: Macmillan, 1992), 1775, citing Stephanie D. Peters, Gail E. Wyatt, and David Finkelhor, "Prevalence," in *A Sourcebook on Child Sexual Abuse,* ed. Finkelhor et al. (Newbury Park, Calif.: Sage, 1986).

37. Ruth Rosen, review of *Neither Victim Nor Enemy: Women's Freedom Network Looks at Gender in America,* ed. Rita J. Simon, *Contemporary Sociology* 26, no. 1 (1997): 19–20. Also found at http://www.womensfreedom.org/books.htm.

38. Christina Hoff Sommers, *Who Stole Feminism? How Women Have Betrayed Women* (New York: Touchstone, 1994), 211.

39. Ibid., 224.

40. Ibid., 222.

41. Ibid., 223.

42. D'Emilio and Freedman, *Intimate Matters,* 374.

43. Stanko, "Naturalizing Danger," 150.

44. Ibid., 149.

45. D'Emilio and Freedman, *Intimate Matters,* 374.

46. Ibid.

47. Lawrence P. Greenfield, "Sex Offenses and Offenders: An Analysis of Data on Rape and Sexual Assault," NCJ-163392 (Washington, D.C.: U.S. Department of Justice, Feb. 1997), 1; and "National Crime Victimization Survey: Questions and Answers about the Redesign" (Washington, D.C.: Bureau of Justice Statistics, Oct. 30, 1994), 1.

48. *Redesign of the National Crime Victimization Survey* (Washington, D.C.: U.S. Department of Justice, Bureau of Justice Statistics, 1997), http://www.ojp.usdoj.gov/bjs/cvict_rd.htm (accessed Mar. 3, 2005).

49. Lawrence P. Greenfield, "Sex Offenses and Offenders," 1; and "National Crime Victimization Survey: Questions and Answers," 1.

50. U.S. Department of Justice, Bureau of Justice Statistics, "Women Usually Victimized by Offenders They Know," news release, Aug. 16, 1995. Also found on Westlaw at 1995 WL 491581.

51. Patricia Tjaden and Nancy Thoennes, *Full Report of the Prevalence, Incidence, and Consequences of Violence against Women: Findings from the National Violence against Women Survey,* NCJ 183781 (Washington, D.C.: Department of Justice, Nov. 2000).

52. Ibid., 47. Note that the percentages add up to more than 100% because some victims had multiple assailants.

53. Tjaden and Thoennes, *Full Report of the Prevalence, Incidence, and Consequences of Violence against Women.*

54. Stanko, "Naturalizing Danger," 149.

55. Keith Kaufman, Michelle Barber, Heather Mosher, and Megan Carter, "Reconceptualizing Child Sexual Abuse as a Public Health Concern," in *Preventing Violence in Relationships:*

Interventions across the Life Span, by Paul A. Schewe (Washington, D.C.: American Psychological Association, 2002).

56. Sommers, *Who Stole Feminism?* 224.

57. Stanko, "Naturalizing Danger," 149.

58. Janice Haaken and Sharon Lamb, "The Politics of Child Sexual Abuse Research," *Society* (May–June 2000).

59. Elizabeth Stanko, "Naturalizing Danger," 153.

60. Ibid.

61. Ibid., 157.

62. Michel Foucault, *Madness and Civilization* (New York: Vintage, 1988), xi, 10.

63. Sharon Lamb, *The Trouble with Blame: Victims, Perpetrators, and Responsibility* (Cambridge: Harvard University Press, 1996), 76.

64. John M. Conley and William M. O'Barr, *Just Words: Law, Language, and Power* (Chicago: University of Chicago Press, 1998), 38.

65. Ibid., 7.

66. Lamb, *Trouble with Blame,* 56.

67. Diana Scully and Joseph Marolla, "Convicted Rapists' Vocabulary of Motive: Excuses and Justifications," *Social Problems* 31, no. 5 (June 1984): 530–544.

68. Quoted in Susan Ehrlich, *Representing Rape: Language and Sexual Consent* (London: Routledge, 2001), 57.

69. Robert Reiner et al., "Casino Culture: Media Crime in a Winner-Loser Society," in *Crime, Risk, and Justice: The Politics of Crime Control in Liberal Democracies,* ed. Kevin Stenson et al. (Chicago: University of Chicago Press, 2001), 173, 177.

70. Eric Silver and Lisa L. Miller, "A Cautionary Note on the Use of Actuarial Risk Assessment Tools for Social Control," *Crime & Delinquency* 48, no. 1 (Jan. 2002): 138–61.

71. Reiner, "Casino Culture," 178.

72. Fay Honey Knopp, "Community Solutions to Sexual Violence," in *Criminology as Peacemaking,* ed. Harold E. Pepinsky et al. (Bloomington: Indiana University Press, 1991), quoted in Lois Presser et al., "Strange Bedfellows: Is Sex Offender Notification a Form of Community Justice?" *Crime & Delinquency* 45, no. 3 (July 1999): 299–315.

Chapter 6 Harbinger of the Preventive State?

1. Carol Steiker, "Foreword: The Limits of the Preventive State," *Journal of Criminal Law and Criminology* 88 (1998): 774.

2. Oren Gross, "Chaos and Rules: Should Responses to Violent Crises Always Be Constitutional?" *Yale Law Journal* 112 (2003): 1017–18.

3. Ibid., 1038.

4. "Top Bush Officials Push Case against Saddam," *CNN,* Sept. 8, 2002, http://www.cnn.com/2002/ALLPOLITICS/09/08/iraq.debate/.

5. "Bush Pledges to Make America Safer," CNN, July 20, 2004, http://www.cnn.com/2004/ALLPOLITICS/07/20/bush.iowa/.

6. Robert M. Chesney, "The Sleeper Scenario: Terrorism-Support Laws and the Demands of Prevention," *Harvard Journal on Legislation* 42 (2005): 26–27, 21.

7. Raneta Lawson Mack and Michael J. Kelly, *Equal Justice in the Balance: America's Legal Responses to the Emerging Terrorist Threat* (Ann Arbor: University of Michigan Press, 2004), 141, 131–32.

8. Ibid., 3.

9. Chesney, "Sleeper Scenario."

10. Mack and Kelly, *Equal Justice,* 3.

11. "Civil Rights Groups Warn against Tipster Training," St. Petersburg Times (Florida), July 9, 2004, http://www.sptimes.com/2004/07/09/news_pf/State/Civil_rights_groups_ w.shtml. James Bamford, "The Agency That Could Be Big Brother," *New York Times,* Dec. 25, 2005, section 4, 1. Adam Liptak, "In Case about Google's Secrets, Yours Are Safe," *New York Times,* Jan. 26, 2006, A1.

12. "Interview by Brook Gladstone with Lucy Dalglish, Executive Director, Reporter's Committee," New York, New York, Sept. 24, 2004, *On the Media,* New York Public Radio, http://www.wnyc.org/onthemedia/transcipts/transcripts_092404_homefront.html; Ann W. O'Neill, "Watchdog Challenges Secrecy in U.S. Court; Miami Docketing System Keeps Sensitive Cases Out of Public Eye; Practice Violates Free Speech, Access Rights, Group Charges," *Ft. Lauderdale Sun-Sentinel,* Jan. 8, 2004, 1A.

13. Mack and Kelly, *Equal Justice,* 118, 152–53.

14. "List of Communities That Have Passed Resolutions," June 10, 2004, http://www. aclu.org/SafeandFree/SafeandFree.cfm?ID=11294&c=207.

15. *Doe v. Ashcroft,* No. 04 Civ. 2614(VM), 2004 WL 2185571, at 1 (S.D.N.Y. 2004).

16. Mack and Kelly, *Equal Justice,* 3.

17. *Hamdi v. Rumsfeld,* 124 S. Ct. 2633 (2004); *Rasul v. Bush,* 124 S. Ct. 2686 (2004) (holding that noncitizens held at Guantanamo can challenge their "enemy combatant" status in U.S. civilian courts).

18. American Libraries Online, "Patriot Act Compromise Announced," Feb. 10, 2006, http://www.ala.org/ala/alonline/currentnews/newsarchive/2006abc/february2006a/ patriotcompro.htm.

19. Karen C. Tumlin, "Suspect First: How Terrorism Policy is Reshaping Immigration Policy," *California Law Review* 92 (2004): 1184; Mack and Kelly, *Equal Justice,* 73.

20. Tumlin, "Suspect First," 1185.

21. Rochelle Olson et al., "Pawlenty Wants Easier Access to Immigrant Data," *Minneapolis–St. Paul Star Tribune,* Sept. 1, 2004, A1.

22. Erwin Chemerinsky, *Constitutional Law* (New York: Aspen Publishers, 2002), 762–889.

23. Mack and Kelly, *Equal Justice,* 123.

24. Barbara Hudson, *Justice in the Risk Society: Challenging and Re-affirming "Justice" in Late Modernity* (London: Sage, 2003), 35.

25. *Dred Scott v. Sandford,* 60 U.S. (19 How.) 393 (1856): 404–5.

26. 163 U.S. 537 (1889).

27. Congress's authorization of compensation for internment victims supports the view that these cases and the principles they applied are now generally rejected, however.

28. *Korematsu v. United States,* 323 U.S. 219–20, 235, 220.

29. *Korematsu,* 323 U.S. at 218–19 (emphasis added).

30. 274 U.S. 200 (1927).

31. Howard Markel, "The Ghost of Medical Atrocities: What's Next, after the Unveiling?" *New York Times,* Dec. 23, 2003, F6.

32. *Buck,* 274 U.S. at 207.

33. 197 U.S. 11 (1905).

34. Markel, "Ghost of Medical Atrocities," F6.

35. *Griswold v. Connecticut,* 381 U.S. 471 (1965).

36. *United States v. Virginia,* 518 U.S. 515 (1996) (requiring "exceedingly persuasive justification" for gender discrimination).

37. 42 U.S.C.A. § 12101 et. seq. (2004).

38. 517 U.S. 620 (1996).

39. 539 U.S. 558 (2003).

40. *Cooper v. Oklahoma,* 517 U.S. 348, 366 (1996) (quoting *United States v. Chisolm,* 149 F. 284, 288 [C.C.S.D. Ala. 1906]).

41. *Foucha v. Louisiana,* 504 U.S. 71, 81 (1992).

42. Anthony Amsterdam, "Federal Constitutional Restrictions on the Punishment of Crimes of Status, Crimes of General Obnoxiousness, Crimes of Displeasing Police Officers, and the Like," *Criminal Law Bulletin* 3 (1967): 33.

43. *City of Chicago v. Morales,* 527 U.S. 41 (1999) (loitering law); *Kolender v. Lawson,* 461 U.S. 352 (1983) (loitering law); *Papachristou v. Jacksonville,* 405 U.S. 156 (1972) (vagrancy law).

44. *Kolender,* 461 U.S. at 352.

45. *Debs v. United States,* 249 U.S. 211 (1919); *Frohwerk v. United States,* 249 U.S. 204 (1919).

46. *Dennis v. United States,* 341 U.S. 494 (1951).

47. *Brandenburg v. Ohio,* 395 U.S. 444 (1969).

48. *Robinson v. California,* 270 U.S. 660 (1962).

49. *Hyde v. United States,* 225 U.S. 347, 388 (1912).

50. *U.S. v. Cintolo,* 818 F.2d 980, 1003 (1987).

51. *In re Blodgett* 510 N.W.2d 910, 913 (Minn. 1994); *In re Young,* 857 P.2d 989, 992 (Wash. 1993).

52. Eric S. Janus, "Civil Commitment as Social Control: Managing the Risk of Sexual Violence," in *Dangerous Offenders: Punishment and Social Order,* ed. Mark Brown and John Pratt (London: Routledge, 2000), 82–83.

53. Eric S. Janus and Paul Meehl, "Assessing the Legal Standard for Predictions of Dangerousness in Sex Offender Commitment Proceedings," *Psychology, Public Policy and Law* 3 (1997): 42.

54. 534 U.S. 407, 412 (2002) (emphasis added) (quoting *Kansas v. Hendricks,* 521 U.S. 346, 360 [1997]).

55. Eric S. Janus, "Sex Offender Commitments and the 'Inability to Control': Developing Legal Standards and a Behavioral Vocabulary for an Elusive Concept," in *The Sexual Predator: Legal Issues, Clinical Issues, Special Situations,* ed. Anita Schlank (Kingston, N.Y.: Civic Research Institute, 2001), 1–1, 2–4.

56. Robert A. Prentky and Raymond A. Knight, "Identifying Critical Dimensions for Discriminating among Rapists," *Journal of Consulting and Clinical Psychology* 59 (1991): 643.

57. Daniel A. Krauss et al., "Beyond Prediction to Explanation in Risk Assessment Research: A Comparison of Two Explanatory Theories of Criminality and Recidivism," *International Journal of Law and Psychiatry* 23 (2000): 98.

58. Robert J. McGrath, "Sex Offender Risk Assessment and Disposition Planning: A Review of Empirical and Clinical Findings," *International Journal of Offender Therapy and Comparative Criminology* 35 (1991): 338.

59. Roy F. Baumeister, Todd F. Heatherton, Dianne M. Tice, *Losing Control: How and Why People Fail at Self-Regulation* (San Diego: Academic Press, 1994), 11–12.

60. Eric S. Janus and Robert A. Prentky, "The Forensic Use of Actuarial Risk Assessment with Sex Offenders: Accuracy, Admissibility, and Accountability," *American Criminal Law Review* 40 (2003): 1457–58.

61. Nikolas Rose, "At Risk of Madness," in *Embracing Risk: The Changing Culture of Insurance and Responsibility,* ed. Tom Baker and Jonathan Simon (Chicago: University of Chicago Press, 2002), 214.

62. J. Arboleda-Florez et al., "Understanding Causal Paths between Mental Illness and Violence," a supplement of *Social Psychiatry and Psychiatric Epidemiology* 33 (1998): S38–S46; V. A. Hiday, "Understanding the Connection between Mental Illness and Violence," *International Journal of Law and Psychiatry* 20 (1998): 399–417.

63. Rose, "At Risk of Madness," 209.

64. Grant T. Harris and Marnie E. Rice, "Actuarial Assessment of Risk among Sex Offenders," in *Sexually Coercive Behavior: Understanding and Management,* ed. Robert A. Prentky, Eric S. Janus, and Michael Seto (New York: New York Academy of Sciences, 2003), 989.

65. Michael Petrunik, Feb. 1994, "Models of Dangerousness: A Cross Jurisdictional Review

of Dangerousness Legislation and Practice, Public Safety and Emergency Preparedness Canada," http://ww2.psepc-sppcc.gc.ca/publications/corrections/pdf/199402_e.pdf.

66. Ortwinn Renn, Eugene A. Rosa, Thomas Webler, and Carlo C. Jaeger, *Risk, Uncertainty and Rational Action* (London: Earthscan, 2001), 18.

67. Hazel Kemshall, *Understanding Risk in Criminal Justice* (Berkshire, Eng.: Open University Press, 2003), 6.

68. Hudson, *Justice in the Risk Society,* 66, quoting Mary Douglas, *Purity and Danger: An Analysis of Conceptions of Purity and Taboo* (London: Routledge and Kegan Paul, 1966).

69. Hudson, *Justice in the Risk Society,* 66–67.

70. *Kansas v. Hendricks,* 521 U.S. 346, 347 (1997) (noting that a civil commitment does not again "affix culpability for prior criminal conduct, but uses such conduct solely for evidentiary purposes").

71. Stephen J. Gould, *The Mismeasure of Man* (New York: W. W. Norton, 1981), 113–45.

72. *State of Minnesota ex rel. Pearson v. Probate Court,* 287 N.W. 297, 301 (Minn. 1939), aff'd, 309 U.S. 270 (1940).

73. Gould, *Mismeasure of Man.*

74. Harris and Rice, "Actuarial Assessment," 208.

75. "Risk Assessment: Discussion of the Section," in *Sexually Coercive Behavior,* ed. Prentky et al., 240.

76. Hudson, *Justice in the Risk Society,* 38, 181, 181–82, 183–84.

77. Rose, "At Risk of Madness," 214, quoting Malcolm Feeley and Jonathan Simon, "The New Penology: Notes on the Emerging Strategy of Corrections and Its Implications," *Criminology* 30 (1992): 452.

78. Hudson, *Justice in the Risk Society,* 44.

79. Kemshall, *Understanding Risk,* 1, noting a "shift from the 'reactive investigation of individual crimes' to a 'strategic, future-oriented and targeted approach to crime control'" (quoting Mary Maguire, "Policing by Risks and Targets: Some Dimensions and Implications of Intelligence-Led Crime Control," *Policing and Society* 9 [2000]: 316).

80. Barton Gellman, Dafna Linzer, and Carol D. Leonnig, "Surveillance Net Yields Few Suspects," Washingtonpost.com, Feb. 5, 2006, http://www.washingtonpost.com/wp-dyn/content/article/2006/02/04/AR2006020401373_pf.html.

81. *New Jersey v. T.L.O.,* 469 U.S. 325, 328 (1985).

82. Kemshall, *Understanding Risk,* 33.

83. Rose, "At Risk of Madness," 214.

84. Kemshall, *Understanding Risk,* 12, quoting D. Carson, "Risking Legal Repercussions," in *Good Practice in Risk Assessment and Risk Management 1,* vol. 1, ed. Hazel Kemshall and Jacki Pritchard (London: Jessica Kingsley, 1996).

85. Kemshall, *Understanding Risk,* 1.

86. Eric S. Janus, "Closing Pandora's Box: Sexual Predators and the Politics of Sexual Violence," *Seton Hall Law Review* 34 (2004): 1233.

87. Hudson, *Justice in the Risk Society,* 60.

88. Ibid., 40.

Chapter 7   There Are Alternatives

1. Karin Brulliard, "Va. Court Limits Committing of Sex Offenders," *Washington Post,* Mar. 5, 2005; http://www.washingtonpost.com/wp-dyn/articles/A8804-2005Mar4.html.

2. Kim English, Suzanne Pullen, and Linda Jones, Jan. 1997, "Managing Adult Sex Offenders in the Community—A Containment Approach," http://www.ncjrs.org/pdffiles/sexoff.pdf.

3. David Chanen, "Cops to Make Do with Less," *Minneapolis–St. Paul Star Tribune,* June 22, 2004, 1B.

4. Betsy Z. Russel, "Worst Molesters Unsupervised: After Prison, Idaho's Violent Sex Offenders Return to Society with Minimal Oversight," *Spokane Spokesman-Review*, July 24, 2005, 1A.

5. Department of Corrections Annual Report (2000), 3, 7, 9.

6. *Sex Offenses in Washington State: 1998 Update* (Olympia: Washington State Institute for Public Policy, 1998), 21.

7. National Center for Missing & Exploited Children, *A Model State Sex-Offender Policy* (Arlington, Va., 1998).

8. D. Richard Laws, "Sexual Offending as a Public Health Problem: A North American Perspective," *Journal of Sexual Aggression* 5, no. 1 (2000): 37.

9. Kathleen C. Basile, "Implications of Public Health for Policy on Sexual Violence," in *Sexually Coercive Behavior: Understanding and Management*, ed. Robert A. Prentky, Eric S. Janus, Michael C. Seto (New York: Academy of Sciences, 2003), 449–50.

10. Ibid., 449, 448, 449.

11. James A. Mercy, Mark L. Rosenberg, Kenneth E. Powell, Claire V. Broome, and William L. Roper, "Public Health Policy for Preventing Violence," *Health Affairs* (Winter 1993): 7–29; summarized in *Research and Advocacy Digest* 5 (Jan. 2003): 9.

12. Keith Kaufman et al., "Reconceptualizing Child Sex Abuse," in *Preventing Violence in Relationships*, ed. Paul A. Schewe (Washington, D.C.: American Psychological Association, 2002), 34.

13. Robert Alan Prentky and Ann Wolbert Burgess, *Forensic Management of Sexual Offenders* (New York: Kluwer Academic/Plenum, 2000), 237.

14. "Working Upstream: A Public Health Approach to Preventing the Sexual Abuse of Children," Stop It Now!, 2002.

15. Basile, "Implications of Public Health," 454, 455, 455–56.

16. Ibid., 453.

17. David Wolfe and Peter Jaffe, 2003, "Prevention of Domestic Violence and Sexual Assault," http://www.vawnet.org/DomesticViolence/Research/VAWnetDocs/AR_Prevention.pdf.

18. Kaufman, "Reconceptualizing Child Abuse," 42, 40, 42.

19. Research Triangle Institute International, "Evaluation Assistance for Projects Designed to Prevent First-time Male Perpetration of Sexual Violence: Final Report on Identification of Programs" (Durham, N.C.: RTI, 2003).

20. Ibid.

21. Prentky and Burgess, *Forensic Management*, 205.

22. Patricia Rozee and Mary P. Koss, "Rape: A Century of Resistance," *Psychology of Women Quarterly* 25 (2001): 304.

23. Governor's Commission on Sex Offender Policy, Jan. 2005, http://www.doc.state.mn.us/commissionsexoffenderpolicy/default.htm.

24. Prentky and Burgess, *Forensic Management*, 241, quoting Kirk Heilbrun and Patricia A. Griffin, "Community-Based Forensic Treatment," in *Treatment of Offenders with Mental Disorders*, ed. Robert M. Wettstein (New York: Guilford Press, 1998), 196. John Q. LaFond and Bruce J. Winick, "Sex Offender Reentry Courts: A Cost-Effective Proposal for Managing Sex Offender Risk in the Community," in *Sexually Coercive Behavior*, ed. Prentky et al., 309.

25. Prentky and Burgess, *Forensic Management*, 241, 242.

26. Ibid., 243.

27. Ibid.

28. Kim English, Linda Jones, and Diane Patrick, "Community Containment of Sex Offender Risk: A Promising Approach," in *Protecting Society from Dangerous Offenders: Law, Justice, and Therapy*, ed. Bruce J. Winick and John Q. LaFond (Washington, D.C.: American Psychological Association, 2003), 265–66.

29. Kim English, Linda Jones, Diane Patrick, and Diane Pasini-Hill, "Sexual Offender Containment: Use of the Postconviction Polygraph," in *Sexually Coercive Behavior*, ed. Prentky et al., 413.

30. Ibid.

31. Ibid., 414.

32. English, Jones, and Patrick, "Community Containment," 272.

33. LaFond and Winick, "Sex Offender Reentry Courts," 309.

34. Ibid., 312.

35. Ibid., 314, 320.

36. Rozee and Koss, "Rape," 295–311.

37. Robert Freeman-Longo, "Challenging Our Thoughts about Sex," Feb. 15, 1998, http://www.selfhelpmagazine.com/articles/sexchal.html.

38. From http://www.stopitnow.com, cited in Basile, "Implications of Public Health," 456.

39. Lois Presser and Elaine Gunnison, "Strange Bedfellows: Is Sex Offender Notification a Form of Community Justice?" *Crime and Delinquency* 45 (1999): 300.

40. Mary P. Koss, Karen J. Bachar, and C. Quince Hopkins, "Restorative Justice for Sexual Violence: Repairing Victims, Building Community, and Holding Offenders Accountable," in *Sexually Coercive Behavior,* ed. Prentky et al., 384, 388.

41. Ibid., 388.

42. Jon Silverman and David Wilson, *Innocence Betrayed: Paedophilia, the Media, and Society* (Cambridge: Polity Press, 2002), 169, 170, 172, 170, 173, 176, 42.

43. Paul Slovic, "Trust, Emotion, Sex, Politics, and Science: Surveying the Risk Assessment Battlefield," *University of Chicago Legal Forum* 1997 (1997): 61.

44. Eric S. Janus, "Minnesota's Sex Offender Commitment Program: Would an Empirically Based Prevention Policy Be More Effective?" *William Mitchell Law Review* 29 (2003): 1102.

45. R. Karl Hanson et al., "First Report of the Collaborative Outcome Data Project on the Effectiveness of Psychological Treatment for Sexual Offenders," *Sexual Abuse: A Journal of Research and Treatment* 14 (2002): 169.

46. "State Looks to Release Sexual Psychopaths," *Minneapolis–St. Paul Star Tribune,* June 22, 2003, 1A.

47. Stephen Huot, director of the Minnesota Department of Corrections Sex Offender and Chemical Dependency Unit, e-mail message to author, Nov. 25, 2002.

48. Prentky and Burgess, *Forensic Management.*

49. Dan Gunderson, Apr. 19, 2004, "Minnesota's Probation System Overloaded," http://news.minnesota.publicradio.org/features/2004/04/19_gundersond_probcaseload.

50. Jim Doyle, "Treatment for Rapists, Molesters under Fire: Cost, Legality and Effectiveness at Issue in Extended Program," *San Francisco Chronicle,* July 11, 2004, 1A.

51. Governor's Budget Recommendations, Department of Education, Prevention, 2004–05; http://www.budget.state.mn.us/budget/operating/200405/rec_rev1/e12_education.pdf.

52. Report of the Interagency Task Force on Domestic Violence and Sexual Assault Prevention, Jan. 2004; http://archive.leg.state.mn.us/docs/2004/mandated/040043.pdf.

Chapter 8 The Politics of Sexual Violence

1. Derrick Nunnally, "Housing Deadline Issued for Pedophile," *Milwaukee Journal Sentinel,* Mar. 24, 2004, http://www.jsonline.com/news/metro/apr05/318523.asp.

2. Steve Schultze, "State Official Apologizes for Morford Placement: Family Services Head Says She Was Unaware of Shelter for Children," *Milwaukee Journal Sentinel,* June 7, 2003, http://www.jsonline.com/news/metro/jun03/146682.asp.

3. Conrad deFiebre, "Psychopathic Sex Offenders Get New Home," *Minneapolis–St. Paul Star Tribune,* Nov. 5, 1995, 1B; Bill Salisbury, "Tab Coming Due on State Sentencing Policies: Prisons, Hospitals Seek $140 Million for Construction," *St. Paul Pioneer Press,* Sept. 6, 2005, A1.

4. Bruce Rind, Philip Tromovich, and Robert Bauserman, "A Meta-Analytic Examination

of Assumed Properties of Child Sexual Abuse Using College Samples," *Psychological Bulletin* 124 (1998): 22.

5. Associated Press, "House Votes 355–0 to Condemn Findings of Child Sex Abuse Study: Journal Article Concluded That Some Victims Suffer Little Long-term Effects," *Baltimore Sun,* July 12, 1999, final ed., 6A.

6. American Psychological Association Executive Vice-President Raymond D. Fowler to United States Representative Tom Delay, June 9, 1999, http://www.apa.org/releases/delay.html.

7. Family Resource Council, "APA Admits Error in Publishing Highly Criticized 'Adult-Child Sex' Study: FRC's Parshall Applauds 'Good First Step' as APA Pledges 'Unprecedented' Independent Review," news release, June 9, 1999.

8. Ofelia Rodriguez-Srednicki and James A. Twaite, "Understanding and Reporting Child Abuse: Legal and Psychological Perspectives. Part One: Physical Abuse, Sexual Abuse, and Neglect," *Journal of Psychiatry and Law* 32, no. 3 (2004): 336.

9. *Call v. Gomez,* 535 N.W.2d 312 (Minn. 1995).

10. American Psychiatric Association, *Dangerous Sex Offenders: A Task Force Report on Sexually Dangerous Offenders* (Washington, D.C.: APA, 1999), 173.

11. W. Lawrence Fitch, "Sexual Offender Commitment in the United States: Legislative and Policy Concerns," in *Sexually Coercive Behavior: Understanding and Management,* ed. Robert A. Prentky, Eric S. Janus, and Michael C. Seto (New York: New York Academy of Sciences, 2003), 493. Anita Schlank, Rick Harry, and Michael Farnsworth, "The Minnesota Sex Offender Program," in *The Sexual Predator: Law, Policy, Evaluation and Treatment,* ed. Anita Schlank and Fred Cohen (Kingston, N.J.: Civil Research Institute, 1999), 10–2 (describing the Minnesota program and noting its national prominence).

12. Roxanne Lieb, "State Policy Perspective on Sexual Predator Laws," in *Protecting Society from Dangerous Offenders: Law, Justice, and Therapy,* ed. Bruce J. Winick and John Q. La-Fond (Washington, D.C.: American Psychiatric Association, 2003), 46–52, table 2.2.

13. Conrad deFiebre, "Psychopathic Sex Offenders Get New Home," *Minneapolis–St. Paul Star Tribune,* Nov. 5, 1995, 1B.

14. Paul Landskroener, in discussion with Moose Lake City Council (notes on file with author).

15. Minn. Stat. § 244.052 subd. 2 (1996); Douglas L. Epperson et al., *Minnesota Sex Offender Screening Tool—Revised: Development, Effectiveness, and Recommended Risk Level Cut Scores,* Dec. 2003, http://www.psychology.iastate.edu/faculty/epperson/TechUpdatePaper12-03.pdf.

16. Eric S. Janus and Nancy Walbek, "Sex Offender Commitments in Minnesota: A Descriptive Study of Second Generation Commitments," *Behavioral Sciences and the Law* 18 (2000): 343.

17. Minnesota Department of Corrections, *Civil Commitment Study Group: 1998 Report to Legislature* (Saint Paul, 2000), 23.

18. Janus and Walbek, "Sex Offender Commitments in Minnesota," 343.

19. Minnesota Department of Human Services, *State Operated Forensic Services, Operational Plan—Fiscal Year 2003: Project/Goal 4* (Saint Paul, 2000) (on file with author).

20. Josephine Marcotty, "State Looks to Release Sexual Psychopaths: Is Concern for Offenders, or the Lock-up Program's High Cost, Driving Change?" *Minneapolis–St. Paul Star Tribune,* June 22, 2003, 1A.

21. Ibid.

22. Ibid.

23. Ibid.

24. Warren Wolfe, "Sex Offender Release Rules Are Changed: Pawlenty's Executive Order, in Effect, Will Keep Psychopaths Locked Up, Chief of Staff Says," *Minneapolis–St. Paul Star Tribune,* July 11, 2003, 1B.

25. Chuck Haga, "High Publicity of Sjodin Case Puzzles Some: Why Has This Abduction Had Such Lasting Attention?" *Minneapolis–St. Paul Star Tribune,* Dec. 7, 2003, 1A.

26. Patricia Lopez, "Governor Cites Bad Judgment on Rodriguez: Pawlenty Faulted Corrections Staffers in Release of Convict," *Minneapolis–St. Paul Star Tribune,* Dec. 19, 2003, 1A.

27. Josephine Marcotty and John Stefany, "Hurdles High for Offender Commitment: Many Most Likely to Commit Sex Crimes Again Are Released after Prison Rather Than Institutionalized," *Minneapolis–St. Paul Star Tribune,* Jan. 11, 2004, 1A.

28. "Rodriguez: What to Do with Sex Predators?" *Minneapolis–St. Paul Star Tribune,* Dec. 4, 2003, 26A.

29. Paul Gustafson, "Level 3 Offender Review Changed," *Minneapolis–St. Paul Star Tribune,* Dec. 5, 2003, 1B.

30. Conrad deFiebre, "Sex Offender Review Criticized: Pawlenty's Action Threatens a State Commitment Law That Protects the Public, DFLers Say," *Minneapolis–St. Paul Star Tribune,* Jan. 13, 2004, 2B.

31. Conrad deFiebre, "Life and Death: Getting Tough on Sex Offenders: Push for Life Sentences Might Cost $1 Billion or More over 20 Years," *Minneapolis–St. Paul Star Tribune,* Apr. 19, 2004, 1A.

32. Minnesota State Legislature, 83rd Regular Session 2003–04, http://www.leg.state.mn.us/leg/legis.asp (search of House and Senate bills for 2003).

33. Conrad deFiebre and Dane Smith, "DFL Fires an Early Salvo at Pawlenty: A TV Ad Blames the Governor for the Release of Hundreds of Sexual Predators," *Minneapolis–St. Paul Star Tribune,* Mar. 17, 2004, 1A.

34. deFiebre, "Life and Death," 1A.

35. Ibid.

36. Ibid.

37. Jessica McBride and Reid J. Epstein, "State Tops in Release of Sexual Predators," *Milwaukee Journal Sentinel,* Sept. 22, 2003, 1A. Ben Steverman, "Prosecutors Promise Aggressive Stance on Sex Offenders," *Minneapolis–St. Paul Star Tribune,* Jan. 21, 2004, 1S.

38. McBride and Epstein, "State Tops in Release," 1A.

39. *Call v. Gomez,* 535 N.W.2d 312 (Minn. 1995).

40. McBride and Epstein, "State Tops in Release," 1A.

41. Ibid.

42. Jessica McBride, "Predator Law Has Officials in a Bind," *Milwaukee Journal Sentinel,* Oct. 26, 2003, 1B.

43. "Sexual-Predator Law Needs Another Look," *Post-Crescent* (Appleton, Wis.), Oct. 1, 2003.

44. Jessica McBride and Reid J. Epstein, "Tougher Sexual Predator Law Sought," *Milwaukee Journal Sentinel,* Sept. 25, 2003, 1A.

45. Reid J. Epstein, "House-Hunting for Sexual Predator Seems Futile," *Milwaukee Journal Sentinel,* Sept. 9, 2003, 1B.

46. Ibid.

47. Tom Held, "Prosecutors Lose Some Input on Sex Predators," *Milwaukee Journal Sentinel,* Feb. 4, 2004, 1B; *In re Commitment of Schulpius,* 678 N.W.2d 369 (Wisc. 2004).

48. Jake Henshaw, "S.J. Follows Soledad: Bay Area Is Next to Fight Settlement of a Sex Predator within Its Borders," *Salinas Californian,* Mar. 20, 2004, 1A.

49. Justin Berton, "Oh, Give Me a Home: The State Says Sexual Predator Cary Verse Is Rehabilitated, But It Isn't the State He Needs to Worry About," *East Bay Express* (Berkeley), Mar. 9, 2005, http://www.eastbayexpress.com/issues/2005-03-09/news/feature.html.

50. Thomas Alex Tizon, "Police Say Idaho Case Inspired Man Who Killed Sex Offenders," *Duluth News Tribune,* Sept. 7, 2005.

51. Mike Carter and Jonathan Martin, "Why State Chose Not to Commit Violent Molester," *Seattle Times,* July 7, 2005, A1.

52. "Rallying against Domestic Violence," *Minneapolis–St. Paul Star Tribune,* Feb. 12, 2004, 5B.

53. Chief Judge Kevin Burke, e-mail message forwarded to author, Feb. 6, 2004.

54. Vicki Haddock, "Molester Multitudes, Police Can't Locate Thousands of Sex Offenders," *San Francisco Chronicle,* Mar. 21, 2004, E3.

Chapter 9   Righting Public Policy against Sexual Violence

1. Robert Alan Prentky and Ann Wolbert Burgess, *Forensic Management of Sexual Offenders* (New York: Kluwer/Plenum, 2000), 150.
2. Patricia D. Rozee and Mary P. Koss, "Rape: A Century of Resistance," *Psychology of Women Quarterly* 25 (2001): 303.
3. Jenny Kitzinger, "The Gender-Politics of News Production: Silenced Voices and False Memories," in *News, Gender and Power,* ed. Cynthia Carter, Gill Branston, and Stuart Allan (London: Routledge, 1998), 186–204.
4. Paul Slovic, *The Perception of Risk* (London: Earthscan, 2000), 411.
5. Lucy Berliner, "Victim and Citizen Perspectives on Sexual Offender Policy," in *Sexually Coercive Behavior: Understanding and Management,* ed. Robert A. Prentky, Eric S. Janus, and Michael C. Seto (New York: New York Academy of Sciences, 2003), 468.
6. E-mail message to author's research assistant, Mar. 30, 2005.
7. Catherine M. Greene, "A State of Emergency on Matters of Sexual Violence in Massachusetts: Progress in Motion," http://www.nsvrc.org/publications/newsletters/summer02 rsrc.htm.
8. Rosario, "GPS No 'Silver Bullet,'" B1.
9. Generation Five, "About Generation Five," http://www.generationfive.org/aboutUs.html (accessed Oct. 16, 2005).
10. Janet Carter, "Family Violence Cries Out for Prevention," *Women's E-News,* Jan. 28, 2004, http://www.womensenews.org/article.cfm/dyn/aid/1690.
11. Telephone interview with Debbie Rogers, Program Director, Florida Council Against Sexual Violence, Mar. 3, 2005.
12. Slovic, *Perception of Risk,* 411.
13. Laurie O. Robinson, "Sex Offender Management: The Public Policy Challenges," in *Sexually Coercive Behavior,* ed. Prentky et al., 5.
14. Doble Research Associates and the Center for Sex Offender Management, *Public Opinion and the Criminal Justice System: Building Support for Sex Offender Management Programs,* Apr. 2000, 6, http://www.csom.org/pubs/pubpinion.pdf.
15. William Edwards and Christopher Hensley, "Contextualizing Sex Offender Management Legislation and Policy: Evaluating the Problem of Latent Consequences in Community Notification Laws," *International Journal of Offender Therapy and Comparative Criminology* 45, no. 1 (2001): 87.
16. Ibid.
17. California Coalition on Sexual Offending, "Using the Internet to Provide Passive Community Notification about Registered Sex Offenders: A Resource Paper Prepared for the California Coalition on Sexual Offending," by Nancy Irwin et al., 2004, 20, http://ccoso.org/papers/InternetNotification.pdf.
18. E-mail message from Carla Ferrucci to David Arons, Mar. 24, 2005.
19. Jenny Kitzinger, "Gender-Politics of News Production," 186–204.
20. Paula Skidmore, "Gender and the Agenda: News Reporting of Child Sexual Abuse," in *News, Gender and Power,* ed. Carter et al., 216.
21. Jenny Kitzinger, "Researching Risk and the Media," *Health, Risk, and Society* 1, no. 1 (1999): 55.
22. California Coalition on Sexual Offending, "Using the Internet," 20.
23. Catherine Donaldson-Evans, "Molesters Often Strike Again," FoxNews.com, Apr. 16, 2005. http://www.foxnews.com/story/0.2933.151999.00.html.

24. Jane Musgrave, "Murders Ignite Frenzied Furor over Molesters," *Palm Beach Post,* May 16, 2005, final ed., 1A.

25. Ibid.

26. Ibid.

27. United Press International, "Analysis: Miami Beach Closed to Offenders," *Washington Times,* May 3, 2005, http://washingtontimes.com/upi-breaking/20050503–021248–2184r.htm.

28. U.S. Department of Health and Human Services, Administration for Children and Families, Administration on Children, Youth and Families, National Center on Child Abuse and Neglect, *Third National Incidence Study on Child Abuse and Neglect,* by Andrea Sedlak and Diane Broadhurst, 1996. California Coalition on Sexual Offending, "Using the Internet," 16.

29. "State's Sex Offender Law Could Have a Few Bad Side Effects." *Times-Republican,* http://www.timesrepublican.com/edit/story/0220202006_edtedit.asp, last visited Mar. 12, 2006.

30. Musgrave, "Murders Ignite Frenzied Furor," 1A.

31. Ibid.

32. Ibid.

33. Jamie Thompson, Leonora Lapeter, and Carrei Johnson, "Sexual Crimes: No Easy Answers," *St. Petersburg* (Florida) *Times,* Apr. 24, 2005, South Pinellas ed., 1A.

34. Ibid.

35. *Doe v. Miller,* 405 F.3d 700 (8th Cir. 2005).

36. Rosario, "GPS No 'Silver Bullet,' " B1.

37. Heron Marquez Estrada, "Tracking Criminals with GPS Welcomed," *Minneapolis–St. Paul Star Tribune,* Jan. 1, 2004, 1B.

38. "We Need a Smart Law on Sexual Predators, Not Just a Tough One: Schwarzenegger's Plan Needs More Time to Give Details on Monitoring Offenders," *San Jose Mercury News,* Aug. 18, 2005, 24A.

39. Ibid.

40. Jordon Rau, "A Bid to Toughen Stance on Sex Offenses: A Proposal to Restrict Where Such Criminals Can Live and to Track Them for Life Is Likely to Go on the Ballot. Some Question Its Usefulness." *L.A. Times,* February 19, 2006, 1.

41. Rosario, "GPS No 'Silver Bullet,' " B1.

42. Stephen J. Lee, "Dru's Law Passes Senate, Dorgan's Legislation Reintroduced after Stalling Last Year in House," *Grand Forks* (North Dakota) *Herald,* July 29, 2005, 1B.

43. "Sex Offenders: The Senate's Smart Strategy," *Minneapolis–St. Paul Star Tribune,* May 12, 2005, 16A.

44. "State Puts Squeeze on Probation Programs, Budget: Lawmakers Prefer to Spend Money on Jails Instead of on Probation Officers," *Duluth News Tribune,* May 8, 2005, 1C.

45. Rosario, "GPS No 'Silver Bullet,' " B1.

46. Kim Petrie, "Uproar Aside, No Level 3 Sex Offenders Live in Area," *St. Cloud Times,* Aug. 8, 2005, 1A.

47. Charley Shaw, "MN Program Offers Stable Housing for Parolees," *Finance and Commerce* (St. Paul, Minn.), Aug. 29, 2005.

INDEX

actuarial risk assessment, 7, 56–58
alternate system of justice
  delineation of rights and, 106
  in sexual predator commitment cases, 32–34
  sexual predator laws as basis for, 5–6, 94, 101–3
Araji, Sharon, 83

Basile, Kathleen, 118
Baumeister, Roy F., 103
Berliner, Lucy, 17, 69–70
bio-psychological model of sexual violence, 88–90
Brownmiller, Susan, 77
Buck v. Bell, 99–100
Burgess, Ann, 51, 68, 70, 117, 121, 146

Canadian Circles of Support and Accountability, 124
Carney, Robert, 130
Chesney, Robert, 95
civil commitment. *See* sexual predator commitment laws
clinical risk assessment, 55–56, 58
Clinton–Lewinsky affair, 76
community notification and registration laws
  design and structure, 66–67
  diminishment of social values, 91–92
  effectiveness, 67–71
  effect on recidivism, 67–68
  impact on offenders, 70–71
  legal challenges, 20–21
  legal framework, 20
  origins, 3, 15–16
  perceived benefits, 66, 68
  punitive intent, 21
  See also Megan's law
community supervision, 126
  containment model, 121–23
  reentry courts, 122–23
  restorative justice model, 123–25
conservative opposition to feminist analysis, 76–77, 82–84
constitutional law
  outsider jurisprudence and, 97–100
  preventive state and, 94, 97–101
  punishment of sex offenders and, 18–20
  sexual predator commitment laws and, 36–41
  substantive due process, 38
containment model, 121–23
control, lack of. *See* inability to control
costs
  community notification and registration laws, 66–67, 71
  sexual predator commitment laws, 61–62, 114–15, 126–27
Crime Victimization Survey. *See* National Crime Victimization Survey
culture war, 75–77, 87

D'Emilio, John, 77
determinate sentencing, 17–18

Dred Scott v. Sandford, 97–98
Dru's law, 158
Dworkin, Andrea, 78

Edwards, William, 152
empirical research, 7
    sexual violence policy and, 43–45, 58–59,
        154–55
eugenic sterilization laws, 99–100
Evans, Sara, 79, 82

Farnsworth, Michael, 133
Feeley, Malcolm, 106
feminist analysis of sexual violence, 6–7, 51,
        75–79, 81–87
    conservative opposition, 75–77, 82–84
    significance of family in, 78–79, 84
Foucha v. Louisiana, 37–38
Freedman, Estelle B., 77
Freeman-Longo, Robert. *See* Longo, Robert

Ghilotti, Patrick, 140–141
GPS tracking of sex offenders, 157–58
Gunnison, Elaine, 124

Haaken, Janice, 87
Hale, Sir Matthew, 80
Hanson, R. Karl, 7, 48
Harris, Grant, 105
Heatherton, Todd F., 103
Hensley, Christopher, 152
Hudson, Barbara, 104, 106, 107

inability to control
    imprecision as defining characteristic, 103
    legal standards for commitment, 29–32,
        38–41, 52
    minimization of responsibility, 89–90
indeterminate sentencing, 17

Jacobson v. Massachusetts, 100
Jacob Wetterling Crimes against Children
        and Sexually Violent Offenders Regis-
        tration Act, 16
Jessica Lunsford Act, 156
judicial limitations on offender commitment
    assurances, 26–27, 31
    compromises, 36, 40–41
justice, alternate system of. *See* alternate sys-
        tem of justice

Kanka, Megan, 3, 15
Kansas v. Crane, 38–39, 102

Kansas v. Hendricks, 37–39
Kitzinger, Jenny, 154
Knight, Raymond A., 103
Korematsu v. United States, 98–100
Koss, Mary, 83, 84, 120

LaFond, John, 122–23
Lamb, Sharon, 87, 89
Lawrence v. Texas, 100
legal outsiders. *See* outsider jurisprudence
Levine, Judith, 47
Linehan, Dennis Darol
    criminal history, 27
    sexual predator commitment trials, 27–
        32, 34–36, 39–40
Logan, Wayne, 67, 70
loitering laws, 101
Longo, Robert, 16, 70

MacKinnon, Catharine, 6–7, 77–78
media and sexual violence policy, 153–55,
        159–60
Megan's law, 3, 16, 20
    See also community notification and regis-
        tration laws
Megan's laws. *See* community notification
        and registration laws
mental disorder diagnosis
    basis of outsider jurisprudence, 102–3
    legal standard for commitment, 38–39,
        52
Minnesota "psychopathic personality" com-
        mitment law, 29
Minnesota Sex Offender Program, 133–35
Minnesota Sexually Dangerous Persons
        Law, 32
Minnesota Supreme Court, 29–32, 36, 39–
        40
MnSOST-R, 57

National Crime Victimization Survey, 45–
        46
    redesign, 85
National Violence against Women Survey,
        46, 86

O'Connor v. Donaldson, 37
outsider jurisprudence
    constitutional history, 97–100
    mental disorder diagnosis and, 102–3
    risk and, 102–5
    sexual predator laws as reconstruction of,
        101–9

patriarchy, 77–78, 81, 84
Pearson standard, 29, 36, 38–39
Petrunik, Michael, 16
Plessy v. Ferguson, 98
policy on sexual violence. *See* sexual violence policy
politics
  release of sex offenders and, 135–40
  sexual violence policy and, 7–8, 132–33
Prentky, Robert, 51, 68, 70, 103, 117, 121,
  146
Presser, Lois, 124
prevention gap, 13–14, 18, 20, 131
  public perception, 16–17
prevention of sexual violence
  community notification and registration
    laws and, 68
  cost-benefit analysis of policy models,
    125–29
  effectiveness of sexual predator laws, 117
  funding, 114–15, 128
  primary prevention programs, 117–20
  recommendations, 129
  role of criminal justice system, 120–21
  sexual predator commitment laws and,
    62–66
preventive state, 4–5, 93–97
  constitutional constraints, 94, 97–101
  risk and, 106–9
  sexual predator laws and, 5–6, 94–95, 97,
    106–9
  terrorism laws and, 94–97
public attitudes and opinions
  punishment of sex offenders, 18
  response to sexual violence, 149–50
  toward rape, 80
public health approach to sexual violence,
  116–20
public policy on sexual violence. *See* sexual
  violence policy
punishment of sex offenders
  constitutional constraints, 18–20
  public attitudes and opinions, 18

Quinsey, Vernon, 105

radical prevention. *See* preventive state
rape
  incidence, 46–47, 83–86, 128
  by intimates or acquaintances, 46, 85–86
  laws, 80–82
  See also sexual violence
rape-murders, 47

rape myths, 79–81
  influence on legal system, 80–81
  public acceptance, 80
rape reform movement, 81–82, 87
recidivism
  effect of community notification and reg-
    istration laws on, 67–68
  effect of sexual predator commitment laws
    on, 62–66
  influence on sexual violence policy, 49–50
  rates, 42–43, 48–50
reentry courts, 122–23
registration laws. *See* community notification and registration laws
release of sex offenders
  community opposition, 140–42
  politics of, 135–40
  standards for, 138–40
residential-exclusion laws, 156–57
restorative justice, 123–25
RESTORE, 124
Rice, Marnie, 105
risk
  basis of outsider jurisprudence, 102–5
  as essentialist attribute, 21, 91, 102–4
  preventive state and, 106–9
risk assessment and prediction, 54–58, 107
risk management, 121
ritual exile, 89
Robinson, Laurie, 16, 152
Rodriguez, Alfonso, Jr., 1, 136
Romer v. Evans, 100
Rose, Nikolas, 107
Rosen, Ruth, 83
Rozee, Patricia, 120
RRASOR, 57
Rush, Florence, 83
Russell, Diana, 83

Safe Dates, 118
Schwartz, Barbara, 70
self-control. *See* inability to control
sentencing
  determinate, 17–18
  indeterminate, 17
  length of sentence, 18, 82
sex offender commitment laws. *See* sexual
  predator commitment laws
sex offenders
  abused as children, 51
  custody status, 47
  mental disorders, 52–53
  recidivism rates, 48–50

sex psychopath laws, 22–23
sexual predator archetype
    construction, 14–15
    effect on public policy, 2–4, 142–43
    in sexual predator laws, 88
sexual predator commitment laws
    adoption, 23–24
    constitutionality, 36–41
    cost effectiveness, 125–27
    costs, 61–62, 114–15, 126–27
    effect on recidivism, 62–66
    history, 22
    legal framework, 20–22
    opposition, 23
    origins, 3, 14–15
    population confined under, 62, 131
    social acceptance, 130–32
sexual predator laws
    antifeminist characteristics, 77, 87–92
    bio-psychological model of sexual vio-
        lence, 88–90
    diminishment of social values, 90–91
    moral neutrality, 90–91
    negative consequences, 143–44
    outsider jurisprudence and, 101–9
    paradoxical characteristics, 145–46
    preventive state and, 5–6, 94–95, 97, 106–9
    social costs, 60–61
sexual violence
    bio-psychological model, 7
    etiology, 51
    feminist analysis, 6–7, 51, 75–79, 81–87
    incidence, 46–47, 83–86, 128
    language of, 89–90
    measurement, 45–46
    See also rape
sexual violence policy
    design recommendations, 146–49

empirical research and, 43–45, 58–59,
    154–55
media influence on, 153–55, 159–60
need for comprehensive strategy, 152–
    53
politics of, 7–8, 132–33
recent developments, 155–60
recidivism and, 49–50
role of public input, 149–52
role of victims and advocates, 150–52
Simon, Jonathan, 106
Sjodin, Dru, 1, 136
Skidmore, Paula, 154
Slovic, Paul, 149, 152, 154
Sommers, Christina Hoff, 84, 87
Stanko, Elizabeth, 84, 87–88
STATIC-99, 56–57
Stop It Now!, 118–19
substantive due process, 38

terrorism laws, preventive state and, 94–97
Tice, Dianne M., 103
Timmendequas, Jesse, 15
treatment of sex offenders
    effectiveness, 53–54, 126–27
    funding, 115
    models, 54

United States Supreme Court, 29, 37–40
USA Patriot Act, 5, 95–96

vagrancy laws, 101
Verse, Cary, 141–42
Violence against Women Act, 86–87
    funding, 114

Washington Community Protection Act, 15
Winick, Bruce, 70, 122–23